D0984526

COUNT-DOWN

COUNT-DOWN

The Polish Upheavals of
1956, 1968, 1970, 1976, 1980 ...

JAKUB KARPIŃSKI

translated by
Olga Amsterdamska
and Gene M. Moore

KARZ-COHL · NEW YORK PUBLISHERS, INC.

Copyright © 1982 by Karz-Cohl Publishers, Inc.
All rights reserved under international and
Pan-American copyright conventions.
Printed in the United States of America

Chapters 1, 2, and 3 of Countdown are adapted respectively
from the following volumes:

Ewolucja czy rewolucja
Copyright © 1975 by Instytut Literacki, Paris

Porcja wolności: październik 1956
Copyright © 1979 by Instytut Literacki, Paris

Krotkie spięcie: marzec 1968
Copyright © 1977 by Instytut Literacki, Paris

Library of Congress Cataloging in Publication Data

Karpiński, Jakub.
  Countdown, the Polish upheavals of 1956, 1968,
1970, 1976, 1980.

  Selected compositions, translated from the Polish.
  Includes index.
  1. Poland—History—1945–   . I. Title.
DK4430·K37   943·8'055   82–203
ISBN 0–918294–14–2   AACR2
ISBN 0–918294–15–0 (pbk.)

published in the United States by
KARZ-COHL PUBLISHERS, INC.
320 West 105th Street, New York, N.Y. 10025

CONTENTS

COUNT-
DOWN

CHAPTER 1

THE ORIGINS OF THE SYSTEM

The Underground State

The present social system in Poland was established primarily as a result of circumstances beyond Polish control: namely, the military situation in Europe at the end of the Second World War and a series of agreements between the Soviet Union, Great Britain, and the United States.

Following the Polish defeat to the Germans in September 1939 and the internment of the former Polish government in Rumania, members of the prewar opposition quickly came to the fore. On September 9, 1939, a National Council was convened in London to replace the Diet and Senate, with Ignacy Paderewski as president and with three vice-presidents—Stanisław Mikołajczyk from the Peasants' Party (SL), Tadeusz Bielecki from the National Party (SN), and Herman Lieberman from the Polish Socialist Party (PPS). These three parties began to play a dominant role within the very first months of the German occupation not only in exile but also inside Poland. The dominant role of the prewar governing faction, Sanacja, was finished.

All this was taking place at a time when the Polish nation was suffering tremendous losses. In September 1939, Poland was divided between the Third Reich and the Soviet Union. The Germans incorporated into the Reich part of their occupied territory; the rest became known as the General Government. And in both those areas incorporated into the Reich and into the Soviet Union, there were mass deportations. Policies regarding the local populations varied somewhat in different areas at different times; but from the beginning, both the German and Soviet authorities directed their activities toward liquidating the Polish state, its offices and administration.

3

With their time advantage, the Germans succeeded in virtually destroying the Polish economy, administration, and education. In the name of collective responsibility, they began rounding up innocent hostages. A passerby on the street could suddenly find himself in a concentration camp, or facing a firing squad. Participation in secret schools was punishable by death, not to mention political or military activity.

From the earliest months of the occupation, leaders of the political parties began their underground work, and military organizations connected with the various political parties sprang up: most important was a part of the Polish armed forces later called the Home Army (AK), which grew to an unprecedented size given its underground conditions.

The exact number of Home Army members is difficult to establish, due to the nature of its activities. It is known that by the end of the war there were between 300 and 400 thousand soldiers. As early as 1940, the Socialist military organization (Peoples' Guard) accepted the leadership of the Home Army, then called the Union for Armed Struggle. The National party's National Military Organization joined the Home Army in 1942, as did the Peasant Battalions, which belonged to the peasant movement, in 1943.

Diplomatic relations between Poland and the Soviet Union, which had been suspended following the Red Army invasion of September 17, 1939, were reestablished on July 30, 1941, shortly following the Nazi invasion of the Soviet Union, only to be broken again on April 25, 1943. The immediate cause of the latter break was the discovery of the graves of four thousand Polish officers in Katyn Forest near Smolensk, which was announced by the German authorities in April 1943. On April 17, a delegate of the Polish Red Cross in Switzerland, acting on instructions from the Polish government, asked the International Red Cross for an investigation. The Soviet Union called this request a "treacherous blow," reflecting a "hostile attitude"; and *Pravda* referred soon afterwards to "Polish cronies of Hitler," and claimed that "the Polish nation condemns the treacherous government of General Sikorski."

On June 30, 1943, the Gestapo arrested the commander of the Home Army, General Rowecki. On July 4, the prime minister and commander-in-chief, General Władysław Sikorski, was killed in a plane crash over Gibraltar.

In Teheran, in November-December 1943, Stalin, Roosevelt, and Churchill decided that Poland would be within the operational sphere of Soviet troops, which were granted exclusive control of Polish territory.

They also agreed that the so-called Curzon Line would mark the eastern border of Poland.

In the spring of 1944, the Red Army entered the territory of the Polish Republic.

It was felt by the Poles that it was necessary both to fight the Germans and to make the presence of the Home Army known to the Soviets. As a result, the underground Polish authorities created "Operation Storm." The goal of the operation conducted by the Home Army on eastern territory was to document the rights of Poles in this area. The government and the Home Army (AK) were committed to territorial integrity, one based on the eastern border established by the Soviet-signed peace treaty in Riga in March 1921 and reaffirmed in the Sikorski-Majski treaty of July 1941, in which the Soviets repudiated "the German-Soviet treaties of 1939 concerning the territorial changes in Poland." But in 1943 the Soviet Union officially returned to its position as outlined in the Ribbentrop-Molotov Pact (with minor corrections in favor of Poland, such as the eventual return of Białystok). This Soviet position was reflected in the attitude of the Red Army and the NKVD towards the Home Army and underground authorities.

At the beginning of July 1944, the AK and Red Army joined forces in the capture of Vilno. After the city was taken, a briefing was held for Polish and Soviet officers; the briefing ended with the arrest of the Polish officers, and several thousand AK soldiers were deported to the interior of the Soviet Union. This was repeated in late July, after the AK had assisted the Red Army in the capture of Lvov: the Polish officers were arrested and their soldiers disarmed.

Even on territory the Soviet authorities recognized as Polish, as with the left bank of the Bug River, Soviet commanders assumed jurisdiction over the Polish population, ordering them, for example, to surrender their arms and making arrests. Soviet military headquarters were established in the cities.

The Warsaw Uprising was a continuation of "Operation Storm." Militarily it was a Polish-German conflict; but politically it concerned Polish-Soviet relations. The question of aid for the Warsaw Fighters was a source of tension between the Soviet Union and Great Britain (and, to a lesser degree, with the United States). But in Teheran it was agreed among the Allies that Poland was to be an area controlled by Soviet troops. The desire to maintain good relations with the Soviet Union, expressed particularly by Roosevelt, limited the degree of effective help the Allies could give to Warsaw. Treaties between Great Britain and Josef Stalin took precedence over prewar treaties between Britain and Poland.

In the meantime, the USSR was entering Poland as a decisive force. The Soviet army was fighting against the Germans, and it became increasingly evident that its presence in Poland would prove crucial in the development of internal Polish affairs.

On September 1, 1944, Commander-in-Chief General Kazimierz Sosnkowski issued an order in which he criticized Great Britain for its insufficient help to the uprising. General Sosnkowski's remarks proved useless, and, in any event, he resigned immediately after issuing the order. For a short time he was replaced by the commander of the Home Army, General Tadeusz Komorowski.

In November, after the defeat of the uprising in October 1944 and following the failure of Premier Mikołajczyk to mend the broken relations between Poland and the Soviet Union, Mikołajczyk resigned. He was replaced by the Socialist, Tomasz Arciszewski, as the third premier of the government-in-exile (after Sikorski and Mikołajczyk).

Early in February 1945 at the Yalta Conference, the leaders of the three great powers agreed that the provisional government in Poland, which was located in Lublin and had in fact been instigated by the Soviets to counter the London government-in-exile, should be "reorganized on a broader democratic basis, including Polish democratic leaders within Poland and abroad." Beyond the fact that this disadvantaged the exile government—recognized by all the Allies with the exception of the USSR—it was unclear to whom the expression "Polish democratic leaders within Poland and abroad" referred. The "reorganized government" was to be recognized by all the Allied powers and was given "the responsibility of holding free and open elections, based on a universal secret ballot, as soon as possible."

The exile government condemned the Yalta agreements, declaring that they were made in contravention of previous international agreements; and it characterized the border adjustments contemplated in the agreements as a "fifth partition of Poland." On February 22, 1945, the Council of National Unity issued the following statement: "The council strongly protests the one-sidedness of the Yalta agreements but is forced to accept them, desiring only to see in them a possibility, given present realities, of saving Polish independence." In view of this situation, the National Council of Ministers and the Council of National Unity decided to join the negotiations for creating a "reorganized government." They assumed that the "democratic leaders from within Poland" mentioned in the Yalta agreements would come from their institutions, which were active in Poland under the occupation. Early in March 1945, Anthony Eden supplied the Soviet government with the names and pseudonyms of the National Council of Ministers members. Further action in this regard was undertaken by the NKVD.

In a matter of time, the NKVD, which enjoyed unlimited freedom of action in Poland, discovered the identities of all the leaders of political parties and the underground authorities. The Government Delegate, ministers, and representatives of the Polish parties in the Council of National Unity were then invited to talks. The last commander of the Home Army, the successor of Tadeusz Komorowski, General Leopold Okulicki, was also to participate in the talks as chief of the military arm of the Government Delegation. These underground leaders barely had time to inform the Polish authorities in London that they were entering negotiations with representatives of the Red Army, when they disappeared. After being transported to Moscow from the initial talks with the NKVD, the invited guests found themselves in prison. For over a month, the fate of the Polish politicians was unknown when, on May 6, 1945, TASS announced: "The group of Poles named in the English press and mentioned in Parliament is composed of 16, and not of 15, persons. The group is headed by the well-known General Okulicki, whose disappearance was not mentioned due to the particular odium attached to his person. General Okulicki and his group are accused of planning and executing diversionary actions in the rear of the Red Army, to which over a hundred Red Army officers and soldiers fell victim. This group of 16 persons did not 'disappear' but was arrested by Soviet military authorities and is now in Moscow, where an investigation is in progress."

Moreover, Stalin declared: "The arrests were made by Soviet military authorities on the basis of an agreement between the Polish provisional government and Soviet military commanders."

The only truth to these statements was that there were indeed 16 and not 15 members of the group. The trial began on June 16, 1945, before a military tribunal of the Supreme Court of the USSR. The verdicts were rendered on June 21.

The commander of the Home Army, General Okulicki, was sentenced to ten years' imprisonment, and, according to information provided later by Soviet authorities, he died in the Soviet Union in 1946.

Government Delegate Stanisław Jankowski, sentenced to eight years, also died in the Soviet Union: according to official information, he died in 1953, only several weeks before his scheduled release.

Members of the National Council of Ministers, Adam Bień, Stanisław Jasiukowicz, and Antoni Pajdak (who was tried separately), were sentenced to 5 years each in prison. Jasiukowicz died in the Soviet Union.

The chairman of the Council of National Unity, Kazimierz Pużak, who was also secretary-general of the Polish Socialist Party (PPS), was sentenced to 18 months; the council vice-president, Kazimierz Bagiński, was sentenced to one year. The other defendants received smaller sentences, and three were acquitted.

The court declared that "the imposition of harsher sentences, including execution, as set forth in the criminal code for the crimes of which the accused were convicted, does not appear to be necessary at a time when we are beginning peaceful reconstruction." *Pravda* declared: "The verdicts rendered by the Military Tribunal of the Soviet Supreme Court against Okulicki, Jankowski, Bień, Jasiukowicz, and others bear witness to the frustration of the criminal aims of the illegal Polish movement, in the interest of peace and the fraternity of nations. They also strengthen Polish-Soviet friendship and thereby further the cause of peace and security in Europe."

The Home Army was dissolved on January 19, 1945, on the orders of General Okulicki before he was deported. The National Council of Ministers ceased to exist after the arrest of "the 16." The Council of National Unity was dissolved on July 1, 1945.

In their place, secret political and military organizations were springing up. A civil war was raging in Poland.

The postwar underground consisted of ever-changing groups with successive leaderships that were generally unable to develop and assume control of regional organizations. Often, armed units took independent action, which was by no means always authorized or supported by the leadership.

As a result of the amnesty of August 2, 1945, some forty thousand former members of the underground came out of hiding. These were primarily members of military organizations, and according to the terms of the amnesty, they were required to surrender their arms. A similar amnesty of February 22, 1947, led to the emergence of another sixty thousand people. Those who took advantage of the amnesties did not have easy lives afterwards. They found themselves imprisoned or worse.

In the political trials, the accusations and sentences were becoming increasingly severe, while the evidence became weaker. These trials followed in the footsteps of the trial of "the 16" and earlier political trials in the Soviet Union. Accusations of membership in underground organizations were linked with charges of having conspired to overthrow the authorities and subvert the system of government. This was punishable by death. The mere gathering of information was easily construed as a violation of state secrets and as activity against the state, that is, as espionage, which was also punishable by death. Initially, the political trials concerned so-called postwar conspiracies; later, trials investigated the wartime underground. AK soldiers and underground activists during the occupation were portrayed as "allies of the Gestapo" and were sentenced for "aiding the German state authorities and acting against the Polish state, against the civilian population or military personnel."

According to Roman Werfel, then a commentator on the political trials, the most important trials of 1947 were those of the association Freedom and Independence (WiN), which was a political organization formed in 1945 and originally headed by Colonel Rzepecki, together with Colonel Ludwik Muzyczka, Colonel Antoni Sanojca, Lieutenant Colonel Jan Szczurek-Cergowski from the AK headquarters, and Captain Józef Rybicki from the Warsaw Leadership of the AK Diversionary Arm. After the arrest of this first staff of WiN in November and December 1945, the leadership then passed to Colonel Franciszek Niepokólyczycki. The second staff of WiN was arrested in the fall of 1946. The trial of the original WiN group took place in January and February 1947. Because elections to the Diet were held before the verdict could be announced, it was officially emphasized that the sentences would be lenient: Colonel Muzyczka was sentenced to ten years and Colonel Rzepecki to eight; others were given smaller sentences. Other, less publicized, trials of this time, involving former WiN members and other underground organizations, resulted in sentences of death or life imprisonment. In September 1947, the trial of the second staff of WiN in Cracow resulted in death sentences for Colonel Niepokólczycki and seven others. Later, Major Wincenty Kwieciński, a subsequent WiN leader, received a sentence of life imprisonment. At the same trial, Colonel Wacław Lipiński, a historian and member of the Piłsudski camp, was sentenced to death, together with Włodzimierz Marszewski, a member of the Presidium of the National party.

Although the civil war persisted, military activity decreased after 1947; and after 1948 virtually all military units had been dispersed. The vicissitudes of the Polish nation during and after the war had deep and lasting effects. Those who had survived the occupation desired calm. The call for reconstruction found a receptive audience, since it was in the national interest. Warsaw, Gdańsk, and Wrocław had been completely destroyed. It was necessary to build housing, cultivate the land, and restore industry. After the war, there were migrations and repatriations on an unprecedented scale, as a result of the changing of borders, the destruction of cities, and later the rebuilding of industry. Re-immigrations were taking place together with escapes to the West and deportations to the East. The Regained (Western) Territories were being resettled, after having been systematically devastated by both the Germans and the Soviets. Investment was slowly being redeveloped in these territories. Farms were taken over, industry and housing were rebuilt. Warsaw was rising from its ruins. Few welcomed the new government with enthusiasm; but active resistance gave way to the hope for change through other means, and finally to apathy. Yet, at the same time, life had to go on, and the conditions of life and of social development had to be maintained. People were no longer reaching for their guns, but for ploughs, shovels, and trowels.

The Other Current

The Communist Party of Poland (KPP)—the Polish section of the Communist International—had ceased to exist in 1938, when it was dissolved by the Executive Committee of the Comintern, and the party leaders had been liquidated. Eighteen years later, it was acknowledged that the party and its leaders had met this fate on the basis of false accusations.

Even before the dissolution of the KPP, the Comintern had attempted to create a new organization in Poland. This was to have been accomplished by people who had been in Spain and France in 1938 and 1939. However, this plan quickly became outdated: the Communist movement respected the agreements stemming from the division of Europe into German and Soviet spheres of influence.

The German attack on Russia changed all this. In July and August 1941, a new Founding Group for Polish Affairs was established by the Comintern in Pushkino, near Moscow.

In late December 1941, six members of this group, including its three leaders, were dropped by parachute near Warsaw. In January 1942, one of the leaders, Paweł Finder, met with several Polish activists in an apartment in the city. This was declared the organizational meeting of the Polish Workers' Party (PPR). The participants in the meeting, former KPP members, disliked this name at first because they found it insufficiently Communist and internationalist; but Finder declared that the name had already been determined in the Soviet Union.

PPR began to develop a regional network, based in part on Communist groups already active in Poland before the creation of the new party.

In November 1942, Marceli Nowotko, the party secretary and a member of the triumvirate, was shot to death supposedly by Zygmunt Mołojec, the brother of Bolesław, another member of the triumvirate. Both brothers were shot in turn by party activists. The party leadership fell to Paweł Finder, and, following his arrest by the Nazis in November 1943, his place was taken by Władysław Gomułka.

In 1942, the Communist movement organized its own military group, which was subordinate neither to the Home Army nor to other Polish underground authorities. This organization originally took the Socialist name of People's Guard, and later, after January 1944, called itself the People's Army. Although such small groups were, as a rule, not very effective militarily, the spoils of victory, nevertheless, were to go to the People's Army.

Other Communist organizations were located in the Soviet Union, but not all the facts concerning the activities of the Communist movement are known. It is not difficult to establish the identity of the leaders of the Union of Polish Patriots, or of the later army divisions: the Soviet Union promoted these activities, after all. But the details of the relationships between the Polish Communist movement and the Soviet authorities have been kept secret. Slowly and gradually, some information has surfaced about Polish activists in the Soviet Union before and during the war: who they were and when, and in what capacity, they were in the USSR. But which of them joined the Communist Party of the Soviet Union or received Soviet citizenship, and when, is not generally known; nor is it known whether those who became members of the Soviet party ever ceased to belong to it, and, if so, when, and whether they ever resigned their Soviet citizenship. It is difficult to establish the identity of their Soviet contacts and the nature of their relationship with the NKVD or Soviet Military Intelligence. What individual instructions did they receive in their direct contacts with the Soviet power apparatus, especially when this apparatus (chiefly the NKVD) by-passed the party? Only fragments of the communications between the party and the Comintern have come to light.

On December 31, 1943, an organizational meeting of the National People's Council was held in Warsaw. It was headed by Bolesław Bierut, a Comintern activist, who, after staying in Byelorussia under the German occupation, returned to Warsaw in 1943 and became one of the most active members of the PPR leadership. After the removal of Władysław Gomułka from the Central Committee in 1949, Bierut succeeded him as secretary-general of the party. Nevertheless, at the time of his activities in the National People's Council, Bierut claimed he was not a member of the party, and others supported his claim. Later, the National People's Council came to be considered a parliament, and its chairman was regarded as a speaker of the Diet and head of state.

In January 1944, another group was formed in Moscow. It was called the Central Bureau of Polish Communists, and it drafted a memo in July 1944 concerning the formation of a new government in Poland. A project of this kind had been suggested by Stalin in his talks with Polish activists in May 1944. Stalin did not use the word "government," but spoke of "an organ of executive power." Following consultations with representatives of the Union of Polish Patriots, the National People's Council (KRN), and the Soviet government, the Polish Committee of National Liberation (PKWN) was created, described as a "temporary executive authority." There were 15 members of PKWN: nine from the Union of Polish Patriots and the Central Bureau of Polish Communists, five from the Moscow Delegation of the National People's Council, and one outsider. On July 21, the committee members signed a manifesto to the Polish nation, dated the following day, and usually associated with the city of Lublin. This "Lublin Manifesto" stated: "The London 'government' in exile and its Home Delegation are an illegitimate and illegal authority." The committee both was and was not a government: in addition to its chairman and two deputies, it was composed of directors of "departments," the names of which corresponded to ministries.

The Soviet Union treated PKWN as a legal Polish government, and signed a treaty concerning relations between PKWN and the Soviet military command on July 26 (this treaty was invoked by Soviet authorities during the trial of General Okulicki). On July 27, most of the members of PKWN traveled from Moscow to Chełm, and early in August they moved to Lublin. At the same time, some members of PKWN held talks with Prime Minister Mikołajczyk in Moscow. On December 31, 1944, PKWN was transformed into a provisional government, and the USSR was the first country to grant it recognition (on January 4, 1945).

It is important to note that the Department of Public Security in PKWN and its later avatars, which was responsible for arrests and repressions and was later transformed into a ministry, was headed by a high functionary of the PPR, Colonel Stanisław Radkiewicz. In actual practice, this department was directed by Soviet so-called advisors, whose activities in this connection ended only many years later, in 1956.

Political Uniformization

Immediately after the war, the Communist movement and an underground opposition were active in Poland. In addition, there was also a legal opposition, although it faced many difficulties. Let us examine the brief history of the legal opposition in postwar Poland. This opposition formed one part of a multiparty system that was of a rather peculiar character, both at the beginning and somewhat later.

While the trial of "the 16" was taking place, talks were held in Moscow between representatives of the Lublin Provisional Government and individuals from Poland and abroad to determine the composition of the new Polish government. In keeping with Stalin's idea, the selection of those from outside the provisional government was made by a commission composed of Molotov and the British and U.S. ambassadors in Moscow, Clark Kerr and Averell Harriman.

As a result of an agreement on June 21, 1945 (the very day the verdict was rendered in the trial of "the 16"), a new Polish government was formed on June 28, which was called the Provisional Government of National Unity, succeeding PKWN and the provisional government. The former premier of the provisional government and chairman of the PPS Central Executive Committee, Edward Osóbka-Morawski, became premier of the new government. Władysław Gomułka (secretary-general of the PPR Central Committee) and Stanisław Mikołajczyk (vice-president, and, after the death of Wincenty Witos, president of the SL Chief Executive Council) were named deputy premiers.

On July 5, 1945, the Provisional Government of National Unity was formally recognized by the United States and Great Britain, which simultaneously withdrew recognition from the government-in-exile of Tomasz Arciszewski. This move was in accordance with provisions of the Yalta Agreement.

Included in the Provisional Government of National Unity was the Polish Peasants' Party (PSL), which was a direct continuation of the Peasants' party. It had changed its name to the *Polish* Peasants' Party after emerging from the underground in order to distinguish itself from the spurious Peasants' party, which had cooperated with the PPR. The PSL membership grew rapidly, and it became more than just a peasants' party. By early 1946, the party had more than 600,000 members and was apparently the largest of all the political parties, with more members than all the other parties combined. PSL activity centered on the Yalta Agreement stipulation that free elections be held in Poland as soon as possible. Its main concern was to guarantee that in future elections a degree of choice would still be possible. At the same time, PSL undertook the defense of democracy and freedom generally; it attempted to limit the activities of the coercion apparatus and to mitigate the more radical acts of the new authorities. Although a part of the new government, the PSL often adopted an opposition position towards the government. Despite difficulties, this opposition found a voice in the PSL press.

The dominant party in the Provisional Government of National Unity was not the PSL, however, but the PPR, whose influence was based neither on the numerical strength of its membership nor on the number of votes it received in elections. (Elections were held only later; the Provisional Government of National Unity was formed solely on the basis of the June 1945 talks in Moscow.) The PPR monopolized the security forces and the army and controlled the formation of organizations and the functioning of the press. On July 5, 1946, a decree was announced establishing the office of censorship, which was called the Main Office for Control of the Press, Publications, and Spectacles (GUKPPiW). Meanwhile physical harassment of the PSL offices and PSL supporters took place unofficially.

The understandings reached at Yalta, initially unknown to the government-in-exile, created a situation in which the USSR held the decisive voice in Poland.

Before the 1947 elections, legal political opposition was being gradually but firmly restricted. This was done through new legislation, but more often without. Arrests were made by both Polish and Soviet security forces, and the ranks of the political opposition, already weakened by the German occupation, were dwindling. Arrests were carried out as early as 1944. People later released were often re-arrested.

One of the first legal acts of the new government was a PKWN decree of October 30, 1944, concerning "Protection of the State." On November 16, 1945, the government issued a "Decree Concerning Crimes Especially Dangerous During the Period of Reconstruction of the State." A second version of this decree, issued on June 13, 1946, and known as the Small Criminal Code, became one of the better-known postwar legal acts. Presumably a provisional document, it remained in force for 23 years. Under this decree, many leaders of political parties and regional activists, along with those who simply—as was said at the time—"didn't like the system," found themselves in jail.

Severely hampered by losses suffered under the occupation, the Polish political leaders were vulnerable to Communist persecutions. At first the new government applied repressions rather evenly: they were directed against all those who had been politically or militarily active and did not intend to cooperate with the Communist-led government. Later, the terror encompassed all political groups even including the Communists, who were suspected of party deviations that, as the charges claimed, led to espionage and treason. Among the parties representing traditional Polish political movements, the National party was refused legalization and was never reconstructed; the PPS was reborn in a form profoundly different from the original; while the PSL was a genuine continuation of the former peasant movement, and, in addition, it broadened the base of its support considerably.

The Labor Party (SP), created in 1937 along traditional Catholic and liberal lines, initially played a far lesser role than the other traditional parties, but it grew during the war. The postwar fate of the Labor Party provides a brief illustration of the methods used by the new authorities against its legal political opposition. In July 1945, the Labor Party held a congress, but it was not officially recognized by the authorities. There were arrests, and the SP leaders were informed that, in order to continue their activities, they would have to unite with their officially sanctioned counterpart. After this unification, there remained a clear division within the party between the old Labor Party and the group with official support. In the summer of 1946, the government prevented the next SP congress from taking place, and thus made it impossible to limit by means of election the policies imposed on the party by the official group. Under these circumstances, in July 1946, the SP leadership decided to suspend further activities, and in September 1946, representatives of the Labor Party (SP) resigned from KRN. The name remained with the officially sanctioned group, which had little to do with Catholicism and was not supported by the Church. And in 1950 this party was incorporated into the Democratic Party. Labor Party leaders and representatives to KRN were arrested and tried in 1951. Two were given life sentences, and three were sentenced to fifteen years' imprisonment. Father Zygmunt Kaczyński died in prison, and Jerzy Braun (the last chairman of the Council of National Unity) spent long years there. Both were prominent SP publicists and activists.

Late in April 1946, KRN adopted "A Resolution on People's Voting," which stated: "Before the elections to the Diet are called, a People's Vote will be held to answer the following questions: a) Are you for the abolition of the Senate? b) Do you want the future Constitution to provide for an economic system introduced through agrarian reform and the nationalization of the basic branches of the national economy, with the maintenance of basic rights of private initiative? c) Do you want permanent recognition of the western border of Poland on the Baltic Sea and the Oder-Neisse line? The People's Vote will take place nationwide on June 30, 1946."

The questions were phrased in a peculiar manner. Voters did not generally know what the "basic rights of private initiative" were. Someone knowing geography would also, for purely geographic reasons, have to take issue with the establishment of the Polish western border on the Baltic Sea. The questions were evidently written in haste. Yet for those who took the questions seriously and disregarded their ambiguity, an affirmative vote was the obvious answer. At the same time, it was clear that such answers would be treated by the authorities not as votes concerning issues, but as an indirect vote of confidence in themselves. Such indirect and conjectural expression of approval for the current government was supposed to take the place of free elections. Under these conditions, PSL, which had been traditionally against the Senate, reluctantly urged its supporters to vote "no" on the first question and "yes" on the others, primarily in order to conduct a straw poll and count its supporters. When the vote was held, many people reasoned like the authorities, but with a result that ran counter to the authorities' intentions: believing that "yes" was the appropriate answer to the individual questions, people voted "no" so as not to give the authorities this conjectural and indirect vote of confidence. In Cracow, 85 percent answered "no" to the first question, 59 percent to the second, and 30 percent to the third. Nationwide, according to the official results, the total "no" votes on the three questions were, respectively, 31 percent, 23 percent, and 9 percent. But according to the calculations of the PSL, the nationwide results were similar to the results reported in Cracow, and the referendum was rigged. However, in Cracow the vote counting was under PSL control.

The basic result of the referendum was to remind the authorities more clearly that PSL was a dangerous opponent; while PSL was reminded that the authorities could not be relied upon to act legally. But both sides hardly needed a referendum for this.

The range of possible actions for the legalized opposition was constantly diminishing, and the referendum was further evidence of this. The Soviet assurances to the West at Yalta concerning Poland were revealing their true colors. The words "democracy" and "democratic" were often used, but it was to be a new form of democracy. Before and during the war, the Comintern had developed the tactic of using popular fronts led by Communist parties. After the war, the Communists organized a Bloc of Democratic Parties, which consisted of fabricated organizations named after the traditional Polish parties—the Peasants' Party, the Polish Socialist Party, and the Democratic Party—with whom they competed and whom they finally replaced.

Under Soviet leadership, the Ministry of Public Security, its official organs and unofficial sectors, were kept busy. An anti-PSL campaign was launched in the press, courtrooms, and back alleys. Regional PSL organizations were dissolved; PSL representatives were removed from local administrations and social organizations. PSL's ability to publish was severely limited, and the activities of those ministries headed by PSL activists (ministries of agriculture, public administration, and education) were hindered.

The date of the elections, which, according to the Yalta and Potsdam agreements, were to take place "as soon as possible" after the end of the war, finally took place on January 19, 1947, following the arrests of candidates to the Diet and members of Electoral Boards. The returns announced by the remaining members of these boards gave the PSL ten percent of the vote and six percent of the mandate. The number of votes the PSL actually received has been estimated at around 80 percent, based on the results in those districts that could be checked by the PSL. Obviously such calculations are only approximate, and exact data is unavailable. PSL contested the validity of the elections. Their protest was not recognized, and a new government, headed by Józef Cyrankiewicz, was installed in February 1947. No PSL representatives were included in the new government.

All of this occurred after electoral experiences in other "people's democracies." The elections in Hungary in 1945 had not been rigged, and the Smallholders' Party—analogous to the Polish PSL—received 57 percent of the vote and an actual majority in the Parliament. Communists and Social Democrats received 17 percent each, representing each about 750,000 votes. Ferenc Nagy became premier, and Zoltan Tildy became president, both from the Smallholders' Party. However, it happened that Jozsef Révai, a leading theoretician of the Communist Party of Hungary, was quite right when he said of his party: "Although we were a minority in the Parliament and the government, we represented the leading force. We had decisive control over the police forces; our strength—the strength of our party and of the working class—was multiplied by the fact that we always could count on the help of the Soviet Union and of the Red Army."

In February 1947, the Hungarian Ministry of Internal Affairs, led by Laszlo Rajk (who was later condemned to death), announced the discovery of a "plot against the security of the Soviet Army" in which deputies of the Smallholders' Party were supposedly involved. Some deputies were arrested; others managed to escape abroad.

However, other opposition parties were organizing to replace the Smallholders' Party. The Hungarian Independence Party was one, and it demanded, among other things, curtailing the activities of the political police and ending the system of "people's tribunals," which delivered verdicts in a hasty and simplified manner.

New elections were held in Hungary in August 1947, and the National Front reportedly received 60 percent of the vote, including 21 percent for the Communists, leaving the opposition parties with the remaining 40 percent. Nevertheless, by the end of 1947, the mandates of the Independence party deputies were annulled, and the party itself was dissolved by the minister of internal affairs.

In June 1948, the Communists and Socialists were united into the Hungarian Working People's Party, and by 1949 they were the only party left in Hungary. Similar events were taking place in the other people's democracies. The Communist parties, with the exception of the Yugoslavian party, were consolidating under the direction of the Soviet-led Informational Bureau of Communist and Workers' Parties (Cominform, created in September 1947 to replace Comintern, which had been dissolved in 1943).

Like the Hungarian Smallholders' Party, the PSL (Polish Peasants' Party) for two years played the role of a national opposition party. The peculiar character of such opposition was perhaps even more clearly expressed in Hungary than in Poland: it was the opposition of a majority against the "leading force" of a minority. Nevertheless, by 1947 the PSL was severely weakened by arrests; its organizational abilities, as well as the personal capabilities of its members, were reduced to a minimum. In Bulgaria, in September 1947, the secretary of the Peasants' Union, Nikola Petkov, was condemned to death. In Rumania, in October 1947, the former premier and leader of the Peasants' party, Juliu Maniu, was sentenced to life imprisonment (it was officially emphasized that he received this sentence only because, at the time, the death sentence had been abolished in Rumania). The situation of the PSL leaders in Poland was becoming increasingly dangerous. Under these conditions, the president of the party, Stanisław Mikołajczyk, decided to abandon political activity, and he escaped abroad in October 1947. Within a short time, other PSL activists also managed to leave, effectively ending the PSL's oppositional role.

On December 15, 1948, the PPS formally merged with the PPR, thus creating the Polish United Workers' Party (PZPR). The screening of members that occurred in connection with this unification involved over 100,000 PPS people and was conducted over the two years preceding the unification.

In August 1948, the PPR itself became a target, centering on the "rightist-nationalist deviation"; and in November 1949, during the Third Plenary Meeting of the PZPR Central Committee under Bolesław Bierut, the purging of this deviation began.

The issue of the "rightist-nationalist deviation" is not entirely clear. The deviation had reportedly originated at a time when, as Stefan Staszewski said at the Third Plenary Meeting, "the party was deprived of contact with Moscow" (as a result of the arrest by the Germans of the only two party leaders who knew the secret code for communicating with the Soviet Union). Gomułka and Marian Spychalski, nominal head of the People's Army intelligence services, were accused of cooperation with representatives from the exile government during the war.

Just before the Third Plenary Meeting, a marshal of the Soviet Union, Konstanty Rokossowski, was named marshal of Poland and minister of national defense and, at the meeting, joined the Central Committee. As expressed by General Marian Spychalski, the official line was that "this strengthened our People's Army, both ideologically and by weeding out our enemies, the nationalists. Today our army has a stronger, more secure leadership with Comrade Marshal Rokossowski at its head."

As with the PPS, the PSL officially ended by unification. In November 1949, the very depleted and reorganized PSL was joined with the SL to form the United Peasants' Party (ZSL). But these were merely symbolic acts. The opposition had been eliminated by 1947, after the elections and Mikołajczyk's escape.

The enthusiasm that had greeted the formation of the Second Republic after World War One was notably absent among the Polish people when the Germans evacuated Polish soil at the end of the occupation. The mood was more similar to that which appeared after the Polish insurrections of 1830 and 1863. The Polish people had survived a war, but it was also yet another unsuccessful insurrection.

The establishment after World War Two of the new system in Poland by the Soviets was preceded by agreements between the Soviet Union, United States, and Great Britain. These agreements, at Teheran and Yalta, essentially provided the Red Army and the NKVD a free hand in Poland. They also enabled the Soviets to undermine the Polish government-in-exile and to organize another government for Poland that would have the full confidence of the Soviet Union. This was followed by the liquidation of political opposition, the standardization of information, and censorship. Permissible opinions ceased to differ one from another. Political standardization was accompanied by organizational standardization in other areas: the cooperative movements, labor unions, local self-government, and higher education all came under the domination of the state and the ruling party. The liquidation of the opposition was rationalized by the statement, "uniformity allows us to conserve social resources." Arrests were supposed to be good for the nation's health.

Poland's sovereignty was further limited by military, political, and economic integration into the Soviet bloc.

The conspicuous presence of the Red Army is no longer necessary for Soviet control of Poland: simply the threat, from time to time and in a more or less veiled manner, of Soviet military force is sufficient. This threat is even officially acknowledged, and it is an important element of propaganda; postwar examples of the use of this force—in the GDR, in Hungary, and in Czechoslovakia—add to it a measure of credibility.

CHAPTER 2

A MEASURE OF FREEDOM

Background: Stalinism and the Consolidation of Power

By 1949, the unification of politics and of social and economic life was already accomplished in Poland. Political opposition had been liquidated, and the direct subordination of the Polish government to Soviet authority was fully apparent.

Since the policy of the Soviet Union at this time was formulated by Stalin, one is justified in speaking of Stalinism not only in the Soviet Union but also in Poland; in this manner, the foreign origins of the socio-political system transplanted to Poland are emphasized.

The bloc of people's democracies was being formed. From the very beginning, the events in these countries exhibited important similarities. Yet it was not "historical laws" that determined this similarity, but rather the effects of common causes: directives issued by the central leadership of the Soviet Union.

Beginning in the spring of 1947, the Polish authorities carried on a "battle for commerce." This consisted of using taxation and administrative and punitive measures to undermine the conduct of private commerce. Over two years, the number of privately-owned stores decreased by half. Cooperatives were centralized and deprived of their authenticity and independence. In April 1949, the Central Planning Office for the Polish economy was dissolved, for promoting ideas that PPR economists claimed were too independent and insufficiently subordinated to the party, and it was replaced by the State Commission of Economic Planning. A one-sector, centrally-controlled economic system was being created. Agriculture was one of the surviving exceptions. The Catholic

Church, embattled and increasingly restricted, was the other independent enclave in the system of state rule.

On November 11–13, 1949, the Third Plenary Meeting of PZPR Central Committee took place. The meeting adopted resolutions in several personnel matters: Władysław Gomułka, Zenon Kliszko, and Marian Spychalski were removed from the Central Committee and deprived of "the right to hold any party positions of authority." (Gomułka had been replaced as secretary-general of the party by Bolesław Bierut in 1948.)

According to the resolution, Gomułka and Kliszko had "declined to help the party unmask enemy agents, who forced their way into various positions partly as a result of their [Gomułka's and Kliszko's] reprehensible toleration." Spychalski, "in his party and state activity both during the occupation and after the liberation, exhibited criminal political blindness which ensued from his falsely nationalistic stance . . . this stance allowed the infiltration into responsible positions of enemy agents who acted against the revolutionary movement in People's Poland and on behalf of foreign intelligence."

At the same plenary meeting, it was resolved to admit to the Central Committee the recently nominated marshal of Poland, Konstanty Rokossowski, a Russian citizen of Polish descent—either Rokossowski had been admitted to the party in the meantime or he became a member by some automatic process. The nomination of Rokossowski, previously marshal of the Soviet Union, as commander-in-chief of the Polish army was a rather rare event in international relations and symbolized the dependence of the Polish army on Soviet authorities. Equally significant was the presence of Russian advisors in the Polish army and the subordination of army affairs to the decisions of the party and the police, which, in turn, were subordinated to Russian directives.

Gomułka, Spychalski, and Kliszko were removed only from their party positions, but in light of Communist practice, one could suspect that they would be arrested and that their lives would be in danger. In fact, in the other people's democracies, terror was no longer limited to the political opposition and had turned against Communists, the very people who had themselves been the persecutors of non-Communists.

Rajk and his codefendants in Hungary had already been hanged by the time Gomułka, Kliszko, and Spychalski were removed from the Central Committee, and Kostov was hanged in Bulgaria shortly after the Third Plenary Meeting. The terror was milder in Poland, but there were those who were killed immediately after the war and in the early fifties. However, those Communist leaders accused of deviations managed to survive.

The purging of the Communist cadres appears to have been part of an overall Soviet policy aimed at isolating the people's democracies from western Europe. In June and July 1947, the Soviet Union and people's democracies, as well as Finland, rejected participation in the Marshall Plan for the reconstruction of Europe after the war. On June 28, 1948, a meeting of Cominform in Bucharest condemned the Yugoslav Communist Party; on September 28, 1949, the USSR annulled its mutual defense treaty with Yugoslavia. The people's democracies followed suit.

In 1949, the USSR backed out of the Berlin conflict, ending its blockade of West Berlin on May 12. That summer, the Communist guerrilla movement in Greece was effectively wiped out. The Soviet sphere of influence in Europe became fixed. At the same time, there was retrenchment against external influences.

In September 1949, TASS announced the explosion of a Soviet atomic bomb. This successful attempt added new confidence to Soviet foreign policy.

In 1949, the reach of Communism was greatly extended in Asia, though this later proved to be a mixed blessing at best, and on October 1, 1949, Mao Zedong officially announced the creation of the People's Republic of China.

On June 25, 1950, the armies of Communist-ruled North Korea crossed the 38th Parallel and rapidly approached Seoul, the capital of South Korea. This was the beginning of the Korean War, which has been considered a cause of the increased military expenditures in the people's democracies.

Clearly, the North Koreans would not have attacked without a prior understanding with the USSR or with the newly-created People's Republic of China. The attack provided the Soviets with a test of the American defenses. The three-year war, in which so-called Chinese volunteers fought on the side of North Korea, while the U.N. armies, composed mostly of Americans, supported the South, only ended in stalemate. The negotiated demarcation line near the 38th Parallel became, in fact, the official boundary between the two Koreas. The war played an important propaganda role for the Soviet camp and was used to heighten a sense of external threat and internal cohesion among the members of the Soviet bloc.

On July 31, 1951, a trial of several generals and higher officers began in Warsaw. General Stanisław Tatar, Colonel Jerzy Kirchmayer, and others were accused of having plotted a *coup d'état* in 1947 and 1948. General Marian Spychalski, arrested in May 1950, testified as a witness that the former secretary-general, Władysław Gomułka, had been informed about Spychalski's contacts with the accused officers. On the opening day of the trial, Gomułka was arrested.

A total of nineteen high officers, mostly from the air force and navy, had been executed between 1951 and 1953. In October 1956, it was officially acknowledged that these officers had been unjustly condemned to death. Their names were made public only in December 1956.

Arrests and trials of Communist functionaries took place in other people's democracies as well. In Prague, from November 20–27, 1952, fourteen Communist activists were put on trial, among them Rudolf Slánský and Vladimir Clementis. They were accused of creating an "anti-state center," of treason, espionage, and sabotage; and they were found to be "Trotskyite-Titoite-Zionist-bourgeois-nationalist traitors and enemies of the Czechoslovak nation, of the system of people's democracies, and of socialism." Eleven people were condemned to death and executed on December 3. Three others were given life sentences.

In Poland, on July 22, 1952, the official name of the state was changed from the Republic of Poland to the Polish People's Republic. Other people's democracies became "people's" or "democratic" republics like the DDR. Until 1960, Czechoslovakia was only a republic; since 1960, it has been a socialist republic.

On October 25, 1952, the second postwar elections to the Diet since January 1947, when the Peasants' Party had participated, were held. In 1952, a single list of candidates was sponsored by the All-Poland Committee of the National Front. It was officially announced that the front's candidates received 99.8 percent of all valid votes, which conformed with the ruling ideology, according to which the correct side should not only win the election but should win in such a way that only a fraction of one percent could be recorded in opposition.

On January 13, 1953, TASS announced the discovery of a doctors' plot in the Kremlin Polyclinic. The doctors were described as "monsters in human shape" and were said to be in contact with "the international bourgeois-nationalist organization Joint, organized by American espionage." It was also announced that some of the doctors were connected with British intelligence and that they were alleged to have planned assassinations of the highest party and state officials and to have murdered several important functionaries. The TASS communiqué augured a resumption of arrests and propaganda-oriented show trials similar to what occurred in the great purge of the thirties. No doubt many Soviet leaders were concerned and anxious to avert such a threat.

1953: Changes in Government and Social Disturbances

On the morning of March 6, 1953, it was announced that Josef Stalin had died at 9:50 the previous evening. The medical reports stated that during the night of March 1–2, Stalin had suffered a cerebral hemorrhage "resulting in paralysis of the right side of the body and permanent loss of consciousness." Respiratory difficulties (Cheyne-Stokes breathing, periodic and intermittent) followed. On March 5, the day of his death, respiration became shallow and very rapid.

After Stalin's death, Grigorii Malenkov assumed the functions of party secretary-general and of premier. However, his career as secretary-general was short-lived. On March 14, Malenkov resigned, and, after several months without a replacement, Khrushchev became secretary-general in September 1953. Malenkov remained premier until February 1955.

On March 14, 1953, Klement Gottwald, the first secretary of the Czechoslovak Communist Party and president of the republic, died. On March 21, Gottwald's previous positions were divided between two men: Antonín Novotný became first secretary of the party and Antonín Zapotocky became president of the republic. Similar divisions of official posts took place later in other people's democracies. The exercise of power was being diffused: power no longer belonged to a single individual. This was true even of the exercise of limited power in countries dependent on the Soviet Union. The principle of leadership was being eroded.

On March 27, an amnesty was announced in the USSR for all those sentenced to less than five years' imprisonment.

On April 4, the Ministry of Internal Affairs issued a statement announcing that the Kremlin doctors arrested on January 19 had been cleared of all charges. This was a public admission of official error, and it raised the issue of culpability.

On April 10, *Pravda* attacked both the former minister of internal affairs, Ignatiev, and the deputy minister and head of the Office of Investigation, Rumin. Rumin was arrested and eventually sentenced to death in July 1954.

Organizational and personnel changes were taking place in the Soviet Union, and one wondered who was in charge. On April 16, it was announced that the country would be governed by a collective leadership composed of Malenkov, Beria, and Molotov (those who had spoken at Stalin's funeral). Within three months, Beria was eliminated. Three years later, Malenkov and Molotov were accused of belonging to an "anti-party" group and were removed from the party leadership and their government positions in June 1957. There was apparently some consensus in the ruling apparatus for a change in operating modes but no clear consensus on the form this change should take.

On May 30, 1953, a painful monetary reform was announced in Czechoslovakia. On June 1, the workers of the Lenin factory in Pilsen (formerly the Skoda armaments factory) organized a march, which quickly escalated into riots and were suppressed by the security forces using firearms.

Living conditions in East Germany also left much to be desired. On June 16, 1953, East Berlin construction workers protested an increase in production norms. Strikes and demonstrations quickly spread from the Berlin factories throughout the DDR. The Berlin demonstrators were fired upon by the police, and the Soviet Headquarters announced a state of emergency and called in Soviet armored detachments. After two days the protest was suppressed. Shortly afterwards, however, the East German government announced changes in its economic policy and promised that the workers' demands would be discussed.

On June 29, *Pravda* published an article criticizing "the cult of personality."

In a Central Committee plenary meeting held from July 2–7, 1953, Malenkov made a speech criticizing Beria. The resolution of the plenary meeting condemned Beria, and an article in *Pravda* claimed that Beria "had plans to seize the party and state leadership in order to destroy *de facto* the Communist party and to supplant its long-standing policy with a policy of capitulation ultimately leading to the restoration of capitalism." According to some sources Beria was killed in July 1953, but others claim a secret trial of Beria and his collaborators took place in December 1953, and Beria was condemned to execution by a firing squad.

In July 1953, prisoners of the Vorkuta labor camp went on strike. Supervisors from Moscow promised the prisoners an improvement in their living conditions. But in one of the camps, the surrounded prisoners refused to surrender, and the guards opened fire killing several prisoners.

Changes were also taking place in the DDR security apparatus around this time, although the nature of these changes was not always clear to outside observers. On July 24, Wilhelm Zeisser, the DDR minister of security, was dismissed.

The June riots in East Germany did contribute to an improvement of the economic situation. A delegation from the DDR visited Moscow from August 20–22, 1953 and arranged for an increase in shipments of food and raw materials from the Soviet Union to Germany. The USSR also returned to the DDR the ownership of German industrial enterprises that had been requisitioned by the Soviet Union immediately after the war. On August 24, 1953, the government of Poland relinquished (effective January 1, 1954) the right to further war reparations paid by the DDR to Poland.

In the area of international relations, the Soviet Union began to relax its self-imposed isolation. After July 27, 1953, a cease-fire was in effect in Korea. Diplomatic relations between the USSR and Yugoslavia were resumed on August 14. The foreign ministers of France, the United States, Great Britain, and the Soviet Union got together in Berlin from January 25 to February 18, 1954, which led to other meetings, such as the Geneva Conference on Indochina, from April 16 to July 21, 1954.

In August 1953, at the meeting of the Supreme Soviet, Premier Grigorii Malenkov spoke of the need to raise the living standard of the population. Similar suggestions could be found in the September 15 speech of the Czechoslovak premier, Široký. Imre Nagy in Hungary had proclaimed a similar policy shortly before.

In Poland in 1953, it was still impossible to detect significant changes in methods of government or even in the membership of the governing group. The trial of the Bishop of Kielce, Czesław Kaczmarek, began on September 14, 1953. The Primate of Poland, Cardinal Stefan Wyszyński, was arrested (officially termed "interned") on September 25. Early in 1954, several hundred priests, including nine bishops, were in various prisons. The Polish Church was called the church of silence, though this was inaccurate: the Church did try to defend itself. It protested against the infringement of its independence with the decree of February 9, 1953, "About the Staffing of Church Positions"; it defended itself against infiltration and the subordination of Church matters to state or party directives. The actions of the Communist party against the Church testified to the permanence of the party's basic principles: namely, to abolish everything independent of the party and the party-state.

Following the USSR and the DDR, Hungary officially condemned the functionaries in charge of the police and the judicial system. On March 13, 1954, a military court in Budapest condemned General Gabor Peter, the minister of security, to life imprisonment. Gyula Decsi, the minister of justice, was given a nine-year sentence. However, in Poland the police still reigned supreme.

In 1954, the functions of premier and party first secretary were separated also in Poland. On March 19, 1954, Józef Cyrankiewicz reassumed the premiership, replacing Bolesław Bierut. Bierut retained his position as party first secretary.

1953/1954. The Respect for Law: the Party and the Security Forces

On December 5, 1953, Lieutenant Colonel Józef Światło, a deputy department director in the Ministry of Public Security, escaped to West Berlin. At a press conference held in Washington on September 28, 1954, Światło spoke about the fate of the Field family, American citizens imprisoned in Poland and Hungary. Światło had arrested Hermann Field in August 1949, when Field came to Warsaw in search of his brother Noel, who had disappeared earlier in Czechoslovakia, and the US Department of State had lodged protests with the Polish and Hungarian governments, demanding that the Field family be freed. In October 1954, following Światło's press conference, Hermann Field was released from a Polish prison. American pressure had certainly contributed to Field's release, but there was something else. The case in many ways resembled that of the Kremlin doctors. From all the evidence collected at the time, there is every reason to believe that the alleged contacts with the Fields were to be the linchpin of a series of upcoming political trials. Here was someone apparently destined to spend a long time in prison—if not his entire life—who was set free.

On September 28, 1954, Radio Free Europe began a daily broadcast program with Lieutenant Colonel Światło speaking about the Polish Communist movement and its methods of wielding power. A selection of transcrips from Światło's programs appeared in the pamphlet, "Behind the Scenes in the Party and Security," published by the Free Europe Committee in 1955–56 and which was reaching Polish readers. Światło dealt mainly with the role of the PZPR, the Ministry of Public Security, and the Soviet agents in Poland. He discussed the connections between the party and police and the police's control of the party. Over both the party and police in Poland were the Soviet authorities. "We must distinguish between two groups," said Światło. "There is the Soviet group: the Kremlin (or, more exactly, the Politburo), the Soviet advisors in the Warsaw Ministry of Security, and the Soviet ambassador in Warsaw. This is the Soviet side, and thus the side of decisions and instructions. On a lower level is the so-called Polish group: its members include Bierut and the PZPR Politburo, Rokossowski, and the Ministry of Security. This is the executive group."

Światło described the intelligence and espionage activities of the Polish Communist movement before and during the German occupation, and he exposed the duplicity of many of the trials in Poland regarding various people accused of contacts with the police or with an intelligence network before or during the war. Światło's report on the cases of Włodzimierz Lechowicz and Alfred Jaroszewicz, who were arrested in 1948 and spent many years in prison, is typical: "The accused claimed that although it was true that they worked in PKB and in 'Start' [underground groups active during the war], and that they worked in the prewar police, they did so as Soviet agents. They referred to Fogelson, an agent of Soviet intelligence in Poland who recruited them before the war, and they cited reports which they had given him. All of this information had been known to the party for some time. Bierut knew Fogelson personally, since they worked in the same sector."

Many of the facts Światło presented were not new; but he made them public. After his broadcasts it was more difficult to claim ignorance about the falsification of election returns, documents, and confessions, about tortures during interrogations, about gangs of party thugs and murders committed by the political police with the full knowledge of their party superiors. Clearly this was more the story of Mafia gangsters than of alleged leaders of the workers' movement.

In late November and early December 1954, when Światło's programs had already been broadcast for a month, a "meeting of central party activists" took place in Warsaw.

In his reminiscences, *Half a Century: The Writers,* Jerzy Putrament quotes his own notes from November 29, 1954: "Historical day: meeting of the Central Committee activists. Bierut's report with suggestions about the reorganization of security." Describing the course of the meeting, Putrament states: "Generally speaking, the security sector was criticized, but not alone: the style of party work, including that of the leadership, was also addressed. Given the importance of the issues concerning the security forces, much higher levels of responsibility could not help but be implicated. For example, for the first time in five years Gomułka's case was discussed. Kłosiewicz, in a long critical speech, said directly: 'either he is guilty and must be tried, or he is innocent and must be freed!' Several days after the meeting, Comrade Gomułka was freed. . . . On December 1, the meeting ended in the same dramatic way, a confrontation between aggressive attacks and a rather helpless defense."

The party historian Władysław Góra, in *The History of People's Poland, 1950–1954* (published by the Warsaw Center for Party Propaganda in April 1967), claims that: "In November 1954, a meeting of the party activists took place in the PZPR Central Committee. . . . For the first time, a very critical attitude was adopted toward the activities of the Politburo and party leadership. The meeting raised the issue of abuses and deviations within the public security apparatus, and it condemned the imprisonment of Władysław Gomułka. There was a discussion of the need for a more humane attitude toward the people and for party policy to strive for greater integration of the problems of building socialism with the immediate interests of every citizen. The participants also spoke of the need to rehabilitate the Communist Party of Poland and to make changes in economic policy."

The November–December meeting was a landmark event vis-à-vis PZPR policies. Party functionaries were already taking certain liberties in criticizing their superiors, though the day was still far off when it would spread beyond a small circle of highly-placed party functionaries.

Institutional changes soon followed. A decree of the State Council dated December 7, 1954, dissolved the Office of the Minister of Public Security and created the Ministry of Internal Affairs and the Committee of Public Security attached to the Council of Ministers. Stanisław Radkiewicz, for many years the minister of Public Security, became minister of State Farms. Even if these changes were on the whole nominal, they were significant as an admission on the part of the leadership that previously something had been wrong in the security sector.

Władysław Gomułka was freed on December 13. The release of Gomułka had political implications that went beyond party affairs. As Gomułka was considered the leader of "rightist-nationalist deviation," the incarnation of evil under Stalinism, his release signified a major policy shift and was not made public. Party members were themselves officially informed about Gomułka's release only on April 6, 1956, almost a year and a half after the fact.

In an unsigned article in the December 1954 issue of *Nowe Drogi* (*New Roads,* a theoretical organ of PZPR), entitled "Let Us Strengthen People's Justice," the public was given its first hint of what lay behind the institutional changes. In the article one could read that "the Party and the government have recently concluded that there were cases involving serious infringements of the law by particular sections of the security forces, cases of activity contrary to the statutes of people's law, to party policy, and to the ideas of humanist socialism. . . ." The article also prepared the way ideologically for Gomułka's rehabilitation. The thesis about the intensification of the class struggle during the building of socialism was reiterated: "The old truth of Marxism-Leninism states that as socialism progresses, the class struggle does not wane, but becomes more intense." At the same time, it was asserted that this process of intensification had various aspects, and it was dangerous to oversimplify the struggle with the enemy. For example, in the case of the Home Army (AK): "Thousands of former AK members are today dedicated workers in all areas of our economic, cultural, and political life, dedicated participants in the building of socialism. . . . Is it not clear that our attitude toward every person should be discerning, that we have to combat all discrimination against those who work honestly for the people's homeland? This concerns not only the former AK members. It also concerns all former members of reactionary parties and groups that were active in Poland before the war and during the occupation—parties and groups that were hostile to the masses, hostile to the Polish nation."

The issue of deviations within the party was stated to be similar. Deviations are "expressions of the pressure of the class enemy, expressions of the pressure of a foreign, hostile ideology on our ranks." But they should not be identified with subversion: "not all deviations are colored and directed by subversion." This relatively moderate formulation may be understood as the beginning of Gomułka's public rehabilitation. It was a long process of gradual ideological concessions culminating in the official admission that the dangerous "rightist-nationalist deviation" never existed.

The December article in *Nowe Drogi* also recalled the essence of the respect for law. "The security forces do not stand above the law. . . . They are constitutionally subordinate to the leadership of the Council of Ministers, just like all the other state agencies. . . . The employees of the security forces are subject to the laws of the Polish People's Republic in the same way as every other citizen. . . ."

There were also reminders about the independence of the courts and the possibility of releasing innocent people: "The court of the Republic has a responsibility to assess the guilt of the accused—this assessment is based on a conscientious examination of all materials provided by the investigation and the court trial; on the basis of this assessment, the court inflicts a punishment on the criminal and frees those who are unjustly accused." Although one might consider this axiomatic, the view that people might be unjustly accused, and that it was the court's responsibility to free those who were, took on added significance when appearing in the PZPR theoretical organ.

The *Nowe Drogi* article also specified the obligations of the party and the prosecutor's office to defend the respect for law. "The Office of the Prosecutor is responsible for monitoring the investigative activity of the security forces. . . . It must be stated that the proper party sectors have not sufficiently reminded the prosecutor's office and the judiciary about their constitutional responsibility with respect to the security forces." These were the first references to the indirect responsibility of the party for lawlessness.

The daily press printed a long speech made by Bolesław Bierut at the Third Plenary Meeting of the PZPR Central Committee, January 21–24, 1955. Bierut mentioned that the "mistakes" in the party resulted from "the tendency to widen the field of activity of the security forces, from attempts to extend their functions, or from their interference in various aspects of state and social activity under conditions which did not justify such interference."

Taking the party's admissions of guilt one step further, the new secretary of the Central Committee, Jerzy Morawski, wrote in a *Nowe Drogi* article (February 1955): "There were cases when innocent people were arrested and illegally detained and cases in which, instead of attempting to establish the objective truth, the evidence was stretched to conform with predetermined false accusations. There were cases when scandalously inadmissible methods were used during investigations. . . . In the course of the past several months, the Politburo has taken a series of steps to remove these deviations and restore healthy relations in the security forces. People who were illegally arrested have been released and rehabilitated. Those guilty of committing or tolerating abuses have been removed from the party and held legally accountable for their actions."

Some parts of Morawski's statement conformed significantly in tone to Światło's formulations. Four months had passed since Radio Free Europe had broadcast the first of Światło's programs about the party and the police. Światło's broadcasts evidently raised an issue that was crucial for everybody: the issue of police terror. They also contributed to the fact that the relationship between the party and the police became a subject of lively interest within the party and—even more importantly—a subject of public party pronouncements. As a result, the party acknowledged its "mistakes" and asserted the need for the party to control the security organs more directly. Jerzy Morawski wrote about the release from prison and rehabilitation of those illegally arrested. Some of them were no longer alive and could be neither released nor rehabilitated in court. The rehabilitations that began at the end of 1954 would continue for two more years. Public attention focused on them especially in late 1956 and 1957, when the names of those who had been posthumously rehabilitated were made public. This rehabilitation had been accomplished through an extra-court procedure and concerned mostly officers of the Polish army who, at the invitation of the Polish government, had returned to Poland from Great Britain after the end of the war.

The International Background

In the summer of 1955 the Soviet government was pursuing a policy of "détente" with the West while simultaneously working toward consolidating its realm. Both the Warsaw Pact and the state treaty with Austria were signed in May 1955. Later in the same month, talks began between the Soviet Union and Yugoslavia. In July the leaders of the four world powers met in Geneva. In September, the Soviet Union established diplomatic relations with West Germany and decided to close down its military base in Porkkala-Udd, near Helsinki.

The signing of the Warsaw Pact was preceded by a conference held in Moscow from November 29 to December 2, 1954. Government delegations from the Soviet Union, Poland, Czechoslovakia, East Germany, Hungary, Rumania, Bulgaria, and Albania took part (this was the order in which they were listed in the official documents of the conference). A representative of the People's Republic of China also participated in the deliberations. The official communiqué called these meetings "a conference of European countries concerning the assurance of peace and security in Europe." It was announced that the participants "examined the situation created in Europe by some Western countries signing the separatist Paris agreements concerning the remilitarization of West Germany and its inclusion in military pacts aimed against peace-loving European states" (the Paris Accords were signed on October 23, 1954). The conference participants stated that in the event of the ratification of the Paris Accords, the countries represented in Moscow "are determined to take common measures in the organization and command of their armed forces, as well as other steps necessary to strengthen their defensive capabilities."

Government delegations from these same eight countries, which made up the European part of the Soviet bloc, met for a conference in Warsaw from May 11–14, 1954. Yugoslavia did not participate in any of these meetings. A *rapprochement* between Yugoslavia and the Soviet Union was imminent, but not to such an extent that the USSR could induce Yugoslavia to join in a military alliance. But the Chinese observer was still there (the Sino-Soviet quarrels began much later).

On May 14, the representatives of the eight countries signed the so-called Warsaw Pact. The pact's aim was to legitimize Soviet intervention in the internal and international affairs of the people's democracies. Occasionally this was viewed as a sign of progress. But very shortly afterwards one could observe a growing desire for even greater progress among pact countries: a desire to leave the pact altogether (as in Hungary and Poland in 1956).

Article 3 of the Warsaw Pact provides for consultations among the parties "concerning all the more significant international affairs involving common interests" as well as immediate consultation when, "according to the opinion of any one of them, there exists the danger of armed aggression against one or several member states." Each particular state is consequently obligated to report on and divulge its political plans and intentions. And the disproportion of forces means that, in reality, it is the Soviet Union that wields all the power, and the other countries must meet its demands and not vice versa (such *de facto* one-sidedness characterizes several other articles of the pact).

Article 4 states that every participating state, "in case of military aggression in Europe against one or several member states . . . will provide immediate help . . . to the country or countries subject to such aggression . . . including the use of military force." It is important that Article 4 specifies "in cases of military aggression in Europe." Thus the pact does not oblige the participants—at least not explicitly—to help the Soviet Union if it were to conduct a war in Asia. If such obligations do in fact exist, they are not stated in the Warsaw Pact.

Article 7 states that "the parties to the pact pledge themselves not to participate in any coalitions or alliances and to abstain from any agreements whose goals contradict the aims of this pact." This article might constitute a pretext for significant limitations on the sovereignty of the signatories, since the final interpretation of the goals of the Warsaw Pact may be imposed on the other countries by the Soviet Union, the strongest member.

On May 15, a "State Treaty Concerning the Reconstruction of Independent and Democratic Austria" was signed in Vienna between Austria, the USSR, Great Britain, the United States, and France. The Soviet Union agreed to the withdrawal by December 31, 1955, of the occupying forces from Austria and to a compensated transfer of Soviet factories on Austrian territory.

From May 27 to June 2, 1955, high-level meetings between Soviet and Yugoslavian representatives took place in Belgrade and on the island of Brioni. On his arrival at the Belgrade airport on May 26, the leader of the Soviet delegation, Nikita Khrushchev, spoke of the "subversive role" which "the now unmasked enemies of the nation—Beria, Abakumov, and others—played in Soviet and Yugoslav relations. We have carefully examined the evidence on which the serious accusations and insults against Yugoslavia were based. The facts prove that this evidence was fabricated by the enemies of the nation, sordid agents of imperialism who infiltrated our party ranks by the use of fraud."

Khrushchev's statement suggested that "the now unmasked enemies of the nation" might also have affected other elements of Soviet policy, not only those relating to Yugoslavia. The Soviet-Yugoslav declaration, for example, stated that "the problems arising from differences in social systems and from differences in the implementation of socialism are the exclusive concern of individual countries." This was the official Soviet recognition of the distinctiveness of the Yugoslavian model of socialism, and such recognition could encourage communists in other countries of the Soviet bloc to choose political variants different from the Soviet model.

On June 7, 1955, the Soviet government approached the West German government with a note proposing the establishment of diplomatic relations. The note, written in a pleasant and friendly style, mentioned that "it is well known that during the period of friendly relations and cooperation between our nations, both sides benefited greatly." From September 9–13, 1955, talks between West German and Soviet delegations took place in Moscow, which resulted in an agreement to establish diplomatic relations. The danger of the Paris Accords, invoked in the Warsaw Pact, did not constitute an impediment.

During his stay in Moscow, the German Chancellor, Konrad Adenauer, inquired about the "release of those Germans who are either still imprisoned in the Soviet Union or within its sphere of influence. . . ." Molotov claimed that there were only several thousand convicted war criminals in the Soviet Union. On September 29, the Presidium of the Supreme Soviet issued a resolution "concerning the early release and repatriation of German war criminals serving their terms of imprisonment in the Soviet Union." This raised questions in Poland about the fate of Poles remaining in the Soviet Union.

From July 17–23, a conference of the four world powers took place in Geneva. The participants were President Eisenhower and prime ministers Bulganin, Eden, and Faure. This was the first summit conference of the Allies since the Potsdam Conference of July 1945 (though France had not participated in the previous conferences), and, however meager the concrete results, the very fact of the Geneva conference was important. "The spirit of Geneva" resounded in the press.

In September 1955, the Finnish president, Paasikivi, and Prime Minister Kekkonen visited the Soviet Union and renewed for the next twenty years the friendship, cooperation, and mutual assistance accord of April 6, 1948. Simultaneously, the Soviet Union relinquished its right to lease the Finnish territory of Porkkala-Udd, which had been granted to the Soviet Union in the armistice agreement of 1944 and reaffirmed in the 1947 peace treaty with Finland. The Soviet Union closed down its military base in Porkkala-Udd and withdrew its troops. It was also announced in September that the last Soviet troops had left Austria. The withdrawal of Soviet troops from Austria and Finland added a measure of realism to hopes for the neutralization of Central Europe. Such hopes were to revive during the following years.

The Thaw

From July 31 to August 14, 1955, "The Fifth World Festival of Youth for Peace and Friendship" (the somewhat unfortunate name was probably concocted in Russian) was taking place in Warsaw. The festival enabled young people from various countries to meet each other, something that had not been easy in the past. Private contacts with foreigners even within the Soviet bloc had been extremely limited until then. Such contacts cast doubt upon the loyalty of the citizen, since they exposed him to life uncontrolled by the local authorities. Contacts with Westerners, not to mention travel abroad, were virtually unthinkable.

The Warsaw Youth Festival was an occasion for numerous cultural events, and the "All-Poland Young Artists' Exhibition" in the Warsaw Arsenal was perhaps the most significant and best known of these. The works of young artists were on the whole still *engagé,* but they had broken with the canons of socialist realism. It was not an academic show.

Soon other works by previously condemned artists were exhibited. Articles, reports, and even poetry about previously unmentionable issues began to appear in literary periodicals. This was "the thaw." This word came to signify a somewhat more daring cultural policy on the part of the authorities. At the same time, intellectuals and artists were exerting pressure to extend further the limits of freedom proposed by the government.

The interdependence of the Soviet camp, or, more exactly, the system of dependence on the Soviet Union, was breaking down. Rehabilitations and the indictments of functionaries of the security organs, first in the Soviet Union and then in Poland, led to a growing public awareness of instability in the previous system of terror. The fairly cohesive ideology was weakened—the vision of society led by the party and its "infallible" leaders was falling apart.

Public cultural life and the media were still controlled by the party and state apparatus. But the subservience of subordinates to their superiors in the party was decreasing.

Many of the party disclosures were no surprise to PZPR outsiders and even to many party insiders. But what was significant was that these disclosures were made public—in newspapers, speeches, and literature. There was now a general commitment to narrow the discrepancy between what was said in public and what was only privately felt.

Adam Ważyk's "Poem for Adults," published in *Nowa Kultura* on August 19, 1955, achieved a certain notoriety. The work was dated June–July 1955. Ważyk wrote about people being forced to lie, about the fact that "there are those waiting for documents, / waiting for justice, / there are those who wait for a long time." His poem ended with a litany of complaints and demands: "we seek redress and ask on our land / for tired people / for keys which open doors / for rooms with windows / for walls without mildew / for hatred of documents / for a holy human time / for a safe return home / for a simple distinction between word and act / We ask for . . . simple truths, the seeds of freedom / the burning reason . . . we demand it daily / we demand it through the party."

The ending lessened the blasphemous nature of the demands. To demand something through the party could hardly be construed as hostile in attitude. But the party overseers of culture did not like the poem anyway. Paweł Hoffman, the editor of *Nowa Kultura,* was fired soon after publication of the poem. The party thaw was taking place fitfully; concessions were sometimes withdrawn. The more daring people were occasionally sharply criticized. But publications continued to extend the previous limits of permissible public expression.

The September 4, 1955 issue of *Po prostu* (*Simply*), a student magazine, appeared with a new subtitle: "A Weekly of Students and Young Intelligentsia." In the introductory article, the editorial board stated its goals: "We are a group of young enthusiasts—students and university graduates, people who cannot help taking part in everything that goes on around them. We are a group of discontented—we want what is greater, wiser, and better. . . . We want . . . to go beyond the problems of our milieu and take a lively part in everything that goes on in our country. We want to express the opinions of the young on all issues concerning politics, morality, and culture."

During the following two years, the journalists of *Po prostu* wrote about issues which had not officially existed. They published articles about the hopelessness of life in small towns and about the local power cliques, about the dim future awaiting the younger generation, about crime and hooliganism. They searched for solutions to seemingly hopeless situations. *Po prostu* was popular and read not only by the young. The periodical spread an attitude of criticism and journalistic activism.

In the fall of 1955, *Po prostu* began to advocate the creation of intelligentsia clubs. Such clubs had been active for some time after the war: for example, there was the Logophagoi Club (word-eaters) in Cracow from 1947 to 1949. It sponsored lectures by professors like Adam Krzyżanowski and Roman Ingarden and held discussions on scientific, artistic, political, historical, and other topical subjects. In the early fifties, there was no longer a place for such clubs.

In 1955, the Club of the Crooked Circle was formed in a private Warsaw apartment. There were rumors that the police and party had been behind its creation, apparently with the intention of sounding out the opinions of the Warsaw intelligentsia. However, the club certainly became independent of this influence and was a genuine center of intellectual and cultural activity.

In late 1955 and early 1956, intelligentsia clubs were forming throughout the entire country. By the spring of 1956, there were approximately 130 such clubs. The club movement contributed to the revival of provincial towns and was becoming socially useful, as a means for the thinking members of society to exercise influence on the authorities, at least on local authorities. The clubs were extending their contacts beyond the intelligentsia to farmers and workers.

The Twentieth
Party Congress

The Twentieth Congress of the Soviet Communist party took place in Moscow from February 14–25, 1956. It was the first such meeting after Stalin's death. The report of the first secretary, Nikita Khrushchev, to the Central Committee, dealt with "socialist legality": "Experience teaches us that the slightest weakening of socialist legality is used by the enemies of the Soviet state in their infamous diversionary activities. Such activities were conducted by the gang of Beria, now unmasked by the party, which had attempted to remove the state security organs from the control of the party and the Soviet government, to put them above the party and the government, and to create there an atmosphere of lawlessness and license. Guided by its own hostile aims, this gang fabricated accusations against honest leading party workers and other Soviet citizens." The issue came down to: who would be more important, the party or the police?

But on the closing day of the congress, Khrushchev made a speech that would become far more famous. The speech was known as the "secret speech," and for a time certain Communist parties (for example, the French Communist party) even denied its existence. Entitled "About the Cult of Personality and its Consequences," it dealt with Stalin's crimes.

Khrushchev began by quoting Marx, Engels, and Lenin to demonstrate their condemnation of the cult of personality, and he revealed Lenin's December 1922 letter to the Thirteenth Party Congress of the All-Union Communist Party (Bolshevik), in which he criticized Stalin by name.

Khrushchev then outlined the dimensions of Stalin's Great Purge (1937–38) against the party, government, and economic cadres. Of the 139 Central Committee members and candidate-members chosen during the Seventeenth Congress in 1934, 98 (70 percent) were later arrested and executed; of the 1,966 Congress delegates, 1,108 were arrested on charges of counterrevolutionary crimes. As noted in the minutes, there was "indignation in the hall." Indeed, the information concerned Stalinist terror directed against the party elite itself.

Khrushchev went on to blame Stalin for the liquidation of the Red Army cadres on the eve of the Second World War, for the country's unpreparedness for war, for his disregard of warnings about German preparations, as well as for the breaking of relations with Yugoslavia in 1949, and for false accusations in the case of the Leningrad party activists, when, according to Khrushchev, "innocent" Communists lost their lives, among them Nikolai Voznesensky, who was killed in 1949. Khrushchev mentioned the case of the Kremlin doctors (the so-called "doctors' plot") and said that at a plenary meeting of the Central Committee in 1952, Stalin was making groundless and ominous accusations against Molotov and Mikoyan.

According to Khrushchev, Stalin was directly and personally responsible for all this. Stalin made decisions single-handedly or in a "roundabout way without collective discussion," and it was, consequently, difficult to protest. As a remedy, Khrushchev called for a return to "the Leninist principles of party leadership, characterized above all by collective leadership." He called for a fight against the willful abuse of power and for a correction of the social evils caused by "violations of revolutionary socialist legality."

During the Twentieth Congress, on February 19, the Communist Party of Poland was rehabilitated (it had been dissolved in 1938 by the Third International—Comintern).

On March 13 it was announced that Bolesław Bierut had died in Moscow the previous evening. The circumstances of his death quickly became a subject of rumors and divergent interpretations. Bierut died shortly after the Twentieth Congress, after which he had remained in Moscow. His funeral in Warsaw was attended by Khrushchev, who, according to party information, had some influence on who Bierut's successor would be. Roman Zambrowski and Zenon Nowak were mentioned as candidates. The fact that in party circles more than one name was mentioned for such a position suggests the existence within the party of factions supporting different candidates. There was talk about Zambrowski's people; there was also a group close to Zenon Nowak, called the Natolin group. The Natolin group was opposed by the Puławy group, which presented itself as a group favoring "democratization" while portraying the Natolin group as opposed to "democratization," or as Polish Stalinists. In reality, both groups had been involved in the realization of Stalinism. Their differences concerned only current policy. As later formulated by Gomułka, at issue were primarily the relationship to the Soviet Union (the understanding of Polish sovereignty) and the attitude towards internal changes (the understanding of democratization). These differences were becoming increasingly public and publicly discussed.

On March 20, 1956, Edward Ochab became the first secretary. He was most likely a compromise candidate, but soon afterwards, it became evident that Ochab supported the advocates of "democratization."

PZPR was, of all Communist parties, the one in which echoes of the Twentieth Congress were the loudest. Khrushchev's so-called secret speech lost its secrecy in Poland. It was published "for the exclusive use of party organizations" by the Central Committee of the Polish United Workers' Party and given the title, "About the Cult of Personality and Its Consequences: The Speech of the First Secretary of CC CPSU, Comrade N. S. Khrushchev, at the Twentieth Congress of the Communist Party of the Soviet Union on February 25, 1956." PZPR members were being acquainted with this fairly long 72-page pamphlet during party meetings. Selected nonparty persons were invited to attend some of these meetings as well. Activists and lecturers were delivering extensive reports, which were then discussed. People were becoming more daring and speaking publicly about important and, until then, even dangerous subjects.

Cominform (the Information Bureau of the Communist and Workers' Parties) was abolished shortly after the Twentieth Congress. The Yugoslavian Communist party had been expelled from Cominform in 1949, and the dissolution of Cominform seemed to be tied to improvement in Soviet-Yugoslav relations. New forms of integration were being forged in the Eastern bloc. Integration between states, previously concealed, was now becoming open (the Warsaw Pact and Comecon); while inter-party contacts were still secret.

More Cultural Freedom

The Polish party's 1954–55 campaign to reform the police was accompanied by some changes (thus far only minor) in the official hostile attitude towards the Home Army (AK). In December 1954, *Nowe Drogi* published an article about those former AK members who were "dedicated participants in the building of socialism," arguing that "it is necessary to combat with intransigence all discrimination against those who work honestly for the people's homeland." After the Twentieth Congress, the case of the former AK soldiers was publicly reopened. At that time, a large number of AK members were still in prison.

The March 11 issue of *Po prostu* carried an article, "Towards the People of the Home Army," dealing with the relevance of a model for "national struggle against the occupying forces." The article reminded its readers about the official treatment of the Home Army: "This injustice must be corrected immediately; it is necessary to accomplish the moral rehabilitation of a great many people of our generation, former soldiers of the AK. It is necessary to reinstate their unblemished moral record under the occupation."

From the discussion this article provoked in the April 1 issue of *Po prostu* and from a *Nowa Kultura* article by Jerzy Piórkowski, "We from the Home Army," published at this time, it became evident that the issue of the Home Army and its place in Polish society had personal, political, and ideological significance. At issue was the rehabilitation of those other than former Communists (from the prewar Communist Party of Poland or from the postwar "rightist-nationalist deviation"). The conclusions of the Twentieth Congress paved the way for journalists to discuss publicly Polish issues that were unrelated to the Communist movement.

Increasingly, the relatively independent voices of intellectuals could be heard. The nineteenth session of the Cultural Council, a group advising the cultural minister, took place on March 24–25, 1956. Jan Kott read a paper, "On Modernism and the Revolutionary Nature of Art." He claimed that Marxist analytic tools had been applied thus far to the past and not to the present. "The perception of the leader in a mythical light is part and parcel of a mythical attitude toward the ideological struggle. . . . This was aided by the thesis of the intensification of the class struggle and the concept of 'enemies of the people'. . . . Art served to legitimize the regime rather than the system; it degenerated into a laudatory, exalting, and decorative art." Kott spoke of various necessities. This fatalism in the critique of the official ideology did indeed reflect some of the characteristics of Marxism.

According to Antoni Słonimski, Kott appeared like an attorney who was haggling with creditors in the name of the bankrupt enterprise. Słonimski was perhaps a better Marxist than Kott or Khrushchev: he was less fascinated with the cult of personality or with Stalin's psychology. He criticized the claim that "the cult of personality is responsible for the faults of the bygone era": "It is not the cult of personality, but a person; and not a person, but a system which permits such harmful action by a person."

Artur Sandauer challenged the thesis that the right to repair a machine belongs only to the man who broke it. He was demanding recognition for people who had not been involved in cultural policy and practice. Stefan Żółkiewski differed, and he declared: "Today we speak openly about these issues. . . . Who started these discussions? They began in the party with Marxists and Communists. And it is they who have the right to shape the future." Żółkiewski believed that the Communist party should continue its "leading role." He noted the special rights of the Communists which followed from the fact that they began speaking openly about issues which others had raised only privately. The party discussions had indeed become open; the leadership was encouraging or merely acquiescing in certain freedoms unleashed by Khrushchev at the Twentieth Congress.

Rehabilitations

A "meeting of PZPR activists of Warsaw" took place on April 6, 1956. The new first secretary, Edward Ochab, having replaced Bolesław Bierut who died on March 12, addressed the meeting. Ochab spoke about the nationalist and opportunist deviation represented by Władysław Gomułka and about Gomułka's opinion that "the nationalist rightwing of the PPS had been correct in their historical disagreement with the internationalist SDKPiL and KPP." According to Ochab, Gomułka also spoke against the party's agricultural policy, geared toward "the socialist reconstruction of the countryside," and he sought to "maintain the existing structure of socio-economic relations in the country." Ochab claimed that the struggle against this deviation was still justified. "But it must be emphatically acknowledged that Gomułka's arrest in 1951, which took place in the atmosphere created by Beria and the trial of Rajk, was incorrect and unjustified." Ochab distinguished between ideological mistakes and personal wrongs: "the acknowledgment of wrongs committed against Władysław Gomułka does not in any way vitiate the correctness of the political and ideological struggle conducted by the party then and now against the false conceptions represented by Gomułka."

Ochab announced the rehabilitation of Wacław Komar, Szczęsny Dobrowolski, and Józef Kuropieska and the restoration of their rights as party members. Marian Spychalski, former vice-minister of national defense, was also released from prison, since the investigation found no proof of his "conspiratorial or diversionary activity." But he was found "responsible for disobeying party and government directives, for deviations in his political and party work in the army, and for deceiving the party leadership."

On April 19, there were government changes. The State Council, acting on the advice of the prime minister, fired Stanisław Radkiewicz, at that time minister of state farms, but formerly minister of public security from 1944–54. He was replaced as minister of state farms by Mieczysław Moczar, who later became minister of internal affairs (apparently Radkiewicz was not the only one to combine agricultural expertise with police work). Also dismissed was the prosecutor-general, Stefan

Kalinowski, "because of serious shortcomings in the work of the Prosecutor-General's Office during the previous years, in the area of supervising the investigative activity of public security organs." Similar reasons were given for firing the chief army prosecutor, General Stanisław Zarako-Zarakowski, who had acted as a prosecutor in the best-known political trials.

On April 21, the State Council dismissed the minister of justice, Henryk Świątkowski, and the minister of art and culture, Włodzimierz Sokorski.

On April 25 it was announced that the Prosecutor-General's Office began an investigation against Roman Romkowski, the former vice-minister of public security, and Anatol Fejgin, the former director of the Tenth Department of the Ministry of Public Security, who were "responsible for breaking the law, imprisoning a number of innocent people, and employing illegal investigative methods in the units of the ministry under their supervision." They had been arrested on April 23. Józef Różański, the director of the Department of Investigations of the Ministry of Public Security, had been arrested earlier and sentenced to five years' imprisonment based on Article 286 of the Criminal Code, for "abuse of power." In June the Prosecutor-General's Office appealed the sentence to the Supreme Court on the grounds it was too lenient. On July 30, the Supreme Court annulled the sentence and returned the case to the lower courts for retrial.

The Eighth Session of the Diet, widely discussed in the press, took place from April 23 to 28, 1956. In an opening *exposé,* Prime Minister Cyrankiewicz encouraged the deputies to participate freely and voice initiatives and criticisms. The budget for fiscal year 1956 and a statute concerning the legalization of abortion were among the issues under discussion. Five Catholic deputies voted against the abortion statute. The custom of unanimity that had prevailed previously in the Polish Parliament was violated.

On April 27, an amnesty statute was announced, mostly concerning political crimes. Close to half of the 70,000 prisoners were released within the following month.

On April 28, convictions were overturned in the cases of Stanisław Tatar, Jerzy Kirchmayer, Stefan Mossor, and others. According to the press communiqué, "it was established that the evidence on which these convictions were based was acquired by impermissible methods of investigation. As a result, the Highest Military Court reopened the court proceedings and annulled the previous sentences; the Prosecutor's Office ultimately discontinued the investigations because of a lack of evidence of guilt."

On May 4, Jakub Berman, the PZPR functionary responsible for security, resigned from his position as deputy premier and from membership in the Politburo. The resolution of the Politburo, made public on May 8, spoke about Berman's errors and deviations.

The Press

Po prostu was extremely popular, as were *Nowa Kultura* and *Przegląd Kulturalny* (*Cultural Review*). Periodicals had become more readable by late 1955. Journalists were rediscovering Poland; their articles were becoming more interesting, and new topics were appearing. After the Twentieth Congress, the Communist movement regained its history. People began to wonder about the circumstances surrounding the deaths of Communist leaders. Hints about the terror in the Soviet Union appeared in the press, and questions arose concerning how it was connected to events in Poland, and what it revealed about Polish sovereignty and Soviet-Polish relations. But these issues were officially discussed (at least in allusions) in reference to the Twentieth Congress and to the murder of Polish Communists in the Soviet Union.

The April 1956 issues of *Nowa Kultura* included an article dissecting the highest state organs, new political poems by Adam Ważyk, and a feuilleton by KAT (Krzysztof Teodor Toeplitz) entitled "Inauguration Speech for the Opening of a New Special Store in Warsaw," in which he discussed the contribution to socialism made by the network of quality stores for privileged people. A piece by Leszek Kołakowski, "Platonism, Empiricism, and Public Opinion," advocated an empirically-based assessment of public opinion as opposed to one deduced from ideological principles. The front page of the May Day issue carried poems by the recently rehabilitated Communist poets, Stande and Wandurski, and the last page carried another feuilleton by Toeplitz, "Your Rights Should Be Your Guide," dealing with the Stalinist system:

> The revolution raised up on its shoulders a new ruling apparatus and spread it over the entire nation. This apparatus included thousands of people whose vital interests became increasingly tied to the apparatus's development and consolidation. Initially, the masses did not control this apparatus; later, the apparatus skilfully rendered any control

impossible. Armed with its own code of honor, and surrounded with its own power, the apparatus defended its own self-interest over the interest of the masses. It created its own mythology, in the form of an infallible leader, and made its own class alliances, with sectors of private initiative and, particularly, with privileged groups of professionals; and, finally, it created its own esthetics in the Zhdanovian version of socialist realism.

Shortly afterwards, the editors retracted Toeplitz's statements (*Nowa Kultura* of May 13): the author had gone too far, and it was considered advisable henceforth to keep a certain distance from him. This was one example of the resistance encountered to widening the margin of permissible expression.

Poznań

It is difficult to determine whether the use of the police and the army against workers has been more common under socialism or under nineteenth-century capitalism.

The Poznań events—officially called "disturbances," and later a "tragedy"—began with a strike by the workers of ZISPO (Stalin Enterprises, formerly and again later called Hipolit Cegielski's Enterprises). The factory employed 15,000 workers. By the end of 1955, the ZISPO workers were lodging complaints about the incorrect method by which their taxes were assessed, depriving them of their entitled rebates. Discontent was especially strong among the 2,000 workers of the shop producing freight cars (W3), and brief work stoppages occurred in this shop in mid-June. On June 26, a delegation of workers left for Warsaw to demand changes in the system of compensation. The workers were promised immediate action and a new system for computing wages, but none materialized. On the morning of June 28, the workers from W3, followed by other ZISPO workers, instead of beginning work, formed a column of marchers and headed downtown. When news of the strike spread, Poznań workers from all over stopped work and came out into the streets. The workers marched in the direction of Freedom Square, where enormous numbers of people had gathered. Reacting to rumors about arrests, several thousand people began to storm the District Office of Security building. Arms were seized in police stations and used in the ensuing battle with the Office of Security functionaries defending their building. The crowd entered the District Party Committee building, and the prison and a jamming station were also stormed. The prison was captured and its prisoners freed. The authorities counter-attacked using armored troops. Battles raged through June 29, and ended with the revolt quelled on the following morning. Because all this was taking place during the International Trade Fair in Poznań, information about the events rapidly reached the rest of the world.

Warsaw radio alleged that the Poznań events claimed 38 lives in contrast to the 200 casualties estimated by Western sources. According to Polish information, approximately 300 people were injured; the number was larger according to Western sources.

A June 28 communiqué of the Polish Press Agency (PAP) stated that on this day "there were serious disturbances in the city of Poznań . . . For some time now, imperialist agents and the reactionary underground have attempted to exploit economic difficulties and resentments in some Poznań factories in order to provoke outbursts against socialist authority. . . . On June 28, enemy agents succeeded in inciting street riots. Several public buildings were attacked, and there were casualties."

The existence of "economic difficulties and resentments" was acknowledged, but according to the communiqué, the riots were provoked by "enemy agents."

At first, the official reaction was along traditional orthodox lines. On June 29 Prime Minister Józef Cyrankiewicz made a speech in Poznań, transmitted by radio and published in the press. He spoke about the amputation of hands raised against the people's power. "The imperialist centers and the reactionary underground, which directly perpetrated these riots, are guilty of the bloodshed in Poznań. . . . Every *provocateur* or madman who dares to raise his hand against the people's authorities must be assured that his hand will be chopped off by the authorities in the interest of the working class, in the interest of working peasants and intelligentsia, in the interest of the struggle for higher standards of living for the population, in the interest of the further democratization of our lives, and in the interest of our Motherland."

Cyrankiewicz claimed that the *provocateurs* profited from the "undeniably real difficulties and discontent in some factories." He also asserted that the Poznań events would not stop the party's and the government's endeavors towards democratization.

On July 2, the Soviet Central Committee accused American monopoly capital of provoking the Poznań events and of financing subversive activities in socialist countries. The US State Department rejected these accusations.

In an interview on July 17 in the Polish press, Prosecutor General Marian Rybicki announced that "323 persons among those detained are under arrest, and an investigation against them is proceeding." They were under "serious suspicion of organizing and committing attacks against public institutions and against soldiers, public security functionaries, and the police. Among those arrested are 64 individuals who committed break-ins, plunder, and theft. Thirty-three criminals who escaped from prison and participated in attacks and robberies have also been arrested."

According to the prosecutor-general, it was not ascertained who fired the first shot in front of the District Office of Public Security. But he claimed that a public security employee was the first casualty and that other employees "resorted to firearms only when the building was under siege and some of the building's defenders had already been killed or wounded."

The prosecutor-general also stated that "the total number of casualties ... rose from 38, as was announced in the first communiqué, to 53 persons. Among them were 5 soldiers and Public Security functionaries, and no women. The youngest—and an especially painful victim—was a thirteen-year-old boy, who probably wandered into the middle of the battle out of curiosity and was killed by a stray bullet." The prosecutor also remarked that "during the incidents in Poznań, over 300 people were injured. . . ."

A second interview given by the prosecutor-general to a PAP reporter was published on September 22. According to Prosecutor-General Rybicki, from the beginning, the investigation conducted after the Poznań events never included the participants in the strike or in the workers' demonstration. No mention was made of enemy agents, and the political aspects of the events were no longer emphasized. There were still claims of organized and hostile actions against the authorities, but the perpetrators were now portrayed as common criminals: "The materials gathered by the investigation show that during the events in Poznań antisocial elements, hooligans and criminals, organized into gangs, were especially active and displayed particularly intense hostility toward representatives of the authorities."

The number of people officially under arrest had shrunk from 323 in

July to 154 by September. According to Prosecutor Rybicki, after the completion of the investigation, indictments against 54 persons were filed in the Poznań district court.

Two trials began on September 27. The proceedings were attended by approximately 200 people, including representatives of the American, French, and Canadian embassies and correspondents from Reuters, Agence France Presse, United Press, *Le Monde,* and the *New York Times,* among others. Also present were Western lawyers and representatives of the League for the Defense of Human Rights from Belgium. At that time, much had already been publicized about the improprieties of legal methods under Stalinism, and the authorities were probably determined to create a good impression. At the same time, the authorities were trying to make the Poznań events look ugly in order to justify the use of the army against the workers.

On October 8, a verdict was rendered in a trial concerning three persons accused of beating a Public Security functionary, Corporal Zygmunt Izdebny, who died shortly after arriving at the hospital. The prosecutor-general had described the beating in an interview as having taken place "in a particularly brutal manner, while [the accused were] shouting provocative accusations that Izdebny had murdered a woman and two children." The accused were sentenced to from four to four and one half years' imprisonment. However, incriminating testimony given by the accused during the investigation was dismissed by the court, which stated that "it is not inconceivable that the atmosphere at the beginning of the investigation could have influenced the psychological state of the defendants." To an extent, then, the complaints of the accused against the police were taken into account.

On October 12, a verdict was reached in a second trial, concerning "ten individuals accused of attacking the Military Department of the Higher School of Agriculture, a prison, and police stations, in order to seize firearms and of using these firearms in violent attacks against the District Office of Public Security and in the looting of stores and apartments." Their sentences ranged from a year and a half to six years in prison, and two of the accused were acquitted. Throughout the trials, Polish journalists reported that "several of the accused . . . retracted their depositions and blamed police beatings for their self-accusations." As a result, "Those guilty of the abuse of power were severely punished, including the leadership of the district police, which did not fulfill its responsibility for sufficient supervision." Also confronted at the trials was the connection between the situation in Poland and the eruption of the Poznań strike and demonstration.

The Poznań trials in September and October were a topic of great interest in the press. At the beginning, the newspaper front pages were almost entirely filled with courtroom details. Every day of the trial was covered, although, of course, not everything was reported. However, the trials were, apparently, not turning out as the authorities had planned, and a third trial was postponed. It was difficult to conduct legal trials and promote intended political propaganda at the same time. Shortly afterwards, other more important events eclipsed the Poznań trials. In the speech of Gomułka on October 20, the party interpretation of the Poznań events became even milder and more favorable for the participants. The hooligans had disappeared just like the imperialist agents before them. All that was left in the propaganda was the working class. But during the following years, the working class again receded into the background until new events recalled the possibility of workers' protests to the minds of the propaganda directors.

Divergencies in the Party

The Seventh Plenary Meeting of the PZPR Central Committee began on July 18, 1956 and lasted nine days altogether (with a two day interruption because of a national holiday). It was the longest plenary meeting ever. And one could suspect that, for once, some serious talk actually took place, in contrast to the ritual programs typical of plenary meetings.

On the opening day First Secretary Edward Ochab delivered a report "On the Political and Economic Situation and the Essential Tasks of the Party." Ochab reminded his audience that their plenary meeting was being held only three weeks after the Poznań disturbances, and he spoke about the direct causes of the Poznań events; namely, there was a significant rise of productivity in the ZISPO factory that was not "properly reflected in wage increases."

Ochab characterized the problem in Marxist terms as a "contradiction between a rapid increase in the productive forces of socialism along with the material and spiritual needs of the nation, on the one hand, and the overcentralized and overbureaucratized forms of managing the economy and entire social life of the country on the other."

On the following day, Premier Józef Cyrankiewicz reported "On the Underlying Principles of the 1956–60 Five Year Plan," in which he discussed the impediments to democratization: "The conservatism of a part of our party and state apparatus delays the process of democratization. This conservatism results partially from the habit of 'governing' through the seemingly expedient use of administrative pressure. . . . A large effort and the political reeducation of many party activists will be required before the party can fully switch to political methods that are perhaps more difficult, but certainly much more effective." Proposing alternatives to "administrative pressure" was nothing new, but the activists, on the whole, tended to stick with older and surer methods.

The Soviets, for their part, were concerned about the plenary meeting. One could claim that the liberalization in Poland was consistent with the line propounded at the Twentieth Congress. This line, however, proved to be short-lived. Events in Poland took on a life of their own, independent of events in the Soviet Union. By July 1956, the Russian comrades clearly wanted to slow down the process of liberalization in Poland, which in their opinion had already gone too far.

On July 21 and 22, the plenary meeting deliberations were suspended in order to celebrate the twelfth anniversary of the PKWN (Lublin) Manifesto. Nikolai Bulganin, Soviet premier, was the guest speaker for the occasion. In his speech, Bulganin claimed that the struggle against the cult of personality legacy was having positive results. Nevertheless, in connection with this struggle, "not only have hostile and opportunistic elements become more active, but also vacillating elements in our own ranks have emerged from their nooks and crannies. . . . It is well known that at times elements hostile to our cause have exploited the press in socialist countries in order to sow their own poisonous seeds. And the press has occasionally succumbed to this enemy influence." Thus, Bulganin had noticed that the press was an important means of exercising social influence. The Russian marshal stated that it was unacceptable to shut one's eyes to "attempts to weaken the international ties of the socialist camp under the banner of so-called 'national specificity,' to attempts to undermine the power of a democratic people's state under the banner of a supposed 'widening of democracy.' . . . The recent events in Poznań, provoked by enemy agents, are a new confirmation that the international reaction still has not abandoned its absurd plans to reintroduce capitalism into the socialist countries." The Russian premier pointed to two mainstays of Russian authority: "internationalism" in foreign relations (read "pro-Sovietism") and "socialist democracy" in internal relations (read "one-party rule").

No doubt Bulganin's speech created a stir at the meeting, at least in the corridors. But Bulganin's speech was to no avail. The Seventh Plenary Meeting adopted a "Resolution about the Political and Economic Situation in the Country and the Tasks of the Party," which stated as its goals "the effective combat against bureaucratism and for the deepening of socialist democracy," to be accomplished by the following: 1) broadening workers' democracy in the factories; 2) broadening autonomy for local governments; 3) strengthening the Diet and improving the efficiency of the government and ministries; 4) fully complying with the socialist rule of law; 5) cultivating criticism from below and openness of political life.

This enumeration clarified what the party understood as democratization and where this democratization would be applied. Democratization was to consist of enhancing extra-party institutional structures such as the Diet, government, ministries, and local governments. Democratization was to rely on the rule of law and on the openness of political life, on freedom to criticize, and on providing workers with some say at their workplaces. In the heading of "socialist democracy," the accent for once was to fall on the word "democracy." However, tension still remained with the adjective "socialist," understood in a very peculiar sense as a social order in which ultimate power belongs to the Communist party.

At the Seventh Plenary Meeting, Edward Gierek, Roman Nowak, and Adam Rapacki became members of the Politburo; Stefan Jędrychowski and Eugeniusz Stawiński became alternate members. The meeting confirmed the resignation of Jakub Berman from membership in this body.

Though full information on the proceedings of the meeting was never made public, word quickly spread concerning the existence of sharply divergent viewpoints within the party leadership. These divergent views were a subject of comment at the following plenary meeting in October, whose proceedings *were* published.

Shortly after the October plenary meeting, an article by Teresa Jankowska appeared in the November–December 1956 issue of *Nowe Drogi*. In this article, one of the few official publications commenting on the existence of party factions, Jankowska states:

"Shortly after the Seventh Plenary Meeting, news about differences of opinion in the party leadership penetrated party activist circles. The lower this information reached, the more distorted it became. Many party members were disturbed by the very thought of differences among the party leadership, let alone that they could be spoken about openly. This was the result of Stalinist education. Many of the almost million-and-a-half party members did not have the slightest idea of differences of opinion in the Central Committee, to say nothing of the issues involved, unless they learned about it—or rather surmised it—from the newspapers." The author mentions "democrats" inside the party who fought with the "conservatives" (or "Natolin" group). However, as she claimed, the available information did not go into any details.

The Seventh Plenary Meeting ended on July 28. An important resolution passed at this meeting was made public only on August 5. On that day, the newspapers carried the following announcement of the Central Committee:

> The Seventh Plenary Meeting has decided to rescind the part of the resolution of the Third Plenary Meeting of November 1949 dealing with the unfair and unjustified accusations made against Comrades Władysław Gomułka, Marian Spychalski, and Zenon Kliszko, who were alleged to have tolerated enemy agents. After the Seventh Plenary Meeting, representatives of the Politburo held a conversation with Comrade Gomułka during which the main problems of the plenary meeting were discussed. A report of this discussion was delivered to the Politburo, which voted to restore the rights of party membership to Comrade Gomułka.

This communiqué may be understood as an announcement of Gomułka's return to power, though it was still unclear what position he would hold.

Also on August 5, it was announced that the "premier has named Comrade Kliszko to the position of Undersecretary of State in the Ministry of Justice." Kliszko was addressed as "comrade," a manner denoting party acceptance. His nomination was the first such instance of a "rightist-nationalist deviationist" returning to an important position (Kliszko had been removed from the Central Committee in November 1949, together with Gomułka and Spychalski).

On the day of these announcements, *Po prostu* published an article by Włodzimierz Godek and Ryszard Turski on the Seventh Plenary Meeting, entitled "Program." The authors began with the questions: "What did society expect from the meeting? What demands did it make?"

Such questions were unusual. By asking them, the *Po prostu* journalists were affirming that society (and not only party members) had a right to expect something from the party, and that it might formulate its own demands. It was no longer a question of "asking *with* the party" (as in Ważyk's "Poem for Adults"); the journalists from *Po prostu* were suggesting that one should demand *from* the party. Some of the things which, in their view, should come out of the plenary meeting were "a program for healing the national economy," a "concrete program to democratize our social and political life," a "strengthening of the rule of law and of citizens' freedoms," and a "thorough, in-depth analysis of mutual relations between the party and the working class and society. . . ." The authors declared their approval of the plenary meeting program, but they called attention to its preliminary character and to the need for supplementing them, particularly regarding "broadening workers' democracy in the factories." It is most likely that in this manner they wanted to support the concept of workers' councils, which was later popularized by *Po prostu* and implemented in some factories.

Godek and Turski's article was characteristic of the then current editorial program of *Po prostu.* The magazine looked to party resolutions for a shield or safeguard for its own views, and it interpreted these resolutions in such a way as to justify the trend towards greater democracy and freedom.

At the beginning of the academic year, on October 9, there was a rally at Warsaw University. The rally passed a resolution formulated as an open letter "to all students in Poland," which was one more example of testing the limits of the publishable and the official. In fact, the rally at the university was not forbidden, and the text was later published. The resolution states that "the distinctive feature of the situation in our country is the struggle between two tendencies: the democratic tendency, demanding a full transfer of leadership to the working class, the intelligentsia, and the peasantry; and the anti-democratic tendency, attempting to maintain the existing state of affairs, which is unacceptable for the entire nation." Under these conditions, "the younger generation should unite and organize itself."

One of the main tasks of the new organization was to engage in a "struggle for openness in political life," and this included fuller information on the intraparty discussions in the plenary meeting, which "concern issues vital for the entire nation." Publication of "the Seventh Plenary Meeting materials and of materials concerning discussions between the party leadership and Comrade Władysław Gomułka-Wiesław and the disclosure of his views" were considered absolutely essential.

The resolution was sharply critical of the censorship. It stated: "we believe that it is indispensable that the Diet discuss the activities of GUKPPiW (the Central Office for Control of the Press, Publications, and Performances) and establish by legislation the competence of this office, which should be allowed to act only in order to protect military and state secrets and to prevent the publication of materials calling for the overthrow of the People's Government. The extent of the authority of GUKPPiW should be determined unequivocally, in such a way that it could not be subject to any elastic interpretations." They also deemed it necessary that the "Diet repeal the paragraph in the Small Criminal Code which makes enemy propaganda a criminal offense, since at this moment the paragraph has become an instrument in the hands of an-tidemocratic forces, especially outside of Warsaw, and is being used for their own purposes."

The students' letter declared that "the struggle of the working class to obtain the real control of the means of production is not only the single true means for increasing the standard of living for the entire nation, but it is also the struggle for the conditions without which true political democracy in Poland is impossible."

The following modes of action were proposed:

> 1) All those who want to act politically should organize their [university] departments into groups, each of which will cooperate with one factory. We want to revitalize the political organization of the younger generation on the basis of these groups. 2) In view of the existing press censorship, it is necessary to use all available means of propaganda to inform the widest possible audience amoung the Warsaw population about the current political situation. This can be done by means of leaflets, flyers, satirical shows, rallies, meetings, etc. 3) The Warsaw students should publish a periodical directed to the entire student milieu, which would constitute an information center and coordinate our movement. 4) We should organize a political Workers' University, which would assist in the formation of the future leaders of the working class. 5) At the university, we should organize meetings with the outstanding activists of the party and government and with deputies to the Diet, in order to gather the best factual information and to present our positions. 6) We should constantly organize mass demonstrations against all attempts to infringe on democracy. 7) In all our activities, we must prepare to take concrete positions in the approaching elections.

Very little in these proposals was new. The students were seeking to create the preconditions necessary for political and economic freedom and democracy. These tendencies would persist for a time in the new youth organizations. Some of the postulates of these days would also be repeated later, for example in 1968 and 1976. And they would reappear not only in Poland.

The Eighth Plenary Meeting
and Demonstrations in Warsaw

The deliberations of the Eighth Plenary Meeting began at 10:00 A.M. on October 19. Edward Ochab, who had been first secretary for the preceding seven months, was presiding. In an impromptu introductory speech (impromptu because rapidly changing events had made any preparations obsolete), Ochab limited himself to discussing recent Politburo decisions to co-opt Władysław Gomułka, Marian Spychalski, Zenon Kliszko, and Ignacy Loga-Sowiński into the Central Committee. The first three had been removed from the Central Committee seven years earlier, and all were now to participate in Central Committee deliberations. The Politburo also decided to decrease the number of its members to nine and to propose the selection of Gomułka as first secretary of the Central Committee. Ochab stated that the situation was complicated by the unexpected arrival in Warsaw of a delegation from the Soviet Politburo, composed of Khrushchev, Kaganovich, Mikoyan, and Molotov. This sudden visit was unprecedented, and Ochab suggested that the deliberations be suspended until 6:00 P.M. to clear things up. There were those who (probably seeking to avoid Soviet pressure) supported continuing on as planned, but Ochab appealed to the members' sense of caution and responsibility, and suspension of deliberations was approved. When asked what would be the subject of the talks with the Soviet delegation, Ochab answered, "the problems of Polish-Soviet relations." This was not very revealing.

What alarmed the Soviets and induced them to make such a sudden visit? What was the subject of the talks? In what way did the PZPR leaders attempt to assuage Soviet fears? What assurances were offered? Answers to these questions remain somewhat conjectural.

Aleksander Zawadzki reported to the plenary meeting about the course of the talks. His statement is the only direct public answer to questions concerning the unusual visit. According to Zawadzki: "Our Soviet comrades explained their sudden arrival as an expression of deep concern in the Soviet Politburo about the development of the situation in Poland. . . . They were especially disturbed by the appearance of anti-Soviet propaganda and our insufficient reaction against this propaganda. . . . The comrades were also interested in the composition of the new leadership to emerge from the Eighth Plenary Meeting of the Central Committee of the party."

This Soviet action had been preceded by articles in the Soviet press condemning Polish journalists. The Soviet articles were accompanied by official pressures aimed at imposing greater constraint on the Polish press.

On October 19, during the talks between the two delegations, Russian troops stationed in Poland began some disturbing movements—armored brigades were moving towards Warsaw and found themselves near Sochaczew. News, occasionally inaccurate, about the Russian troop movements spread quickly. It was in the interest of Poles to spread the news quickly, since this lessened the bargaining power of the troop movements as an argument in the inter-party talks.

On October 20, the issue of the troop movements was raised at the plenary meeting, and frustration was expressed at the inadequacy of governmental sources to clarify the situation. Rokossowski then reminded the Politburo "of the partial centralization of some units due to experiences that followed the Poznań events." Rokossowski was referring to preparations being made for anticipated disturbances in Warsaw. But this concerned the Polish army. As far as the Russian troops were concerned, Rokossowski stated that "it is true that Russian troops have made some movements. They were involved in fall maneuvers where they were stationed. These troops, however, have moved in the direction of Bydgoszcz and of Łódź, and I have consequently asked Marshal Konev, who is directing these exercises, to halt the eastward movement of the northern troops." The easterly direction of the march of these northern troops, through Łódź, pointed the direction: Warsaw.

After Rokossowski's clarifications were entered into the agenda, Gomułka addressed the plenary meeting on October 20. He gave a report on the current economic and political situation, paying great attention to the relationship between Poland and the Soviet Union. He spoke about necessary changes in the method of governing. Gomułka, who had not participated in the development of the party's policies in the early fifties, now criticized these former policies and, from the Central Committee lectern, formulated a program of reforms to be executed by the party. Gomułka's speech was broadcast on radio and read at a rally at Warsaw Polytechnic on the same day.

Rallies in Warsaw factories and in the universities began on Friday, October 19. This was a day of troop movements and of Soviet-Polish talks at the highest level, a day on which the Eighth Plenary Meeting suspended its deliberations. For the previous several days, rumors about impending arrests had been circulating in Warsaw.

Information in the press suggested that important party and state officials (a Central Committee secretary, the president of the Union of Polish Youth [ZMP], the First Secretary of the Warsaw Party Committee) were using the mass meeting to rally support for their intra-party squabble and outmaneuver the Natolin group, which was just then rumored to be trying to contact Soviet authorities behind the party leadership's back. Supposedly, those who addressed the Polytechnic rally were included on the lists of those to be arrested. This resort to popular support went beyond accepted party practice, and this group was later taken to task for such a breach of etiquette.

The Eighth Plenary Meeting closed on Sunday, October 21, with a new party leadership, which ended a series of personnel changes. Removed from the Politburo were Władysław Dworakowski, Franciszek Jóźwiak-Witold, Zenon Nowak, Franciszek Mazur, and Konstanty Rokossowski, as well as Edward Gierek and Roman Nowak (these last two entered the Politburo only three months earlier). Of the old members, six remained: Józef Cyrankiewicz, Edward Ochab, Adam Rapacki, Roman Zambrowski, Aleksander Zawadzki, and Stefan Jędrychowski, who until then had been a substitute member. Newly chosen were Władysław Gomułka, Ignacy Loga-Sowiński, and Jerzy Morawski. The highest party leadership had changed, but not completely.

In the special edition of *Życie Warszawy,* published before midnight on October 21, that announced these changes, one could also read a tribute to the Warsaw Committee and their mass rally. In response to criticism from certain groups of party activists for attempts to inflame the public mood, the paper reported, people of Warsaw organized protest meetings in factories, at the universities, and in other institutions. "With general applause, these meetings confirmed that the so-called 'pressure' expressed only the unconditional support of society for the democratic and progressive tendencies of the Eighth Plenary Meeting. The Warsaw Committee aspires consistently to realize the demands of the workers of Warsaw. . . . Our society is grateful to the Warsaw Committee for its organizational work, for the maintenance of absolute discipline and peace, and for its decisive opposition to all attempts at provocation and disturbance."

A resolution of Warsaw party activists published the same evening in the special edition of *Życie Warszawy* stated that "the work of the Warsaw party organization has drawn the great working masses of Warsaw around the party, and at the same time has made it impossible for the reaction to direct the discontent and the impatience of the people against the party and the people's authority."

According to information in the press, on October 22, "delegations of workers, intelligentsia, and youth from the capital visited the Central Committee building and delivered resolutions in support of the newly elected party leadership and the policies it represented." On October 23, *Życie Warszawy* announced that "rallies are taking place across the entire country expressing full support for the Eighth Plenary Meeting and for the program outlined by Władysław Gomułka." Below the text were two photographs captioned: "Soldiers of KBW (Internal Security Corps) Passing a Resolution" and "Cadets of WAP (Military Political Academy) Speak with Students at a Rally." *Życie Warszawy* also published at great length fragments of resolutions by open party meetings of army, army intelligence and security, and navy groups. Never before in the history of the PRL (Polish People's Republic) had the political role of the army been so clearly demonstrated. *Życie Warszawy* also mentioned non-army resolutions from the Committee for Public Security, from employees of the Prosecutor's Office of Warsaw, and from the National Bar Association. Thus, the political activity of the police and the army, and their support for the new party leadership, were being widely publicized. At the very end of the article, there were references to resolutions passed by various workers' and peasants' groups.

The army resolutions called for "principles of absolute equality and sovereignty" as the basis for Polish-Soviet relations and demanded "public rehabilitations of convicted but innocent officers of the Polish army and the underground," and they asked for "suitable conditions for the further development of Polish military thought, which will undoubtedly increase the fighting readiness of the army and the defense capability of our country."

Życie Warszawy of October 23 published statements from groups outside the party, thus far absent from political life. On the front page there was a "Declaration by Catholic Writers and Activists," in which support was expressed for Gomułka's program and for the political direction advocating democracy and sovereignty.

In the same issue, Jan Rzepecki published a letter "To Colleagues from the Home Army" advocating political involvement and expressing trust in the new party leadership: "The character traits evident in Władysław Gomułka and his closest comrades for the past thirteen years guarantee that he means what he says and that the influence of those who persecuted us and who perpetrated wrongs against us will be truly eliminated." In a rather unfortunate manner, Rzepecki requested a new amnesty: "Now, the gates of prisons will surely open for those of our colleagues who, from lack of experience and political savvy, have allowed themselves to be recruited to commit serious crimes."

On October 23, General Kazimierz Witaszewski was recalled from his positions as vice-minister of National Defense and as head of the Main Political Board of the Polish Army. Witaszewski was rumored to be preparing arrests of party activists and even of journalists suspected of liberalism. His departure was therefore connected with the defeat of the hardline party faction (the so-called Natolin group).

Various demonstrations of strength accompanied Gomułka's accession to power. Armies marched and the workers at Żerań were given arms. Even fraternal political organizations made their voices heard, and, several days later, Catholics and Home Army soldiers also made their appearance. There were hopes of a different political road for Poland, for a greater share of independence and self-determination.

On October 24, "an all-Warsaw rally of the working people" took place, called by the Warsaw Committee. Approximately 400,000 people participated. Gomułka was the main speaker, introduced by Stefan Staszewski, first secretary of the Warsaw Committee. Gomułka's speech was transmitted by loudspeaker throughout the Parade Square, where the rally was held, and was broadcast on radio throughout the entire country. Gomułka spoke at length about relations with the Soviet Union, particularly relevant in view of the recent march of Russian troops in the direction of Warsaw and the furtive sudden visit of Russian leaders to Poland. Gomułka stated: "Comrade Khrushchev has assured us that he does not perceive any obstacles to basing our mutual party and state relations on the principles established at the Eighth Plenary Meeting of our party." (In the published version of the speech, "prolonged ovation" was noted at this point.) "All questions concerning our internal affairs will be decided by our party and government. It depends only on us, whether, and for how long, the Soviet specialists and military advisors will be necessary in our army" (the text notes, "prolonged applause"). "At the same time, comrade Khrushchev has assured us that in the course of the next two days the Soviet troops in our country will return to where they are stationed according to international agreements of the Warsaw Pact" (here again, "ovation").

Gomułka's assurances were understood as evidence that Poland was regaining freedom and independence. Gomułka ended his speech with a farewell to rallying Warsaw: "Today we call upon the working people of Warsaw: enough of rallying and demonstrating! It is time to return to our daily work, animated with faith and consciousness that the party, united with the working class and the nation, will lead Poland on a new road to socialism."

But not everybody at Parade Square shared Gomułka's faith in the unification of the party with the working class and the nation. A column of marchers had formed along Nowy Świat on their way to the Central Committee building. There were cries of "Free Wyszynski! Rokossowski back to Moscow!" Not everyone believed that everything was now in order. Cardinal Wyszynski returned to Warsaw on October 28, and, on November 13, Konstanty Rokossowski was relieved of his position as minister of national defense. Admittedly, these concessions had been indicated some time before, but there was concern they might be withdrawn if nobody demanded their realization.

The unauthorized part of the October 24 rally was described in *Życie Warszawy* on the following morning in a note entitled, "Irresponsible Escapades."

> In the evening in Warsaw—following the rally of nearly 400,000 residents warmly expressing their support for the new leadership—small groups of mostly frantic teenagers, in addition to gangs of hooligans, demonstrated in several places in the city. Individuals in these groups shouted provocative slogans. These irresponsible demonstrations were met with a decisive posture on the part of the workers and the workers' police. In some instances, the Citizens' Police had to intervene.

Orchestrated demonstrations of support for the new leadership were held more than once. The official propaganda let it be understood that politics does not belong to the realm of free public discussion: one has to speak only what and when the party instructs one to. Spontaneity and free initiative are discouraged. What is important is not so much the issues as who is in the party leadership. One has to trust them with one's own and the nation's fate, and one should not prompt them. They know what is good for whom. Of course, one should have one's own opinion, provided it is the same as the party leadership's. And if some (though few) have a different opinion, these are at most only hooligans and teenagers. The propaganda typically contrasted these hooligans with the workers, and the press reassured the public with references to the workers who displayed a decisive and correct attitude.

After October, much was written about how the party stood at the head of a social movement and gained the people's confidence. Nevertheless, questions were asked publicly about whether the party should direct social changes without discussion, or whether social critique is necessary, even if the rulers do in fact enjoy a certain confidence. The November 8 issue of *Po Prostu* carried a text by Jerzy Płudowski discussing a resolution by the Presidium of the Polish Academy of Sciences directed to young scholars and students. The Presidium appeal had called for intensive work, cautious consideration, peace, and for full confidence in the party leadership and the government (not unlike Gomułka's statement in Parade Square). Płudowski wrote that this call "for full confidence in the government and Party leadership has an embarrassingly loyalist character. This is the way we used to speak. But not today. Confidence without conditions, passive, blind confidence, belongs to the past."

The street disturbances later portrayed as incidents of hooliganism did not end on October 24. In Bydgoszcz on November 18, a crowd demolished the District Police Headquarters and then a radio station used for jamming foreign broadcasts. A trial "against 16 perpetrators of hooliganish incidents" took place in the Bydgoszcz district court from January 2-15, 1957. Three of the accused were acquitted and the others were sentenced to imprisonment ranging from six months to six years. On December 10, there were street disturbances in Szczecin and demonstrators entered the Soviet Consulate.

Referring to these events, and their "openly reactionary, chauvinistic, and anti-Soviet character," the prosecutor general called them "examples of how hooliganism may transform itself into provocative, reactionary outbursts." Assaults on jamming stations, the Soviet Consulate, and the Poznań Security Forces building and prison made it only too clear what the people were against.

The Hungarian Example

Hungary was a country in which the new party course began shortly after Stalin's death. In July 1953, First Secretary Mátyás Rákosi relinquished his other position as premier, like Bierut did later in Poland. As the new premier, Imre Nagy announced new policies, including economic and social reforms and an amnesty for political prisoners. In 1954, higher officials of the Hungarian political police were sentenced to prison terms, while some previously imprisoned Communists and Social Democrats, including the future premier and first secretary of the party, János Kádár, were released. Though Nagy ran into party resistance and was replaced as head of government by Andras Hegedüs in April 1955, it was only a temporary setback.

By February 1956, it was evident that the criticism of Stalinist policies at the Twentieth Congress was not to be limited to the Soviet Union. Around this time the Communist Party of Poland was rehabilitated in a resolution by five other Communist parties, and a Russo-Hungarian economist, Yevgenii Varga, published a text devoted to the seventieth anniversary of the birth of Bela Kun, a Hungarian Communist leader executed in the Soviet Union in the thirties.

In Poland, when the repercussions of the Twentieth Congress were being felt, the party was led by a new first secretary, Edward Ochab, who assumed control after Bierut's death and who had not belonged to the inner circle of leaders in Stalin's heyday. It is difficult to say whether the fate of Hungary would have been any different had Mátyás Rákosi, the first secretary of the Hungarian Communist Party, also died at that time. In Hungary, in contrast, the leadership remained unchanged, and the party leader, Rákosi, was probably none too keen on liberalizing the country. Nevertheless, on March 19, 1956, he announced the rehabilitation of Laszlo Rajk and other Communist activists condemned in 1949, and he released from prison former Social Democrats.

In May, news reached the West about the releases of Archbishop of Kolocs, Josef Groesz, Zoltan Tildy, former president of Hungary and leader of the Smallholders' party, and Arpad Szakasits, another former president and a leader of the Social Democrats.

The role of intellectuals—of writers and journalists above all—in Hungary and Poland was similar. Petöfi's Club, organized by the Union of Democratic Youth as a discussion forum for young intellectuals, was active in Budapest after 1954. Following the Twentieth Congress, the speeches at club meetings became increasingly outspoken, and the number of listeners rose. At a club meeting on June 27, the writers Tibor Déry and Tibor Tardos demanded the abolition of censorship and Rákosi's resignation. Those present at the meeting demanded that Imre Nagy be allowed to answer the accusations directed against him. On June 30, both writers were thrown out of the party, and further meetings of the club were suspended.

Soon thereafter, at a Central Committee plenary meeting, held July 18–22, Andras Hegedüs announced that the first secretary of the party, Mátyás Rákosi, had requested the Central Committee to relieve him of his duties as a member of the Politburo and first secretary for health reasons (high blood pressure) and because of his advanced age (Rákosi was 65 at the time). At the same time, Rákosi admitted having committed mistakes "in connection with the cult of personality and violation of the socialist legality."

Rákosi was replaced by Ernö Gerö, who read a paper at the meeting entitled, "The Unified Party in the Struggle for Socialist Democracy." In the paper, Gerö attributed the events in the Petöfi Club, which he denied was comparable to "Poznań," to mistakes committed before June 1953 in connection with the cult of personality and with the violation of socialist legality, as well as to subsequent mistakes by the Rákosi leadership, which were unfortunate for the party.

Also, in the course of the meeting a resolution was passed to exclude Mihaly Farkas, former minister of national defense, from the party, along with a motion to deprive him of his military rank.

On October 6, a national holiday, a funeral was held in honor of the exhumed remains of Communist activists Laszlo Rajk, Tibor Szöny, Andras Szalai, and György Falffy, who had been executed in 1949. A crowd of approximately 150,000 participated, with party and government leaders at the head of the procession.

On October 14, Imre Nagy was readmitted to the Hungarian Working People's Party. In Poland, on the following day, Władysław Gomułka was invited to participate in a Politburo meeting. Events in both countries seemed to be following the same course.

On October 23, students in Budapest called for a demonstration of solidarity with Poland. After initial attempts by the authorities to prohibit such a gathering, it finally took place near the monument of Bem (the Polish general who was a hero of the 1848 Hungarian revolt). Towards evening a growing crowd filled the Budapest streets and a provocative speech by Gerö, broadcast over the radio, further inflamed the mood of the people. On the following morning, Soviet troops intervened, and on October 25 shots were fired by Hungarian security police and Soviet troops into an unarmed crowd in front of the Parliament building. The fighting soon spread to the provinces, and Imre Nagy, who resumed the premiership on October 24, promised the withdrawal of Soviet troops from Hungary.

On October 26, the Presidium of the National Council of Labor Unions appealed over the radio to workers to form workers' councils, which were supposed to decide all issues of production and management in the workplace. These workers' councils were being created across the country.

During the last days of October the situation in Hungary appeared to be growing calmer. On October 25, János Kádár became first secretary. On October 27, a new government was formed, including among its members two leaders of the Smallholders' party. On October 28, Premier Nagy announced an amnesty for the participants in the fighting, the dissolution of the security police, and the withdrawal of Soviet troops from Budapest as soon as new police units could be created.

On October 30, the Soviet government issued a declaration "About the Basis for Development and the Further Strengthening of Friendship and Cooperation between the Soviet Union and Other Socialist Countries." The declaration made general statements about Soviet readiness to have a new arrangement regarding economic relations with other socialist countries, "which would protect against any violation of national sovereignty." It was also imperative "to consider, together with other socialist countries, the question of maintaining Soviet advisors in those countries."

A separate section of the declaration was devoted to the situation in Hungary:

> At the request of the Hungarian people's government, the Soviet government agreed to introduce detachments of Soviet troops into Budapest to aid the Hungarian army and civil authorities in restoring order in the city.
>
> Because a longer stay of Soviet troop detachments in Hungary might contribute to a further inflammation of the situation, the Soviet government has ordered the army to withdraw from Budapest as soon as the Hungarian government decides this is necessary.
>
> At the same time, the Soviet government expresses its readiness to begin talks with the government of the Hungarian People's Republic and with other Warsaw Pact signatories about the stationing of Soviet troops on Hungarian territory.

On October 30, Premier Nagy announced the return to a multiparty system and called for the complete independence and neutrality of Hungary. That same evening, the primate of Hungary, Cardinal Mindszenty, was released from prison, and he arrived in Budapest the following morning to assume his office.

On November 1, Premier Nagy also became minister of foreign affairs. That evening, journalists in Budapest were informed of a protest Nagy had delivered that day to the Soviet embassy in connection with the dispatch of new Soviet troops to Hungary. Nagy demanded the withdrawal of all Soviet troops from the country. "At the same time, Imre Nagy declares that the Hungarian government is withdrawing fom the Warsaw Pact and proclaims the neutrality of Hungary."

On November 3, in the Parliament building in Budapest, talks began between representatives of the Hungarian and Soviet armed forces. They were to be continued at ten o'clock the same evening.

The same day, Nagy's cabinet was changed drastically: 20 members of the cabinet were dismissed, and a new government was formed with representatives from four parties (Social Democrats were included for the first time): there were three members each from the Smallholders' Party, the Social Democratic Party, and the Hungarian Socialist Workers' Party (previously known as the Hungarian Working People's Party), along with two representatives of Petöfi's party (the former National Peasants' Party). A truly multiparty government was created in a country previously governed by the Communist party alone.

The changes in Hungary did not meet with the approval of the Soviet government. Not altogether in accord with their October 30 declaration, the Soviet government sent troops into Hungary a second time early in the morning of November 4.

At 5:15 A.M., Imre Nagy made a short appeal on the radio: "In the early morning hours, Soviet troops launched an attack against the capital of Hungary with the clear goal of abolishing the democratic government of the Hungarian People's Republic. Our troops are fighting with the Soviet forces. The Hungarian government remains at its post."

A little later on the same day, it was announced that in the town of Szolnok, "a Hungarian revolutionary peasant and workers' government" had been created under the leadership of János Kádár. It was also announced that this government had asked for Soviet help, confirmed later by the Soviets, who also referred to the Warsaw Pact, which supposedly authorized military intervention on the territory of member states.

Before noon, with Soviet tanks approaching the Parliament building, Imre Nagy, together with several of his colleagues, asked the Yugoslavian embassy for asylum. Cardinal Josef Mindszenty found asylum in the United States embassy.

The fighting between Russian detachments and ill-prepared insurgents lasted throughout the following week and then gradually subsided.

International opinion, preoccupied with British and French actions in the Suez Canal, was relatively muted regarding the Soviet intervention. The United Nations took up the Hungarian case at a special session of the General Assembly from November 8–10, and three resolutions were adopted. The first demanded the immediate withdrawal of Soviet troops and the cessation of Soviet actions in the country which, according to the resolution, constituted a violation of international law and moral principles. The second resolution demanded that the Soviet Union stop preventing economic and medical aid from reaching the Hungarian people. And the third called for all countries of the United Nations to render aid to Hungary. The Polish delegation voted against the first two resolutions and abstained from the third, along with the entire Soviet bloc, which at that time had nine votes.

On November 21, the General Assembly passed two more resolutions. The first called for ceasing deportations of the Hungarian population; the second demanded that UN observers be allowed into Hungary. The Polish delegation voted with the Soviet bloc against the first of these resolutions; on the second resolution, however, Poland parted company with the rest of the Soviet bloc and was among the thirteen countries abstaining. Although the Polish delegation did not on the whole show great insubordination, this abstention is noteworthy nevertheless. Perhaps this was one of the rare instances in which public opinion was able to exercise some influence on PRL's international behavior.

In December 1956 there were demonstrations and strikes in Hungarian cities. Workers' councils, which had been formed on October 26, with official sanction, to manage the factories after the earlier Soviet intervention, were still active, and the government was forced to negotiate with them. Also, mimeographed periodicals were still appearing. The resistance of the Hungarian nation was not broken. As late as January 1957, there were strikes and demonstrations on the island of Csepel in Budapest, which often turned into battles with the police. Shortly afterwards, the state authorities dissolved the writers' and journalists' unions, and the prosecution of illegal periodicals and hostile propaganda lasted throughout 1957. The playwright Jozsef Gali and the journalist Gyula Obersovszky received death sentences, later amended to life imprisonment. In December 1957, two Hungarian writers, Tibor Déry and Gyula Hay, were sentenced to nine and six years in prison respectively.

The Polish press extensively and objectively covered the Hungarian events. The term "counterrevolution," used in the press of other Soviet bloc countries, was absent from the Polish press. It was also absent from official speeches. The Hungarian attempts to regain self-determination were welcomed in Poland with general sympathy, and the Soviet intervention in Hungary was experienced in Poland as a personal blow. Food and money were collected for the Hungarians, and there were blood donations for the wounded. There was a general feeling of horror.

The Soviet military intervention in Hungary was generally treated as a warning, and for a long time it was the subject of many discussions about the limits of possible freedom and independence in Poland.

Imre Nagy lived until June 1958. On June 17, it was announced in the Soviet Union and Hungary that the trial of Nagy and his comrades had taken place. Nagy, General Pal Malater, Jozsef Szilagy, and Miklos Gimes were sentenced to death and executed, and Geza Lasonczy was announced to have died in prison. Other codefendants were sentenced to prison terms.

On June 28, 1958, Władysław Gomułka refrained from commenting on the fairness of these sentences, claiming that they were an internal Hungarian matter.

Perhaps the deaths of Nagy and his comrades were a warning to his potential imitators. Soviet domination in Eastern Europe is possible now only because of the cooperation of the local Communist parties. The death of Imre Nagy could have been a warning to the East European Communist leaders not to increase freedom and independence in their nations to any great extent, though this warning did not stop Czechoslovak Communists from trying to reform their system ten years later. The specter of freedom haunts even Communists once in a while. Despite this, as long as the Communist parties retain their present structure, or as long as they remain Communist parties, the appearance of a Rákosi, or of a Kádár in the best of cases, is more probable than the appearance of a Nagy. A policy of realizing Soviet interests in the name of proletarian internationalism is more probable than a decisive defense of the interests of their own countries.

The postwar experiences of Eastern Europe, including the Polish and Hungarian experiences in 1956, indicate how difficult it is under communism to reconstruct a free society. Such an attempt is threatened by external intervention or by the incompatibility of independent social structures with a Communist system.

Changing Polish/Soviet Relations

During the Stalinist period, the people's democracies certainly did not have any independent foreign policies. The relationships between the Soviet Union and the people's democracies were based on exploitation (on the Soviet side) and dependence (on the other). Poland was no exception, and it had the added problems created by having a relatively large territory and population and by experiencing the greatest territorial losses to the Soviet Union during the Second World War, the deportation of its citizens to the Soviet Union from 1939 to the postwar years, and the periodic extermination of its population, for example, the execution of Polish officers at Katyn.

With the de-Stalinization of 1956 the reconsideration of the basis of Soviet/Polish relations became a public issue after the Twentieth Congress. The ruling party, whose activists had learned the hard lessons of proletarian internationalism from the USSR at first hand, was under pressure to take a position.

During the Eighth Plenary Meeting of the Polish Central Committee, with the arrival of the Soviet delegation and the unexpected negotiations over the movement of Soviet troops toward Warsaw, the issue of sovereignty became particularly significant. In this setting, the issue of Rokossowski's participation in the party leadership assumed symbolic importance. What would in the past have been an intraparty issue was now discussed on the plane of relations between the USSR and Poland.

Missing from the planned membership list for the new Politburo, Rokossowski's candidacy was proposed from the floor and seconded by Bolesław Rumiński, who said: "The most important issue is how the masses will understand the significance of not electing Comrade Rokossowski. The masses, given the recent atmosphere, will take this as action against the Soviet Union." At the heart of Rumiński's statement was concern over what impression this would make on the Soviets. Rokossowski did get 23 votes out of 75 as a result; but this was not enough for election to the Politburo.

On October 24, Gomułka reported Khrushchev's assurance that within two days the Soviet troops would return to the places where they were stationed. Gomułka did not mention military bases per sé, perhaps because the Soviet Union disavowed having military bases in other countries: the Soviet troops in Poland had "places where they were stationed" rather than "bases." Gomułka also stated that according to Khrushchev, the presence of Soviet specialists and advisers in the Polish army depended entirely on the Polish government.

In an October 30 declaration, the Soviet government elaborated its position by stating that "in order to assure the mutual security of the socialist countries . . . the Soviet government is proceeding on the general principle that the distribution of troops of one or another state signatory of the Warsaw Pact on the territory of any other signatory be decided on the basis of agreements among all the signatories, and only with the permission and agreement of the state on whose territory troops have been placed or might be placed."

In November, Soviet army advisers returned to the USSR, and in farewell, on November 12, they were decorated with Polish state medals.

On November 13 there were changes in the government. The Diet dismissed Konstanty Rokossowski as vice-chairman of the Council of Ministers and as minister of national defense. *Pravda* announced on November 20 that Rokossowski "arrived in the USSR on November 15, and by a decision of the Soviet government was named Deputy Minister of National Defense of the USSR." In this manner, the Polish stage of his army career was terminated.

Also in November the Soviet government announced that it would deliver 1400 thousand metric tons of grain on credit to Poland, and moreover that it would grant long-term credits to Poland in the amount of 700 million rubles.

On December 17, 1956, an agreement was signed "on the legal status of Soviet troops temporarily stationed in Poland" (the meaning of "temporarily" was never defined). Article 1 of the agreement stated that the stationing of Soviet troops in Poland "can in no way infringe on the sovereignty of the Polish state nor lead to interference in the internal affairs of the Polish People's Republic." According to the agreement, the number and location of Soviet soldiers would be decided between both governments; troop movements outside their locations would require the permission of the Polish authorities (Article 2). According to Article 3, Soviet troops, accompanying personnel, and members of their families would be required to honor Polish law.

Given the October action of Soviet troops in Poland and the Soviets' use of troops in Hungary, the Poles felt that some agreement with the Soviets was necessary. Does the December 1956 agreement in fact protect Poland against Soviet military agression? It can only be said that such agression would be contrary to the provisions of this agreement (and to those of various other international treaties). At any rate, this agreement makes it more difficult for the Soviet Union to invoke the Warsaw Pact as a justification for possible intervention.

The issue of Poles still living in the USSR was another thorn in Polish/Soviet relations. And in November 1956, it was declared that Poles living in the USSR would be allowed to move to the Polish People's Republic. This was called repatriation, as opposed to reimmigration (from France, for example), because those who were returning had never emigrated: they did not move eastwards, rather the borders moved westwards. According to information released on November 5, 1957, in the course of three years (1955–57), 103,000 Poles returned from the USSR; of this number, over 66,000 returned in 1957 alone.

The fact that Poland is ruled by a Communist party means that Polish/Soviet relations are not limited to relations between two states, but are dependent on general processes within the Communist movement. The Soviets may have allowed for a separate Polish "road to socialism" in October, but there was soon a tendency to level these differences and increase interstate unity in the name of Communist internationalism.

If, after October, one can speak of Polish foreign policy, it was largely Gomułka's policy. He attempted to work out a compromise between what he considered to be Polish interests and the interests of the Communist movement (i.e., Soviet interests). After Gomułka's second loss of power in the seventies, the close Polish/Soviet connections became even more evident.

The Economy

The year 1955 concluded the Six Year Plan, touted as a tremendous and successful effort and even exceeding its goals in the area of industrial production. Regarding investments and the growth of employment, the results were slightly lower than predicted. However, the Six Year Plan was a total failure in increasing the gross national product, agricultural production, and real wages—that is, in those areas directly felt by workers and consumers.

Changes in agricultural policy were clearly necessary, and the Poznań events demonstrated the need for a new policy in the area of consumption and wages. In 1956 these changes were actually taking place.

Already in 1947–49, Gomułka had been opposed to rapid collectivization, and this position was one of the reasons for his removal as secretary-general of the party.

In his speech to the Eighth Plenary Meeting, Gomułka spoke about improving the socialist model, and he dwelt at length on economic matters, specifically regarding more accounting in enterprises based on changes in the price structure. He mentioned making things easier for artisans and liquidating the so-called surtaxes, payments with which the state authorities burdened private producers in an unpredictable manner.

Gomułka opposed the opinion that "socialism in the countryside can be built only by impoverishing and ruining peasant farms." According to him, cooperatives of producers had a future only if they were voluntary, which presupposed the absence of economic compulsion.

In 1956 most of the cooperatives dissolved spontaneously. From the 10,203 cooperatives registered as of September 30, 1956, only 1,534 remained by December 31, 1956.

By the end of 1956 resolutions were adopted affecting the management of the economy and, specifically, of enterprises. Workers' councils were being formed in many factories, and on November 19, 1956, the Diet legalized these councils, stating that they "rule in the name of the workers of the enterprise, which is national property" and that they are "responsible to the workers of the enterprise and report to them."

Two years later, the law concerning the workers' councils was replaced by a workers' "self-government" law, in which the workers' councils lost the legal status accorded them in 1956. However, the actual significance of the workers' councils was never very great, and it had been declining gradually in the intervening two-year period.

There was general recognition in 1956 of the need for decentralization in economic management but not of how best to achieve it. A model of the functioning of the economy had to be elaborated, and much was written about this need.

An act of the Council of Ministers on December 21, 1956, called for the creation of an Economic Council. This was a structure similar to later committees of experts. In late 1956 and early 1957 it seemed that the Economic Council would act as an advisory organ to develop a new method of organizing the Polish economy. But such a model was never clearly formulated, and no serious changes actually took place in the organization of the Polish economy after October 1956. The party functionaries probably believed that the risks involved in such changes were too great. The result was to maintain the *status quo*.

Culture

The year 1956 left lasting marks on Polish culture. Yet this turning point need not be understood too narrowly: cultural changes occur gradually, and what impact external events have is rarely immediate. Signs of change were evident earlier—not everything began in 1956, and they did not end there.

Starting in 1955, books began to appear that had not previously been published by the state monopoly. In the early fifties, translations of Balzac, Stendhal, Zola, and especially Russian literature (excluding Dostoevsky) were available. After 1955, translations of contemporary American literature (not only of Howard Fast, but also of Hemingway) began to be published. And the works of Sartre and Kafka made their appearance.

Single poems by non-socialist realists, such as Miron Białoszewski and Zbigniew Herbert, had been printed in the periodical *Twórczość* (*Creativity*) in 1955, and in 1956 book-length collections of their poems appeared. It was also in 1955 that Leopold Tyrmand's lively novel about Warsaw, entitled *Zły* (*Nasty*), was published, which, against the backdrop of socialist realism, came as a revelation. There was also the shocking realism of Marek Hłasko's short story, "Pierwszy krok w chmurach" ("The First Step into the Clouds"), published in *Nowa Kultura* in November 1955 and later in a collection of Hłasko's stories in May 1956.

The names of emigrés began to appear in print. *Captive Spirit,* by Czesław Miłosz, was discussed, even if in a distorted way. Koestler, Orwell, and Miłosz were discussed in a *Nowa Kultura* article of October 7, 1956, entitled "The Wastepaper of the Great Conflict," even if critically. A little later a fragment of *1984* appeared in the weekly *Swiat* (*World*). And such unorthodox authors from prewar Poland as Stanisław Ignacy Witkiewicz and Bruno Schulz were now being reprinted.

Writers who had more or less conformed to the conventions of socialist realism now began some soul searching. In January 1956, *Twórczość* published Kazimierz Brandys' "Obrona Grenady" ("The Defense of Grenada"), dealing with the problems of some young people attempting to stage a production of Mayakovsky's "Bath-House." And in 1957 Jerzy Andrzejewski's topical novel, *Ciemnośi kryją ziemię* (*Darkness Covers the Earth*), about the Spanish Inquisition was released. Books written in the late forties and early fifties appeared for the first time: for example, *Rojsty,* by Tadeusz Konwicki, *Głosy w ciemności* (*Voices in the Dark*), by Julian Stryjkowski, and *Czas nieutracony* (*Time Never Lost*), by Stanisław Lem. These books could not be published before 1956.

Roughly speaking, 1956 also saw a reawakening of Polish theater, painting, music, and architecture. In all cultural areas, artists were abandoning socialist realism with visible relief. Still, there were those, mostly theoreticians (Stefan Zółkiewski being one), who tried to revive this doctrine. But even they were seeking to broaden the concept of realism, evidently to the eclipse of the "socialist" dimension. To this day, however, this literary trend is unclear, apart from the fact that it was supposed to be a portrayal not of the existing reality (which would be normal realism) but of the ideal reality—what should exist. But what does a "realistic portrayal" mean in such circumstances? This was a problem. The valuable works, whether from before 1956 or after, were created beyond such doctrinaire concerns.

Professional theater was discovering contemporary drama: the plays of Ionesco, Beckett, and Dürrenmatt were staged. There were productions of "Winkelried's Day," by Jerzy Andrzejewski and Jerzy Zagórski, and of "Yvonne, Princess of Burgundy," by Gombrowicz. Witkiewicz's plays appeared as well, as did such Polish classics as "Forefathers' Eve," "Kordian," and "The Un-divine Comedy," which had not been performed in previous years. There was also a grassroots theater emerging of student cabarets and theaters combining poetry, song, and politics. Polish jazz, previously banned as a manifestation of the "American life style," came out of hiding.

In the *Po prostu* gallery were exhibited the paintings of Tadeusz Kantor and Maria Jarema, who had been vocal critics of socialist realist painting (the exhibition in December 1956). The Polish *avant-garde* from the interwar and immediate postwar period returned to public attention. In June 1957, an exhibition of Józef Czapski's work opened in Poznań, and later moved to Cracow. Banned by the censorship before, Czapski, a painter and writer living abroad, was also banned soon afterwards, and his name was even expunged from footnotes.

The "Second All-Poland Exhibition of Modern Art" opened in the Zachęta Gallery in Warsaw in October 1957 (the first such show took place in Cracow in 1948). New magazines began to appear specializing in particular areas of art; for example, *Projekt,* concerned with applied art (posters, scenic design, industrial art, etc.).

In film, the years of the German occupation could now be portrayed in a manner resembling the truth. The so-called Polish school consists predominantly of movies about this period (Andrzej Wajda's "Canal," 1957; Andrzej Munk's "Eroica," 1957). Later, both these directors also made films about the early years of People's Poland, though not without suffering censorship (Wajda's "Ashes and Diamonds," 1958; Munk's "Crosseyed Luck," 1959).

The first music festival, "Warsaw Autumn," was organized in 1956, featuring first performances of works by Witold Lutosławski, Krzysztof Penderecki, and other contemporary Polish composers whose international fame began after 1956.

Architecture too was being revitalized. The simple and functional structure of the Tenth Anniversary Stadium, built in 1955, constituted one of the signs of the break with socialist realism. And the reconstruction of Warsaw in the early fifties, based on nineteenth-century models, remains a testament to the preceding epoch and serves as a supplement to historical Warsaw architecture destroyed during the German occupation.

Throughout 1956 intelligentsia clubs were being formed, assisted by the editors of *Po prostu,* who also attempted to organize exchanges. The clubs attracted previously isolated people to social, cultural, and often political, activities. They constituted an independent meeting place where valuable new ideas and initiatives were born. The clubs organized discussions and sought to enliven the provinces and were even involved in local economic matters (as, for example, with the Club of Ziemia Sądecka [the Club of Nowy Sącz County], where a program for the autonomous development of Nowy Sącz and its district was discussed and developed; later approved by the government in a special resolution of the Council of Ministers). Culture was no longer restricted to a few cities, namely Warsaw and Cracow, and was becoming, at the same time, more independent.

New periodicals began to appear in places previously considered provincial.

Between October 1956 and January 1957, the censorship relaxed. Newspapers and periodicals were readable for a change , and new issues of *Po prostu, Nowa Kultura, Przegląd Kulturalny,* or the new regional periodicals were quickly sold out.

The Seventh General Meeting of delegates to the Polish Union of Writers took place in Warsaw in late November and early December 1956. The delegates called for the abolition of preventive censorship, for the elimination of prohibitions against certain publications in reading rooms and libraries, for the widening of contacts with Polish émigré writers, and for the repeal of limitations on the distribution of émigré publications, especially of the Paris periodical *Kultura.* Antoni Słonimski was elected chairman of the Writers' Union.

On November 25, 1956, it was announced that jamming radio stations would cease in Poland. According to the communiqué, "the remaining cases of disturbances in reception are caused by jamming stations operating outside Poland. Talks with governments of neighboring countries about this matter should result shortly in a further improvement of reception." This communiqué was issued a week after the Bydgoszcz events, during which demonstrators had destroyed the jamming equipment. Initially, the party or the government had no intention of stopping jamming. At a meeting with editors on October 29, Gomułka said, "As far as some broadcasts are concerned, which distort the truth, especially those of Radio Free Europe, we will not stop jamming." The party leader probably intended to study the accuracy of broadcasts before jamming them. But when the broadcasts are jammed to begin with, it is difficult to decide whether they are true or not. So out of concern for the truth, they simply jammed everything.

The changes in culture and in the dissemination of information were accompanied by changes in education. Required elementary and high-school textbooks of general history, translated from Russian, were withdrawn, and Polish literature and foreign-language textbooks were changed. During the early fifties, the required high-school English textbooks included conversations in English between Polish peasants in a cooperative, to protect students who were allowed to study a nonprogressive language from the influence of "the Western lifestyle." The October changes influenced even biology. Genetics ceased to be regarded as a "bourgeois idealist science" and was introduced into the schools. Less space in school handbooks was devoted to such Soviet scientists as Trofim Lysenko, Ivan Michurin, and Olga Lepieshynskaya.

The ninth session of the Diet (September 5-11) legislated changes in higher education which increased the organizational diversity among institutions of higher education and left many detailed statutory issues to the discretion of individual schools. According to the new law, rectors, prorectors, deans, and assistant deans were to be elected rather than nominated by the education minister, as had previously been the case. The minister was also required to consult with institutions of higher education before reaching decisions. Rectors were required to seek the advice of the university senate in all important matters. These changes significantly increased the autonomy of the universities, and they survived until 1968.

These changes in higher education also carried over to the academic institutes. The Scientific Secretary of the Polish Academy of Science (PAN), Professor Henryk Jabłoński, asserted in an interview (December 1956) that PAN should become more autonomous and less bureaucratic. This involved limiting the role played by the PAN Presidium in the work of the individual departments and increasing the role played by the scientific councils within each research institute. At the PAN General Assembly meeting on January 11-12, 1957, Tadeusz Koparbiński became president of the academy. It seemed that Polish science would gain some independence from party decisions. The post-1956 history of the organization and functioning of science in Poland is a history of partial autonomy and of increasing subjugation.

The State and the Church

In the early fifties the authorities attempted to neutralize and circumscribe the Catholic Church's religious activities (since immediate liquidation was problematic). Towards this end, the authorities sought to make the Church an adjunct to the party; for example, the Church was allowed to take part in the movement for the defense of peace. Denominational organizations (such as fraternities, congregational groups, etc.) were dissolved. Schools, kindergartens, and hospitals were removed from religious orders. Caritas, a charitable organization, was infiltrated and controlled by state athorities. Religion classes were dropped from schools. Priests were persecuted, and the resisters were imprisoned. Despite these things, the religiosity of Polish society persisted, which hampered the authorities' efforts to limit Church influence.

The primate of Poland, Cardinal Stefan Wyszyński, suffered imprisonment in a series of monasteries, and he remained imprisoned for two years after Władysław Gomułka was freed in 1954. He was still imprisoned when the Eighth Plenary Meeting took place and when Gomułka made his speech on Parade Square in Warsaw. However, the October political relaxation soon included Church-party-state relations.

On October 28, 1956, Cardinal Wyszyński was released from imprisonment and returned to Warsaw to resume his official duties. On October 29, he addressed a crowd of faithful gathered in the courtyard of the Primate's Palace and appealed for calm and caution, saying:"Our motherland demands now from you much calm, much caution, and many, many prayers."

On December 8, the Bilateral Commission set up to review Church/state relations, asserted that a new legal act regulating the staffing of Church positions was needed: one that would guarantee state influence while respecting the requirements of Church jurisdiction. In the communiqué, the commission also made recommendations supporting the "full freedom and voluntary character of religious instruction in schools for those children whose parents so desire. The teaching of religion will be conducted in schools as an elective subject. School authorities are required to allow the teaching of religion by an appropriate scheduling of school classes." Religious care for those who were sick or imprisoned was also provided for by the commission.

On December 31, 1956, the State Council passed a new decree on the staffing of Church positions, replacing the one of 1953. In the 1953 decree, the state organs received extensive influence over the personnel policies of the Church. For example, Article 6 of the decree stated that "any social activity against the law and public order, or the support and concealment of any such activity by a person holding a pastoral position in the Church, will lead to the dismissal of this person by the superior

Church organ or by the request of the state organs." This was changed in the new decree (see Article 7) to read: "If an ecclesiastic engages in activity harmful to the state, the appropriate state organ will appeal to the superior Church authority to issue appropriate orders; and in the case of the inefficacy of such orders, the state may ask that the ecclesiastic be dismissed from his position."

On December 28, the Highest Military Tribunal repealed the September 22, 1953, sentences for Bishop Czesław Kaczmarek (12 years imprisonment), three priests (10, 9, and 8 years), and one nun (5 years). Bishop Kaczmarek had been in prison since January 1951. In defense of its decision to repeal the Kaczmarek sentence, the Highest Military Tribunal stated that this sentence was "based on confessions by the accused that were extracted under investigative conditions which infringed on the principles of legality."

On January 14, the same day Premier Józef Cyrankiewicz received the primate of Poland, Cardinal Wyszyński, to discuss Church/state relations, the Polish episcopate issued a statement that Catholics were to "fulfill their duty of conscience and participate in voting." In this way, the Church expressed a certain support for the authorities. But it was a limited support. The statement urged people simply to participate in voting and did not specify voting without deletions, as Gomułka had demanded from voters in the name of the party.

Very shortly after the primate's assumption of his official duties, unresolved disagreements began to appear between the state and the Church. Among them was the problem of reviving the Theological Faculty at the Jagiellonian University in Cracow.

In the postwar history of Church/state relations in Poland, October 1956 was certainly a period of normalization. But the state did not formally recognize the jurisdictional identity of the Church: there was no normalization of relations with the Vatican, and the possibilities of establishing and conducting active denominational organizations were still limited. Still, the difference between 1953 and 1956–57 was striking.

Catholic Associations

During the early fifties, Pax was the official Catholic lay organization. It preached both Catholicism and socialism and supported the Communist regime. Before March 1953, there were also the independent sociocultural Catholic periodicals, *Tygodnik Powszechny* (*Common Weekly*) and the monthly *Znak* (*Sign*). Both were published in Cracow, both shared a similar political outlook and remained much more reticent than Pax in their praise for the existing system, and both published works by the same authors. Both also ended publication (for a time) in 1953. As recounted in the December 25, 1956 issue of the revived *Tygodnik Powszechny,* the final causes of their earlier demise were "our negative attitude toward the methods used at the time against the Church and the Episcopate and our refusal to publish an article commemorating the death of Josef Stalin. . . ."

Pax was formally organized in 1952 and grew out of a group centered around the weekly, *Dziś i Jutro* (*Today and Tomorrow*). This group also ran the daily, *Słowo Powszechne* (*Common Word*), and a publishing house, also named Pax.

The leading force on the *Dziś i Jutro* editorial board and in Pax was Bolesław Piasecki. His publications formulated the ideological position of the numerous Pax ventures. In 1954, Piasecki published a book entitled *Zagadnienia Istotne* (*Important Issues*), which presented a theological argument for why Catholics should support the building of the socialist system in Poland.

In June 1955, Piasecki's *Important Issues* and *Dziś i Jutro* were both placed on the Index (of proscribed literature) by the Church authorities. As a result, Pax decided to suspend publication of *Dziś i Jutro,* and shortly thereafter began the publication of a new journal, *Kierunki* (*Directions*).

In response to the discussion at that time about democratization and freedom, Pax leader Bolesław Piasecki published an article in *Słowo Powszechne* shortly before the Eighth Plenary Meeting, entitled "The State Instinct." Piasecki called for a responsible discussion or else, "instead of democratization, it will become necessary for the reasons of state to be brutally asserted, in a way similar to a state of emergency." This was understood as a threat against the proponents of democratization and an encouragement for the authorities to adopt a hardline posture.

Shortly afterwards, condemnations of Piasecki began to appear in the press. One of the first came from the Club of the Crooked Circle, which demanded that Piasecki be excluded from the All-Poland Committee of the Front of National Unity.

In general, the Polish October was not an auspicious time for Pax. New possibilities for political action were opening up for lay Catholics, and the Pax membership was consequently decreasing. (Perhaps Piasecki's only consolation was that he was relieved of unreliable members.) Piasecki was aligning himself with the more permanent features of the political system and did not let himself be swept up in the wave of liberalization.

But after October 20, 1956, those elements of Polish Catholicism that had been persecuted during the Stalinist era again became active.

A "Statement of Catholic Writers and Activists," published in *Życie Warszawy* on October 23, asserted that "Polish Catholics appreciate the moral significance of the new directions in internal policy, which are to be based on sovereignty and oh the extension of democratization in our lives." The signatories expressed their "full support for the program of the first secretary of the party, Władysław Gomułka," and distanced themselves from the "opinions of Bolesław Piasecki contained in his famous article, 'The State Instinct,' which strike out at the democratization of political life in Poland." This statement was signed by 22 persons, mostly former collaborators of *Tygodnik Powszechny* (from before the Pax takeover) and Pax renegades. It was individuals from such a background who formed the All-Poland Club of Progressive Catholic Intelligentsia, inaugurated on October 27, and who were received by Gomułka on October 30. It must be said that at this time the party conducted a "pluralist" policy toward Catholic associations. In this area, there was room for the toleration and support of many different groups and tendencies.

After a break of almost three years, *Tygodnik Powszechny* was back on the stands Christmas Day 1956. It was edited by Jerzy Turowicz and former staff from the pre-1953 days. The first issue contained "A Dialogue about Idealism and Realism in Politics," by Stefan Kisielewski and Stanisław Stomma. The issue included a map of Poland with only the borders marked and the names of the surrounding countries listed. This clearly illustrated the geopolitical orientation of the texts.

Stefan Kisielewski's article called for "an honest and conscious alliance with the Soviet Union and people's democracies and the idea of full solidarity with the entire Eastern bloc, despite the justified psychological resistance of our society. . . ." And it stressed "that a departure from the socialist forms of economy would bring to Poland an incalculable catastrophe, and that the only option is the road proposed by Gomułka of repair, reform, and improvement of socialism, despite the fact that the majority of people in Poland are neither Marxist nor socialist." As

Stanisław Stomma put it: "Apart from people of ill will, there is another enemy: political idealists. When such people do not see immediate and complete results or have to make compromises necessary in life, they become demoralized and apathetic. This is an echo of the former 'all or nothing' mentality."

Clearly such opinions expressed at this time were heavily influenced by the Soviet invasion of Hungary. The fate of Hungary stimulated such realist tendencies in Polish political thought.

This so-called "neopositivist" program was not directed at party members and did not postulate the party's leading role. It spoke about realities, which, according to the authors, had to be taken into account and were to constitute a frame of reference for the independent social and cultural life of Poland.

In *Tygodnik Powszechny* of January 20, 1957, five (Catholic) candidates for deputy to the Diet answered the question: "Why am I a candidate to the Diet?" Apparently the answer was not obvious. Stefan Kisielewski answered, "One can and must try. When one does not try, and does not take risks, one can never win."

After the election, the Catholic deputies, associated with *Tygodnik Powszechny,* formed a parliamentary group called Znak. The group was also joined by certain other nonparty deputies, filling its ranks during the 1957–61 Diet session to eleven members.

In the next session (1961–65), the Znak deputies obtained only five mandates, and in the following session (1965–69) Stefan Kisielewski was replaced by Janusz Zabłocki, who came to deviate from the Znak position. By 1976, the Znak membership had changed to such an extent that when the Diet voted on revisions of the Constitution, only one Znak deputy, Stanisław Stomma, abstained from voting. And in the next Diet elections Stomma lost his seat.

Apart from publications and from the necessarily isolated activity of the Znak group in the Diet, lay Catholics close to *Tygodnik Powszechny* were also socially active in the clubs of Catholic intelligentsia. On March 10, 1957 a meeting of representatives of 26 such clubs, took place in Warsaw, at which an organizational committee was selected. Soon after, the clubs were registered as the Club of Catholic Intelligentsia in each of five cities: Warsaw, Cracow, Wrocław, Poznań, and Toruń.

Despite efforts by the party, state, and police authorities to infiltrate and undermine the groups gathered around *Tygodnik Powszechny, Więź,* and the Club of Catholic Intelligentsia, and despite the growth and extension of Pax, these groups survived. Their beginnings went back to the early postwar period, but their revival and growth are among the remnants of October 1956.

New Youth Organizations

Between October 1956 and January 1957, the party youth organization, the Union of Polish Youth (ZMP), was disintegrating. At the Fourth Plenary Meeting of the Main Board of ZMP held on November 1-2, attempts were made at infusing some new life into the organization: fourteen new members were enlisted and eleven older members were removed. The Fourth Plenary Meeting also appealed to the young people of Poland for support of the Eighth Plenary Meeting. But the concern expressed in the letter about the threats to socialist democracy both from "conservative" forces and from forces "opposed to the building of social-ism" and about the international situation was evidence of limits to the change. The letter supported the demand that Soviet troops be with-drawn from Hungary, but it also supported the nation of Egypt, which, it claimed, was a victim of aggression. The letter expressed support for "creative attempts to revive the youth movement," but it also asserted that "today, our priority is the unified action of all progressive forces within Polish youth." This emphasis on the need for unity was reaffirmed in a declaration "About the Need for Unity," passed by the Main Board of ZMP on November 13. It stated: "We are for the organized activity of youth in one union." The declaration was in response to the growing trend towards dividing the youth movement. At that time, various groups and clubs of young people were being created, and the continued usefulness of ZMP was being increasingly questioned.

Po prostu published a two-page response to the declaration, entitled "What more should be done?" and signed, "The *Po prostu* group." In the authors' view, the declaration was aimed at the liquidation of "the real socialist and patriotic movement of the youth, in the name of a mystical idea: a miraculous resurrection of the deceased ZMP." "The unification of youth organizations in 1948 spelled the defeat of the youth movement—it was one of the first serious successes of the Stalinist offensive in Poland." In the article three tendencies were identified in the youth movement. The first was "provisionally and conventionally" called the Revolutionary Union of Youth (RZM). "The second tendency is the reactivation of the rural youth organization, Wici." "The third tendency, the weakest, and still in a very embryonic state, consists of the attempts to create the Union of Democratic Youth . . . favored by a large part of the progressive Catholic youth."

The Revolutionary Union of Youth (RZM) was formally created on December 7, at "a conference of representatives of revolutionary, socialist, and communist youth groups from the entire country" in Warsaw. It was organized jointly by the editors of *Po prostu* and *Walka Młodych* (*Young Struggle*), as well as by the Warsaw committees of the Revolutionary Union of Youth and the Union of Socialist Youth. In a letter to young people, the organizers stated that they "support the full independence of the Union" and that they recognize the necessary leadership role of the party in the nation. RZM soon united with the Union of Working Youth to form the Union of Socialist Youth (ZMS), whose fate clearly demonstrated that in the case of a conflict between independence and the party's leadership role, the latter won out.

The National Conference of Rural Youth took place on February 10–11. As stated by the preparatory committee on December 6: "The Union of Rural Youth will be an independent and a nonparty organization. Union members should have the possibility of choosing their party membership—they can freely join PZPR and ZSL [The United Peasants' Party]. . . . The religious question will be considered the private matter of each member."

There was also an All-Poland Convention of Scout Activists in Łódź from December 8–10. A resolution passed on December 10 restored to the organization its traditional name, the Polish Scouting Union (ZHP), and its medal, the Scouting Cross. The ideological declaration of ZHP asserted that "ZHP works under the leadership of the United Polish Workers' Party, that is, it educates its members in the spirit of socialism."

The Union of Young Democrats attempted to maintain its independence and rejected the party's leading role. As a result, the union came under fire in a *Życie Warszawy* article and was finally dissolved by order of the authorities on January 16, 1957, just before elections to the Diet. The communiqué about the dissolution of the union stated that "The Union of Young Democrats made the decision to dissolve the union at all levels of the organization. Former members of the Union of Young

Democrats will be able to participate in the Youth Circles of the Democratic Party." This shortly followed the decision of the Main Board of ZMP "to dissolve itself in view of the dissolution of most parts of the organization."

Even with the official harassment of independent youth organizations, as with the Union of Young Democrats, the period of complete uniformity in the official youth movement was over. The idea of ZMP was not revived for 14 years, and it was not until 1976 that the Socialist Union of Polish Youth (SZMP) was created as a surrogate.

The Diet Elections

The April 1956 session of the Diet was greatly publicized in the press and demonstrated the Diet's existence to the public. Decisions may not have been made in the Diet, but at least it was a place where one could hear interesting speeches. The press discussed the new parliamentary system, and consideration was given to ways in which the Diet's role could be increased.

The session of the Diet was to end in 1956, and new elections were scheduled for December 16. On October 24 the Diet adopted a statute of "Electoral Law for the Diet of the Polish People's Republic" to replace the Electoral Law of August 1, 1952. However, in fact there were few changes in the new electoral law; in many instances the new articles were identical with the old, even carrying the same numbers.

Both laws agreed that the right to nominate a candidate "belongs to political, union, and co-operative organizations, to the Union of Peasant Self-Help, to the Union of Polish Youth, and to other social organizations of the working people" (Art. 33). The right to nominate candidates belonged both to the central and to the regional organs of these organizations (Art. 35), and candidates were to be registered in the districts (Art. 34).

The maximum number of candidates was defined differently in the two laws. The 1952 electoral law stated: "The number of candidates in the ballot cannot be greater than the number of deputies for the given district" (Art. 39). The corresponding article of the 1956 law read: "The number of candidates on the ballot should be greater than the number of deputies for the given district, but not greater by more than two-thirds" (Art. 39).

Both electoral laws allow for the existence of many electoral lists; even the law 1952 did not automatically eliminate the possibility of real elections. "The order in which the lists are placed on the ballot is determined by the order in which they are registered with the regional electoral commission. The size and style of type used to print the ballot should be identical for all lists" (Art. 48.2 of the 1952 law, corresponding with Art. 47.2 of the 1956 law).

According to both laws, if the ballot comprised two or more lists, the voter was to mark the appropriate box to indicate his vote for a specific list. If the voter did not mark the ballot at all, or if he marked two or more lists, "the ballot is counted as a vote for the un-crossed-out candidates of the list printed first on the ballot" (Art. 60.2 of the 1956 law). Thus the first list was automatically privileged. The law also explicitly excluded the possibility of a valid vote for candidates chosen from among several different lists.

In actual fact, after 1952 there was never more than one list of candidates in Diet or local elections. Nevertheless, the very existence of laws favoring the first list could some day be useful legally and even politically to the authorities and could have, in practice, been used in the elections of 1947.

The electoral law of 1956 also specified that "when the number of candidates who are not crossed out is greater than the number of deputies for a given district, the ballot is counted as a vote for those un-crossed out candidates whose names are printed first on the ballot" (Art. 60.3).

Both the law of 1952 and the law of 1956, if they were to be taken literally, required that the act of casting one's ballot be secret. They stated that the voter was supposed to go into the voting booth behind a curtain and to acquaint himself with the ballot.

The October legal changes were not profound. They consisted of a recommendation, and thus of legal permission, for a list to contain a larger number of candidates than the number of deputies for a given district (Art. 39, cited above). But the voter could abstain from choosing, which did not render his vote invalid: candidates whose names were printed first would automatically be recorded.

The electoral law of October 1956 was altered somewhat in the law of December 22, 1960. The rule requiring the voter to make his choice behind a curtain was deleted, although it was stated that secret voting should be made possible: "The polling place must be equipped in such a manner as to insure secrecy of voting" (Art. 6). Further changes were introduced almost 20 years later, in the electoral law for the Diet and local governments of January 17, 1976. The rules permitting the registration of many electoral lists disappeared, and the Front of National Unity was designated as the only organization with the right to establish lists of candidates for deputies and aldermen for local councils. Gradually, the law was being adapted to reflect political reality.

The date of the Diet elections was moved from December 16, 1956 to January 20, 1957, and in December, lists were published of the candidates for deputies registered by the Front of National Unity (replacing the former National Front). The Front of National Unity, like its predecessor, was responsible only for sponsoring the electoral lists for the Diet and for local governments, though this role was legally recognized only after 1976.

On January 9, the candidate for deputy from Warsaw, Władysław Gomułka, answered voters' questions in a Warsaw textile plant. Gomułka demanded that people vote for the candidates of the Front of National Unity (there were no other candidates!) and that they vote without crossing out names. The point was to elect candidates from the first places on the list according to the election law. In this way, all electoral competition was to be eliminated, even within the one existing list of candidates. "Although no one has asked me how he should vote," Gomułka admitted, "let me share with you my view and the view of the party leadership. Vote for the first candidates on the list. Return your ballots without crossing out names. . . . We call on all members and sympathizers of the party: do not cross out any candidates of the Polish United Workers' Party."

So Gomułka was demanding, in effect, that the electoral process be completed with the selection of candidates for the first slots on the ballot. These were called "mandated places," and getting such a place virtually assured the candidate a seat in the Diet. The concept of mandated ballot places is characteristic of Communist legal and political practice, whereby the necessity of maintaining certain legal appearances clashes with communist principles, specifically the principle of the party's so-called "leading" role.

As a practical measure to help ensure the election of reliable candidates the Consultative Committee of Political Parties adopted a resolution stating that "during the electoral campaign, some candidates for the Diet have used disloyal procedures against candidates of allied parties, and have made demagogic promises exploiting human naiveté and the credulity of voters. . . . Condemning such methods during the campaign, we recommend that all consultative committees of parties in the country oppose such disloyal behavior and, if necessary, withdraw by January 17—according to the law—the names of [these] candidates from the list of the Front of National Unity. . . ."

The resolution was signed by the first secretary of the PZPR Central Committee, Gomułka, by the chairman of the National Committee of the United Peasants' Party (ZSL), Stefan Ignar, and by the chairman of the Central Committee of the Democratic Party, Stanisław Kulczyński. Unfortunately, it was not at all clear what laws governed "the withdrawal of candidates from the list of the Front of National Unity." The electoral law did not include anything about such procedure. Only in December 1960 was the law supplemented with a rule stating: "In especially justified cases, on the recommendation of an organization that registered the list of candidates, the regional electoral committee can, according to the recommendation, change the order of candidates on the list or delete a candidate and introduce another one; this must be done not later than 10 days before the elections." This rule legalized a procedure which in 1957 was used in an extra-legal or even illegal manner.

On January 12 it was announced that some candidates to the Diet had shown a lack of discipline and had been removed from the ballot. On January 14, the first name on the list in Lublin, that of former Premier Edward Osóbka-Morawski, was removed from the ballot. Apparently he had been "disloyal" or was using "disloyal procedures" or making "demagogic promises," or perhaps he did not oppose "provocative statements."

On January 14, in the Warsaw Palace of Science and Culture, there was a meeting with candidates for the Diet. In his speech on this occasion, Gomułka stated: "The elections do not address the question of whether the people's government and our party, together with the other parties of the Front of National Unity, will remain in power. The revolutionary party of the working class—and PZPR is such a party—will never return power to the reaction or to those who want to restore capitalism in Poland." This was an official announcement that PZPR was not planning to honor the election results if they should prove to be adverse to the party. One has to admit that in this case Gomułka spoke rather openly.

The day before the election, on January 19, Gomułka spoke on the radio and repeated his appeal for general participation in the elections and for voting without crossing out names. He warned against the consequences of crossing out the names of party candidates. He was letting it be known that only Communist rule could defend Poland against the intervention of the Soviet Union: "Only socialist Poland can exist on the map of Europe as a sovereign and independent country." Society should therefore trust the party. Only its rule could insure the existence of Polish statehood. "Calling for the crossing out of PZPR candidates on the ballot is not just equivalent to calling for the destruction of socialism in Poland. The crossing out of candidates of our party is equivalent to crossing out the independence of our country, and crossing out Poland from the map of Europe."

Gomułka was making the elections into a plebiscite, comparable to the referendum of 1946: "Are you for or against the continued existence of Poland on the map?" was meant to be interchangeable with, "Are you for or against the candidates who, as has already been decided, should have seats in the Diet?" The nature of this threat to continued existence was not made explicit; however, the recent Hungarian experiences contributed to a certain uniformity of conjecture: Gomułka was warning against the friendly intervention of the USSR and was linking its likelihood with the behavior of the voters.

This was not the position of the *Po prostu* editors, however. Committed to the "program of the Polish October," they felt it was the voters' duty to see it was carried out by *choosing* the best candidates from the Front of National Unity list.

In the special edition of January 20, *Po prostu* reminded its readers of the main banner of the Poznań demonstration: "Bread and Freedom." In an article entitled, "What Does Polish Society Expect from the Diet *Anno Domini* 1957?" the editors wrote: "A country that is subject to the economic favor or disfavor of another country cannot be fully sovereign. And this is why Polish society, which desires both liberty/independence and bread . . . appeals to the Diet . . . with a categorical demand: develop a constructive economic program for our country!"

This *Po prostu* issue also stated that public opinion demanded above all that "state capital be invested on the basis of maximum financial effectiveness . . . that industry turn as much as possible from production for military defense to civilian production . . . that the work force artificially employed in the national economy be moved to agriculture and to new areas of production requiring relatively small investment. . . ."

According to *Po prostu:* "Public opinion attaches enormous importance to changing the socio-economic model in Poland, to overcoming the Stalinist system. This demand, addressed generally and categorically to the Diet, means:

- socialization, with the working class taking over the means of production, which were taken over by the state in 1946–47: this should be done mostly through the movement of workers' self-government, which the bureaucracy is presently opposing;
- directing the economy according to economic laws;
- adding a second chamber to the Diet, a chamber of producers, with the task of coordinating the workers' self-government . . .
- reduction in the number of ministries and general limitation of the government apparatus;
- subordination of the government to the Diet, with the government accountable to the Diet;
- reform of the constitutional system, according to the political traditions of our country. . . ."

Po prostu was committed to having at least somewhat authentic elections. They were to be based on what the voters, and not the authorities, wanted, on their understanding of the "program of the Polish October," and on their selection from among the candidates of the Front of National Unity.

The elections took place on January 20. According to official sources, 94.1 percent of the population participated, 98.4 percent of whom voted for the Front of National Unity list. The Diet was composed of 288 PZPR members, 114 members of the United Peasants' Party, and 41 Democratic Party members, as well as 64 independents, including, as was officially announced, 12 Catholic activists, from Pax and elsewhere.

In the 37th District, comprising Nowy Sącz and its county, the voting results were anomalous and had to be repeated. The voters were to select three out of five candidates for the Diet. However, only two achieved the absolute majority required by law for election. Nowy Sącz was the only district in which a candidate with a mandated place lost the election (however, neither of the two "non-mandated" candidates achieved the required majority). On March 17, 1957, additional elections were held in the district. The ballot contained two names (the person who had lost the first time was not renominated). The candidate who received 62 percent of the vote was elected (the second candidate received 37 percent).

The Diet chosen in 1957 did not play an important role; but PZPR's preelection preparations themselves were significant since they demonstrated the extent to which the party leadership was willing to tolerate democratic mechanisms. The Electoral Law of October 1956 gave voters certain possibilities. Yet the manner in which the elections were conducted enabled the PZPR, in practice, to insure itself against democratic mechanisms allowed by the law, mechanisms which only later gradually disappeared from the legal order.

Poland and China

In June 1956, the director of the propaganda division of the Chinese Communist Party, Liu Ting-i, delivered a speech entitled, "Let a Hundred Flowers Bloom, Let a Hundred Schools of Thought Compete." This was the beginning of the Chinese campaign of the Hundred Flowers, which, as it was described in China at the time, was to be based on party support for freedom of opinion and freedom and independence in art and science. Later, this very call for free discussion by the Chinese was seen by many as a mere prelude to the cultural revolution, as a way of facilitating the selection of future victims. Whatever the hidden meanings of the Chinese policy may have been, the Chinese policy had a large resonance in Poland. The name of "Hundred Flowers" was even adopted by one of the discussion clubs.

The Polish press published more information about the internal and foreign policy of China, about principles of peaceful coexistence and about the Hundred Flowers policy. At the end of December 1956, the newspapers published a very extensive Chinese declaration about the issues of the workers' movement, "A Contribution to the Historical Experience of the Dictatorship of the Proletariat." This very diplomatically formulated text contained praise for Stalin's achievements while denouncing his "errors"; it accepted the leading role of the Soviet Union in the socialist bloc while condemning great power chauvinism. It is likely that the Chinese leaders were at that time interested in the unity of the socialist bloc, "with the Soviet Union as its leader" and China as an arbiter or mediator. Four years later, they would be far less inclined to emphasize the leading role of the USSR, and Gomułka would attempt to arrogate the role of arbiter, though he became merely a spokesman for the Soviet position.

The Chinese premier, Chou En-lai, visited Poland from January 11–16, stopping in Moscow both before and after his visit, with a short interlude in Budapest on his return to Moscow. On January 14, during the visit of the Chinese guest, Premier Cyrankiewicz declared that the Chinese fully understood the direction of Polish changes. Cyrankiewicz also spoke about the need for equality in international relations between large and small countries.

At a farewell reception in the Chinese embassy, Chou En-lai stated: "We want to assure our Polish brothers that the nation of six hundred million Chinese will always be an ally of the Polish nation in its struggle for peace and socialism." In this accepted style of political propaganda, Chou En-lai was officially giving support to the new authorities in Poland.

The common declaration of both delegations asserted that "relations between socialist countries . . . should be based on the principle of respect for sovereignty, noninterference in internal affairs, equality, and mutual benefits."

It would be an exaggeration, however, to regard the Chinese policy of this time as supporting all freedom movements in Eastern Europe. The divergencies between the Soviet Union and China had not yet fully emerged. In January 1957, both in Budapest and Moscow, the Chinese condemned the Hungarian uprising as strongly as any Soviet bloc country, with the sole exception of Poland (it is difficult to count Yugoslavia as a member of this bloc). A Chinese-Hungarian communiqué on January 17 spoke about "subversive activities aimed at the destruction of the system of people's democracies and the annihilation of socialist achievements in Hungary." It also asserted that the Hungarian working people, relying on the help of Soviet troops, had "thwarted a counter-revolutionary military uprising incited by the reactionary forces of imperialism." The Sino-Soviet declaration of January 18 went even further, declaring that aggressive imperialist circles and counter-revolutionary Hungarian elements had attempted to abolish the socialist system in Hungary and to revive a fascist dictatorship, and thus to create in Europe a breeding ground for future war. The joint declaration went on to say that "by providing help to the Hungarian nation and liquidating the counter-revolutionary *putsch,* the Soviet Union has fulfilled its international responsibility towards the working masses of Hungary and towards other socialist countries by serving the interests of peace for the entire world." This defense of peace and fulfillment of international responsibility was to be repeated twelve years later in Czechoslovakia. By that time, however, the Chinese position had changed, and China did not support the intervention of the Warsaw Pact in Czechoslovakia.

The Party and the People

Reigning Communist parties generally fear the independent voice of the street. And in 1956, the people were beginning to assert themselves and were forcing the party to hear their demands. Under this pressure, the Communist authorities went from blaming the Poznań events on the provocations of imperialist agents to merely blaming hooligans. Later, even references to hooligans disappeared from the press. On October 20, Gomułka addressed the plenary meeting: "The working class has taught the leadership of the party and the government a painful lesson. The Poznań workers, by resorting to the strike and to street demonstrations on this black June Thursday, have called out in a great voice: Enough! This cannot continue! We have to abandon our false path! . . . We, the party and government leadership, are responsible for the Poznań tragedy. . . . The Six Year Plan, widely advertised as directed toward increasing the standard of living, was a disappointment to the working masses. Attempts to prove there had been a '27 percent increase in real pay over 6 years,' were unsuccessful and only irritated people. We had to retreat from the position taken by lousy statisticians."

However, this conciliatory mood on the part of the authorities quickly began to change after the elections of 1957. On March 22, 1957, the Diet passed a resolution invalidating all overdue additional salary claims granted in the Diet law of November 19, 1956. It was a partial (and thus a fictitious) declaration of the bankruptcy of the state. Those to whom the state owed money could expect to receive nothing.

In May 1957, at the Ninth Plenary Meeting, Gomułka's attitude toward workers' strikes had changed significantly. Strikes were not to be tolerated by the party. "Without taking the right to strike away from the workers, we have to tell them: a strike is not a way of improving the standard of living; it does not increase but decreases the national ration of bread. Thus, it is better not to strike."

But the workers kept striking. From August 12–14, 1957, there was a street-car strike in Łódź. In his speech of August 17 in Cracow, on the twentieth anniversary of peasant strikes, Gomułka praised the earlier peasant strikes while calling the Łódź strike "wild" and those who provoked it "hoodlums." This last epithet, employed later in 1976, has thus a substantial history.

For Gomułka, the Poznań strike was important as evidence of the inefficiency of the ruling group, which had previously excluded him. A year later, however, the strikes were said to have been instigated by hoodlums and brought to a halt by the attitude of the working class.

The *Trybuna Ludu* issue with Gomułka's speech about the Łódź strike also had a front-page announcement entitled, "Notorious Shirkers Expelled from Mines." It asserted that "the struggle undertaken last month by the Ministry of Mining and Energy against an unusually high rate of absenteeism in the coal mines continues. In July and the first half of August, over one-and-a-half thousand notorious shirkers were fired from the coal mines. A series of orders have been adopted aimed at increasing worker discipline and the quality of their products."

The workers, and society generally, did achieve certain improvements in their standard of living, but the official attitude towards them very quickly became stricter. The danger of strikes demanded preventive measures.

The policy towards peasants changed a little more slowly. In 1956 it seemed that the party leaders had withdrawn from the collectivization program. There were promises of redress for injustices committed against the peasants. And when Gomułka spoke at the harvest celebrations in Tenth Anniversary Stadium in Warsaw on September 8, 1957, he claimed that the new agricultural policy inaugurated eight months earlier had already shown positive results. He announced that "land illegally taken from its owners, or expropriated from the owners by economic pressures . . . has by now been almost completely returned." According to Gomułka, the peasants' trust in the future was confirmed by their reclaiming their land from the state.

Twenty years later, in contrast, the authorities would be happy when peasants relinquished the cultivation of land to the state. Government policy was then designed to induce abandonment of individual land cultivation (for example, the 1977 retirement law for farmers). The times were long past when not reclaiming land from the state was regarded as a lack of trust in the government.

Nevertheless, in 1957 the government policy towards peasants was much more conciliatory than the policy towards workers; though Gomułka still insisted on "discipline, order, and respect for social property" and warned the peasants about hoodlums and hostile instigations, and about delaying their deliveries of livestock.

To the intelligentsia, October 1956 was a time of increased possibilities for creative and useful work. The role of "political criteria" and censorship subsided, and there were possibilities for social action in organizations enjoying at least a limited degree of autonomy. This was short-lived, however. Censorship soon made a comeback, and the political police soon intervened in the affairs of the intelligentsia clubs. The authorities attempted to coopt these clubs via the National Center of Cooperation of Clubs of Intelligentsia, attached to the Front of National Unity. Nevertheless, the Club of the Crooked Circle remained active and independent in Warsaw for quite some time, and the Clubs of Catholic Intelligentsia survived even longer.

This change in party policy toward workers' strikes and intellectual freedom corresponded with changes in internal party policy. At the Ninth Plenary Meeting that reaffirmed the *Polish* road to socialism and condemned the mechanistic imitation of the Soviet Union (associated with the Stalinist period) and the petrification of Marxist thought, the party's commitment to proletarian internationalism was also reaffirmed, which meant that the Polishness of the road to socialism did have certain limitations. In the party there should be a struggle on two fronts: against dogmatism and against revisionism.

In 1956 much was said in the party about dogmatism. But this time the main danger was said to come from revisionism. The warning about the revisionist danger was directed against those party members who were counting on the further development of the October changes. And it could certainly count on the support of the party apparatus, which was disoriented by the outspokenness of the various party publicists.

At the Ninth Plenary Meeting, Gomułka spoke on "The Central Problems of Party Policy." This covered a whole range of issues, including, as it turned out, the views of "Party Member Comrade Leszek Kołakowski," expressed in the February 3, 1957 issue of *Życie Warszawy*. Gomułka's critique exemplified the attack against revisionism: "What does Kołakowski want? He wants a so-called integral democracy. . . . Under the conditions of any class society, integral democracy is nonsense. . . . For this revisionist hangover, Comrade Kołakowski was celebrated by the Trotskyist and bourgeois press, which publishes articles of his not cleared by the censorship for publication in Poland."

The policy against the revisionists adopted at the Ninth Plenary Meeting was later systematically implemented, and the suspension of the weekly *Po prostu* during the summer was one of the results. The disappearance of *Po prostu* was met by a protest demonstration of students in Warsaw on October 3, 1957, on Narutowicz Square, which lasted several days.

On October 4, there was an extraordinary meeting of the Warsaw Section of the Union of Polish Writers (ZLP), which passed a resolution protesting the suspension of the weekly *Po prostu* and "the current activities of the Main Office for the Control of the Press and of Spectacles [which] violate the freedom of expression guaranteed by the constitution." The resolution criticized the suspension of *Po prostu* as "a very serious limitation of the freedom of democratic criticism, which makes the consolidation of the progressive forces very difficult and constitutes a dangerous signal of return to the old methods. We, the assembled, protest against this administrative order, and we stress its dangerous political and moral consequences."

This was one episode in the long fight of the intellectuals against the censorship, and the fight continued well into the sixties. For over thirty years, censorship has been one of the constant supports of the system, and its abolition in Czechoslovakia in 1968 was considered by neighboring countries to be one of the most anti-socialist acts of Dubček's group.

The October 17, 1957 issue of *Trybuna Ludu* carried a resolution of the Central Commission of Party Control announcing the expulsion from the party of ten members of the editorial board of *Po prostu* and the official reprimand of six persons. The resolution stated that "for many months, the party members and candidate-members working as editors of *Po prostu* have expressed a political line in the periodical that is contrary to the resolutions of the Eighth and Ninth Plenary Meetings. Since the resolution of the secretariat approving the suspension of *Po prostu* by the Main Office of the Control of the Press, two open letters have been addressed to the first secretary, Comrade Gomułka: one from the party organization of *Po prostu* employees protesting against the dissolution of the weekly and another from the editorial board of *Po prostu* defending the illegal student demonstration that took place on October 3, and protesting the action of the People's Militia against the demonstrators. . . . Protesting with open letters to party organs against resolutions passed by other party organs is contrary to the principles of

democratic centralism governing our party and to party statutes. . . .
Defending illegal demonstrations directed against the party and the
people's authority is also contrary to the attitude of party members."

In a speech addressed to students at the inauguration of the academic
year, Cardinal Wyszyński stated that he understood their aims and
desires, but that they in turn should understand that the country was in
a difficult situation.

A film club, Po prostu, associated with the weekly, had to change its
name to Zig-zag. Public speaking simply became increasingly difficult.
There was still the Club of the Crooked Circle (until 1962), the Clubs
of Catholic Intelligentsia, *Tygodnik Powszechny, Znak,* and *Więź,* and
some standards were still maintained by such periodicals as *Przegląd
Kulturalny* and *Nowa Kultura* (which existed until 1963). But increasingly things were said and written in zig-zags, as the film club's name
says.

October 1956 ended slowly. It was still ending in October 1957, and
remnants of October lasted until March and August 1968 (e.g., independence of the intelligentsia, some relative national independence, and a
certain amount of decency in the media). Some remnants of October
have persisted to this day, despite the tendency to unify the social situation in the Communist bloc. October was only one stage in the struggle
for freedom and independence. The changing fate of this struggle constitutes the postwar history of Poland.

The Origins of Change

The changes of October 1956 were influenced by various events, groups,
and individuals. We have discussed the situation among the Soviet leaders and in the other Soviet bloc countries, the divergencies within the
PZPR, the actions of the workers and intellectuals, and the situation of
the Church and the peasants. The changes of 1956 took place, not
because of any one circumstance, but because of the convergence of
circumstances.

When Gomułka spoke to the party assembly on October 20 on the
situation in Poland and his program for change, he was speaking not only
to party members and their needs and desires but to society at large. Just

as 1956 cannot be characterized as primarily a party movement, nor can it be characterized as primarily a product of the workers' councils or student movements.

Within the party elite itself, there were distinct coalitions and differences of political opinion. Changes in the staffing of important party and government positions can be interpreted as signs of internal party struggles. Some activists condemned the press; others praised it or even, one may surmise, encouraged it through their instructions to the censors, editors, and authors. Some attacked the Warsaw Committee of PZPR for inciting popular unrest; others cooperated with it or defended it. Some demanded that Rokossowski be elevated to the Politburo; others took issue with this. Orders given by Kazimierz Witaszewski, chief of the Main Political Board of the Polish Army, differed from the orders given by Wacław Komar, chief of Internal Security, recently released from prison. These divergencies within the party became visible during the Seventh and Eighth Plenary Meetings of the Central Committee, and later Gomułka mentioned them, specifically the Natolin and Puławy groups.

These differences, however, revolved around shared interests. In a Communist society, this is especially the case when the authorities decide for some reason to limit their power, widen the margin of freedom, decentralize some decisions, or decrease the terror.

But even in a system very close to totalitarianism, the power elite does not have complete control over the external environment nor over the consequences of its actions, which in turn can further limit its power. All this pertains to the situation in Poland in 1956, but for the beginnings of this process one must look outside of Poland.

With the liquidation of Beria and perhaps even earlier, the members of the highest power elite in the USSR made a contract guaranteeing mutual security from the fear of arrest and liquidation. This was the beginning of the process of liberalization. Inside the party, this process began in Poland in late 1954 and early 1955 (as evidenced in the meeting of central party activists and the Third Plenary Meeting).

At the beginning of 1956, the Twentieth Congress of CPSU constituted one of the events favoring liberalization. The main issue in the so-called "revelations" of the Twentieth Congress was not the activities of Stalin and the power apparatus under his control. Information on the police, the false accusations, the camps, and the mass deportations under

Stalin and Lenin could be obtained if desired, though it was not publicly circulated. What was new about the Twentieth Congress was the acknowledgment by the Communist authority itself of its past crimes and the implication that others could now speak of these crimes openly, without fear.

Khrushchev took a risk. But the idea evidently was that by spreading information about "the cult of personality and its consequences" from the party lectern, the opponents of liberalization would be hamstrung. Khrushchev wanted to present them with a *fait accompli,* or rather with a spoken word. In the Communist political rituals, the words spoken by the leader from a party lectern during a congress play a very important role. Either it is necessary to accept them, or the speaker must be explicitly condemned, stripped of his party position, sunk into oblivion, and officially disavowed. There are reasons to believe that Khrushchev did have some opponents and that a condemnation of Stalinism was treated as a dangerous and risky venture.

The "secret" speech of Khrushchev was widely popularized in Poland during party meetings in which outsiders participated in discussions on the speech—troublesome questions were asked, demands were publicly formulated. By popularizing this speech, the party leadership sought to strengthen the liberalizing tendencies in Poland begun in 1954–55.

For whatever reasons, though the liquidation of Beria and of his collaborators may well have played a role, Lieutenant Colonel Światło defected to the West in December 1953. And it was his broadcasts from the West that contributed to the initial lessening of party and police discipline in Poland and to a certain civilizing process at the top of these institutions. Światło had earlier arrested Gomułka, but his broadcasts helped to present Gomułka as a national hero and victim of Stalinism. It was obviously important that Gomułka survived at all, but several other Communist leaders, such as Janos Kadar or Gustav Husak, also survived Stalinist prisons. Gomułka's release began a slow process of freeing other prisoners, eventually even non-Communists, of public rehabilitations and admissions of illegal police action. Party control of the police became a very important issue both for the PZPR and the CPSU. Higher officials of the political police—Różański, Romkowski, and Fejgin—were officially accused of abuse of power. This abuse centered on the police being above the party and threatening not only regular party members but especially those who occupied exposed positions. Motivated by similar concerns, party activists moved for greater sovereignty—even if it were not connected with democracy. Aware of the murder of KPP leaders in the USSR in the thirties and of later Soviet plans to organize a show trial of Communists arrested in Poland in the late forties and early fifties, party activists saw the issue of sovereignty to be directly related to personal safety. As a result, in the process of safeguarding their own security, party activists were reducing the element of fear within society as a whole. This in turn led to increased public pressure for further democratization.

In 1956 Polish society differed from today's society in the extent of its living historical memory. Members of the Home Army (AK) generation were born around 1920 and grew up in an independent Poland; during the Warsaw Uprising they were approximately 24 years old. In 1956, those who survived were approximately 36, and they still had a long future ahead of them. They had experienced the Second Republic, the war, and after. Indeed, memory of the Warsaw Uprising and its defeat may well have constrained, as many authors suspect, the Polish society of 1956 from undertaking significantly risky acts. The immediacy of the Stalinist period could well have made people content with a greater share of freedom and unconcerned about increasing democracy.

Khrushchev, Lieutenant Colonel Swiatło, Edward Ochab, the Poznań workers, and the officials who chose at some point not to lower the taxes of these workers, all contributed to some extent to the events called the Polish October. October was not just a creation of the "Puławy group," nor was it a creation of party revisionists.

During the Ninth Plenary Meeting, Gomułka condemned party advocates of the continuation of the October changes, and at that time he called them revisionists. However, this distinction was lost on those outside the party, to whom the term revisionists usually referred to German supporters of border revisions, and not to members of the PZPR, whose groups were not widely known.

It was decided in the PZPR that submission to events taking place outside of the party is dangerous; the history of 1956 is consequently not remembered eagerly by the party. For the party, 1956 was tainted by a serious sin: that of acting according to the expressed needs not only of party activists but also of wider social circles. However, the program of such action was very poorly formulated and realized by the party. This was so not only due to diehard Stalinist attitudes among the leaders of this party. The resistance of the party apparatus also impeded the changes of October 1956. Democratization threatened the *raison d'être* of the party apparatus. People connected to it risked losing their source of income and privilege. If the October changes were continued in Poland, the Communist party would have to limit seriously its "leading role" and probably also weaken its centralized and monolithic structure. October 1956 constituted one of the proofs that there are great difficulties in radically changing the role and structure of the Communist party. Such changes are made even more difficult by the external presence of the USSR.

Fear of Soviet intervention contributed to the slowing down of liberalizing changes. The possibility of such an intervention was demonstrated dramatically in Hungary. Hints about the danger of the disappearance of Poland from the map of Europe hit a sensitive nerve. The so-called considerations of the "reasons of state" psychologically hindered the activities of the opposition. With the reins of state power generally acknowledged to be safely in Gomułka's hands, people did not remember the need to have checks on the activities of the party apparatus. Generally, the news about the party's liquidation of independent initiatives and social activities was accepted rather quietly.

However, the attempts to reconstruct in Poland a political culture with the active participation of society, to create conditions for sovereignty and democracy, did not end there. These attempts are not hopeless, although the complex of systemic, psycho-social, and international conditions makes these attempts as difficult today as they were years ago.

CHAPTER 3

SHORT CIRCUIT

Foreshadowings

The closing of *Po prostu* in the summer of 1957 sparked a series of student demonstrations. The police responded with clubs and tear gas.

For many, the events of October 1957 constituted an end to the hopes of October 1956, hopes connected with the supposedly new leadership and personally with Władysław Gomułka. After October 1956, the program of the intelligentsia was quite often limited to simple trust and hope. Gradually these feelings turned to disappointment.

In late 1958 and early 1959, a court action was brought against Hanna Rewska, who was accused of distributing books published by the Literary Institute in Paris. This was the first trial of its kind after 1956, and the charge in such cases was "distributing" and "storing in order to distribute"—or only "storing"—materials that "contained false information which could significantly harm the interests of the Polish state." Press notices about the trial of Hanna Rudzińska, arrested in 1961, stated that she "slandered Poland for dollars." This slander supposedly consisted of storing a Polish translation of a book by Feliks Gross, a professor at the City University of New York. This book, originally published in English, dealt with the subject of political power.

The first trials after October in which the writing or borrowing of disloyal books was regarded as a crime were important in establishing judicial precedents. The authorities believed that if some prosecutors could be found who would sign warrants and indictments dictated by the Ministry of Internal Affairs (MSW) and judges who would hand down dictated verdicts, others would follow suit. Submission and subordination are infectious. Though, at the beginning of the sixties, it may have been more difficult to control judges than prosecutors, judges could still be found who would zealously follow the advice or the recommendations of the MSW or PZPR.

These early trials were to influence the future administration of justice. But they were also, no doubt, intended to have an exemplary influence on intellectuals as a deterrent. The intelligentsia had to be shown that freedom should not be taken too literally.

However, despite such crackdowns, some freedom did persist. The Club of the Crooked Circle, active in Warsaw, survived until February 1962. Founded before October 1956, it expanded during the relative freedom of the October period.

The Club of the Crooked Circle engaged in many different activities: the club organized art exhibits and had a section on social analysis and a theater section. Discussions at club meetings ranged from social, literary, and scientific issues, and there were talks on history, economic life, and the legal system in Poland. Outstanding writers and scientists were among the lecturers and discussants. Non-party members were in the majority, but party members also participated in the club's activities.

At the end of the fifties and early sixties, the Club of the Crooked Circle was an enclave of intellectual freedom, and it was so atypical that many wondered why the authorities tolerated its existence for so long. But there was an advantage for the authorities in allowing the intellectuals to speak freely to small and narrow audiences: in a relatively cost-free manner, the authorities could examine the mood among the intellectuals. Several humanities departments at Warsaw University constituted similar enclaves of freedom and were tolerated for an even longer time. The university survived from October 1956 to March 1968 in an essentially unchanged form.

In March 1964, almost eight years after October, Polish intellectuals again acted as a group. Thirty-four writers and scientists addressed a short letter to Premier Cyrankiewicz. In two sentences they condemned the activities of the censorship (and the paper shortage) as dangerous to the national culture. Clearly, this was far from a complete political program.

In response to the unpublished letter of the 34, The daily press published in May what was called a counter-letter, signed by several hundred members of the Union of Polish Writers (ZLP). They protested against "the campaign of Radio Free Europe and the Western press slandering Poland." Its signatories asserted: "We are against foreign interference in our national problems and cultural policy; this is a concern shared by the creative intelligentsia and the political and state leadership of our country." Cyrankiewicz, the addressee of the letter of the 34, also publicly condemned it, and several signatories recanted in a letter to the London *Times.*

The basic tactic was to stress the internal nature of the issue. Perhaps there were some shortcomings somewhere in Poland, but they could be discussed with "the political and state leadership of the country" (if the leadership cared to discuss it). By taking complaints to the outside, one was only serving anti-national goals (and "forces").

In the spring of 1964, students gathered in the courtyard of Warsaw University. Information was provided on the letter of the 34, and the silence of the press was noted. However, the rector of the university, Stanisław Turski, said a few reassuring words, and the students dispersed shortly thereafter. This was the only demonstration organized by students between October 1957 and March 1968, and the mild reaction of the authorities is in stark contrast to their behavior in 1968 and with predictably different results.

To discourage further contacts with the West (and especially with the Polish émigré community) among intellectuals, one of the signatories of the letter of the 34, Melchior Wańkowicz, was tried in the fall of 1964. He was accused of "spreading false information that could be harmful to the interests of the Polish state." This "false information" was contained in a letter to his daughter. Wańkowicz was sentenced to three years' imprisonment but never went to jail. Legal action was also brought against Stanisław Mackiewicz and Jan Nepomucen Miller, who were accused of publishing articles in the Polish émigré press.

In March 1965, Jacek Kuroń, a doctoral student in the Education Department of Warsaw University, and Karol Modzelewski, an assistant professor in the Department of History, were arrested. Both had written an "Open Letter to Members of PZPR and ZMS in Warsaw University," which provoked much discussion and interest. The authors provided a Marxist analysis of the ruling system in socialist countries, analyzing the contradictions and concluding that a conflict existed between the working class and a class which they called the "central political bureaucracy." Under such circumstances, revolution was inevitable: the working class would be forced to overthrow the bureaucracy and thus join the world revolutionary movement. In July 1965, Jacek Kuroń was sentenced to three years' imprisonment; Karol Modzelewski to three and a half years.

At the beginning of the 1966/67 academic year, ZMS organized a meeting in the Department of History at Warsaw University which was addressed by Leszek Kołakowski, professor of philosophy, and Krzysztof Pomian, an associate professor in the same department. The topic was Polish culture in the last decade. Though both party members, Kołakowski and Pomian were critical of the fate of culture during this period. Kołakowski also criticized legal conditions and practices (based in part on the Small Criminal Code, which facilitated severe sentences for numerous rather vaguely defined crimes), and Pomian presented his views on the need for independence of the youth movement. The remarks of the lecturers and discussants formed a pessimistic assessment of the changes that had taken place in the last ten years since October 1956. The upshot was the expulsion of both lecturers from the party. Several writers who were party members protested this decision, but most were either expelled themselves or resigned of their own accord. These events constituted one stage of the process by which the party leadership was parting company with representatives of the movement or perspective known in party parlance as revisionism.

It is not easy to establish what views are revisionist per se. Revisionism must be seen in contrast to the so-called party line. One is not a revisionist in general, but only in relation to the current party line, which changes and is not always clear. It is perhaps easier to assemble a list of persons who have been described as revisionist than to compile a list of revisionist views. It is certain, however, that among the required revisionist opinions was a proclaimed belief in Marxism and socialism (understood in a manner different from that of the official ideological spokesmen); and party membership (at least for a time) was also a prerequisite.

Etymologically speaking, anyone who attempts to modify his ideology or its implemenation might be called a revisionist. Thus, any party member who attempted to revise the party practice or ideology, no matter how, could be called a revisionist. In the Communist movement, however, revisionists are only considered to be those who, once the party has seized power, support—if only verbally—the reduction of party and state repression and omnipotence. Those who desire opposite kinds of changes in the party are called dogmatists (hardliners). But dogmatists are mentioned much more rarely than revisionists and are generally considered by the party leadership not to constitute a serious threat. Dogmatists desire that party power be strengthened, and their error is merely tactical (they would like to achieve the aims of the party more rapidly, which occasionally might involve greater danger and risk). On the other hand, Communist parties pay great attention to the revisionists, who are assiduously expelled from the organization. PZPR revisionists (and not only the revisionists) attached great hopes to October 1956; they were involved in cultural movements, in the protest movement, and in the renewal of social life. Already in 1957, with the closure of *Po prostu,* the party began to part company with the October revisionists.

During the academic year 1966/67, tension in Warsaw University increased and there were disciplinary proceedings against students accused of improper behavior at university-organized discussions. At that time there were Student Discussion Centers affiliated with ZMS. Well-known lecturers took part in open meetings, and there were rather open and unrestrained polemics. The students' improper behavior supposedly lay in making remarks that insulted lecturers. No one wanted to declare these remarks politically improper, and even Mieczysław Rakowski, the editor of *Polityka* and a prime target of "insults," disclaimed being insulted.

As a result of these disciplinary proceedings, the student rights of Adam Michnik were suspended. This triggered the first mass petition at the university in many years: over 200 Warsaw University employees and approximately 1000 students signed a letter to the rector protesting this decision.

During the Arab-Israeli conflict of June 1967, the Warsaw Pact took a pro-Arab stance. In June 1967, Gomułka, speaking at the Fifth Congress of Labor Unions, mentioned an Israeli Fifth Column allegedly operating in Poland. His speech was followed by various half-official actions within the party, but these actions did not at first form a well-defined pattern. One such action was the publication of a work about West German/Israeli friendship, which, given the long-standing hostility of the propaganda toward West Germany, was clearly designed to compromise Israel. The cover of the book featured a picture of two joined flags: the Israeli flag with the star of David and the German flag. Today, it would probably be considered that West Germany, rather than Israel, would be compromised by such a connection.

Shortly afterwards it became clear that these activities were omens of things to come. Before March 1968, the official attitude towards the so-called Zionists had not yet been openly declared.

"Forefathers' Eve"

The academic year 1967/68 began in an atmosphere of discussions. The students and young faculty of Warsaw University were discussing theoretical issues and the current situation.

Information was reaching Poland about economic reforms in Yugoslavia and Hungary and about the political changes in Czechoslovakia, which, in particular, constituted a reference point for Polish students and intellectuals. But Czechoslovakia must not only have been a topic of conversation among students and the intelligentsia. The Polish authorities were clearly following events in Czechoslovakia, though with much anxiety.

During the winter, the authorities ordered the closing of a popular production of Mickiewicz's "Forefathers' Eve," which takes place in tsarist-occupied Poland and is full of biting anti-Russian lines. The last performance was set for January 30, and young people came *en masse.* Applause was frequent and long-lasting. After the performance, people marched toward Mickiewicz's monument bearing a banner, "We Demand More Performances!" which was laid under the monument. Later, police cars appeared and some student demonstrators were taken to police stations. They later suffered disciplinary action by the university and administrative courts. The courts sentenced the students to heavy fines.

The authorities' ban of "Forefathers' Eve" was seen as a very drastic action. Although, as Stefan Kisielewski later pointed out, considering the twenty-odd years of previous censorship, it was not an altogether unprecedented event. Yet the last time that Mickiewicz had been censored in Poland was in the nineteenth century under the tsarist partition. Even in People's Poland, a prohibition against performing Mickiewicz was an unusual event.

The very next month, students protested the ban with a petition. Despite police harassment, over three thousand signatures were collected in Warsaw, and on February 16 they were sent to the Diet. The petition was also signed by people outside Warsaw, but the exact number of these is difficult to determine.

The collection of signatures was not easy, since the security service functionaries conducted an ostentatious surveillance of certain persons, and some activists of ZMS and PZPR snatched the petitions from students gathering signatures. Security forces also circled the university, although on the whole they restrained themselves from entering university buildings. The students were kept fully informed about these police methods in fliers hung on the bulletin boards and walls.

In the meantime, an Extraordinary General Meeting of the Warsaw chapter of the Union of Polish Writers was called for February 29.

Stanisław Witold Balicki, the director-general of the Ministry of Culture and Art, spoke at the meeting and defended the ban of "Forefathers' Eve." Balicki wondered, "Who was affected by the ban, for better or worse? Who might have been hurt by it? Adam Mickiewicz, or Kazimierz Dejmek?" (the director of the banned production of "Forefathers' Eve"). The fact that such a ban harms the entire nation does not often occur to censors. Balicki stated, "Already during the opening night and first performances, certain individuals attempted to interrupt the performance by demonstrating applause, as if to isolate certain of Mickiewicz's lines from their context and impose on them a different, contemporary meaning. . . ."

As a result of all this, "The Ministry of Culture and Art, which has the statutory right to direct the National Theater, decided on January 16 to cancel further performances of 'Forefather's Eve' as of February 1 —the end of the previously sold-out performances."

Balicki's explanation could hardly be regarded as satisfactory, and in a final effort to rally support for the party's actions Jerzy Putrament, secretary of the ZLP party cell, took the floor. He encouraged the writers to "dissociate themselves from attempts by specific diversionary centers to exploit our meeting. I am not refering to the students but to Radio Free Europe, which has been dwelling on this meeting."

It is not always clear why party activists are so concerned with what Radio Free Europe will say. Sometimes it seems as if activists listen to nothing else and consider its opinions as other governments would public opinion. In any event, by focusing attention on Radio Free Europe, Putrament was employing the same tactic used against the letter of the 34. Clearly even Putrament found it difficult to expect writers to praise the authorities for censoring Mickiewicz. So better to condemn supposed common enemies and at least send a message to the authorities that, despite everything, "we are still with you." Putrament said: "If we adopt the resolution of our party organization, it would create an opportunity for a dialogue. . . ."

There are those who like to speculate about what would have happened if the past were different. But had the writers in fact taken Putrament's advice, it seemingly would have made little difference. In the March attacks against the writers, the resolution of the General Meeting was hardly mentioned. The only difference would have been that the writers would have lost face. Maybe this was what Putrament desired (a political victory). Or perhaps Putrament really believed in the prospect of fruitful talks with the authorities. The fact of the matter is that policy toward the intellectuals is often devoted to compromising potential leaders of opinion (even if the party gains no direct benefits from this).

The General Meeting of the Warsaw Chapter of ZLP adopted a four-point resolution:

> 1. For a long time, there has been increasing interference on the part of the authorities charged with overseeing cultural and artistic activity; this interference concerns not only the content of literary works but also their distribution and reception by the public.
>
> 2. The system of censorship and control of cultural and artistic activity is arbitrary and secret; the jurisdictions of particular authorities have not been defined, and no appeal procedures have been specified.
>
> 3. This situation threatens national culture, hampers its development, removes its authentic character, and condemns it to gradual impoverishment. The ban against performances of "Forefathers' Eve" is an especially glaring example.
>
> 4. The demands of writers, presented . . . by the ZLP leadership and by the leading representatives of the literary community, have thus far been ignored.
>
> Led by our concern as citizens, we call upon the government of the Polish People's Republic to return to tolerance and creative freedom, in accord with our age-old traditions. We demand the return of "Forefathers' Eve" as staged by Kazimierz Dejmek, whose removal from the stage brought about understandable bitterness on the part of the inhabitants of the capital.

The resolution of the General Meeting was to some degree an extension of the letter of the 34, and it expressed the will of the writers' professional union. Before then, it had not been common for such collective resolutions to express the true opinions of those it represented.

In the speech mentioned earlier, Putrament, while on the one hand advocating talks with the authorities, on the other criticized Gomułka's character: "He is difficult to talk to, has no sense of humor, has a grudge against writers, and a number of other infamous traits." One wonders whether, when Putrament said this, he expected the Warsaw Party Committee to distribute the minutes of the General Meeting containing his speech. If Gomułka indeed bore a grudge against writers, it would have been thanks to Putrament, and one wonders what Putrament was really up to.

Meanwhile, at Warsaw University, disciplinary proceedings were initiated against the students detained by the police at the protest on January 30 against the "Forefathers' Eve" ban. On March 4, two students, Adam Michnik and Henryk Szlajfer, were expelled from the university by the minister of education, Henryk Jabłoński. The minister's right to effect expulsion was defended on the grounds of his "general powers of supervision." But according to this claim, the minister had free rein within his jurisdiction regardless of the existing laws. The minister was free to apply his "general powers of supervision" in a completely arbitrary manner. This was a dangerous precedent.

Equally significant, as this relatively new peremptory style, was the source of information on which the minister's decision was based. Obviously Minister Jabłoński had no personal contact with the expelled students. In the official statements of youth organizations disseminated several days later, the minister's decision was linked with an investigation initiated by the Ministry of Internal Affairs. Jabłoński must have acted on the information (and suggestions) of the police possibly transmitted through the office of the rector of the university, which was in contact with the Warsaw Committee of PZPR. In this manner, the party, police, and administration acted in concert. But the information prompting the decisions had come from the police, and this indicated that the police, and not the party, played the leading role.

A demonstration at Warsaw University was called for March 8 "in defense of democratic freedoms." A handbill distributed before the demonstration announced "Citizens' Rights Again Threatened." Also distributed was Article 71 of the Constitution: "The Polish People's Republic guarantees its citizens the right to free speech, to publication, to assemblies and rallies, and to marches and demonstrations." This text may very well have reminded the students, as well as representatives of the authorities, that Poland indeed had a Constitution. It was not to be soon forgotten.

The demonstration began at noon in front of the university library. A resolution was read and adopted demanding the reinstatement of the expelled students Adam Michnik and Henryk Szlajfer, the dropping of disciplinary proceedings against eight other students, and returning a scholarship to one of them. The resolution also demanded that the minister of higher education, Henryk Jabłonski, and the rector of Warsaw University respond within two weeks, directly to the student body.

During the demonstration, ZMS activists shouted continually, "Troublemakers out of the University!" but this was about it. There were also middle-aged men, dressed in sheepskins and forage caps, who descended from buses marked "Excursion" and whom the students regarded as plainclothes policemen. The official version of the events described them either as members of the Voluntary Reserve of Citizens' Militia (ORMO) or as "worker activists" or "sociopolitical activists." When the demonstration moved from the library to Kazimierzowski Palace (where the rector's office was), these strangers surrounded the demonstration and grabbed individuals from the densely-packed crowd. Students had their grade books and ID cards confiscated, and some were dragged into the buses. The students tried to keep together and shouted for the students to sit down, so that the strangers still standing could be singled out.

The prorector of Warsaw University, Zygmunt Rybicki, appeared on the balcony of Kazimierzowski Palace and agreed to talk with a delegation of students, who entered the building. Rybicki also complied with student demands to dismiss the "newcomers," though it was with the words, "Thank you, comrades," that he bid the newcomers farewell. The buses then left the courtyard.

Police patrols continued outside the campus area, but the university area itself appeared to be free of any police. Meanwhile, in the talks with the student delegation, the prorector insisted that the expelled students could not be reinstated at the moment and not in Warsaw. A date for a second meeting was set for Monday, March 11.

Around two o'clock in the afternoon, as the students, escorted by their professors, were moving towards the exits, squads from ZOMO (a paramilitary police force) appeared in the main gate of the university and proceeded to run through the courtyard with truncheons beating the students. Some students attempted to hide inside the surrounding buildings. A crowd of onlookers gathered around the university and began chanting, "Gestapo! Gestapo!" As others later noted, this chant was not wholly accurate; after all, the Gestapo had been a secret police.

In a speech delivered by Gomułka on March 19 to the Warsaw party activists, the following fragments touched on the events of March 8: "The courtyard was entered by worker activists who had been previously mobilized by the leadership of the Warsaw party organization, which was ... rightly concerned that the demonstration should not lead to disturbances. ... The situation became increasingly tense and dangerous. Anxious to control the situation, the leaders of the team concerned with safeguarding public order decided to call in the Citizens' Police, who restored order."

It is significant that, according to Gomułka, the forces mobilized for the occasion, which played such an important role in the events of March 8, were ordered by the Warsaw party organization. Thus, the intervention in the events at the university was conducted neither by the state authorities nor by the administration, but by the organs of a political party. This must be understood as extremely characteristic of the manner in which decisions are made and power is exercised in the Communist system.

A University Senate Commission was convened on March 11, which called students to testify on the events of March 8, especially the incidents of student beatings (either by the police or unidentified persons). The commission displayed good faith, but it did not publish any report of its activities, nor is it known what happened to the materials it collected. There have been many such instances of commissions set up to investigate abuses of the authorities that are not heard from again.

Arrests had been made in the university community at six o'clock on the morning of March 8, and again in the afternoon. Those arrested were later tried for violations of Article 36 of the Small Criminal Code, which dealt with participation in secret organizations. It was on the afternoon of March 8 that Jacek Kuroń and Karol Modzelewski were arrested, and their (second) trial took place in January 1969.

On March 9 unsigned notes appeared in *Życie Warszawy* and *Sztandar Młodych* (*Banner of Youth,* a ZMS periodical) about "disturbances in street traffic and communications" the day before in the university vicinity, and *Sztandar Młodych* described the appearance of "representatives of the Warsaw workers and an ORMO group, which arrived because of excesses." *Życie Warszawy* declared that "since persuasion failed, first ORMO and then the Citizens' Police had to intervene." According to *Życie Warszawy,* "groups of students stopped traffic during the evening rush hour." There were also references to the "banana youth—those unfamiliar with material worries, the realities of life, and the needs of our society," and to "hooligan elements" who joined the students.

This depiction of the events provoked rather widespread indignation, but it was only the beginning of the press campaign: the "anti-Zionism," for one, evident on handbills distributed before March, had not yet found its way into the newspapers, at least not until Monday, March 11.

At noon on March 9, in an overflowing auditorium at the Polytechnic, a second student rally began. This one affirmed its solidarity with the university and condemned the brutal police action and the first press notices. After the rally, students formed a march and headed towards the editorial offices of *Życie Warszawy* but was dispersed by the police.

At seven o'clock in the evening of March 9, students of the Electronics Department of Warsaw Polytechnic adopted a resolution condemning police action and tendentious press information, and they demanded an end to repressions and correction of misinformation.

On Sunday, March 10, news of these events was spreading by word of mouth across Warsaw and Poland, and Western radio broadcasts were also covering the events. But it was not until March 12 that newspapers outside Warsaw mentioned them, when they reprinted a March 11th text from *Trybuna Ludu.*

On March 10, *Życie Warszawy* published in its "City" section an unsigned notice stating that university students "had been expelled for organizing notorious political disturbances and for transmitting false information to anti-Polish propaganda centers and violating the orders of the university authorities. . . . Yesterday certain groups of students again attempted to provoke excesses in the streets, which necessitated the intervention of the forces of order."

People from various departments and colleges met to consider what to do next. Some response had to be made to police actions and press lies. It was decided that another demonstration at Warsaw University was to be held on March 11. Meanwhile, they prepared drafts of resolutions to define what had taken place and to formulate the necessary demands.

Three Weeks in March

Monday, March 11

On March 11, two Warsaw newspapers, *Trybuna Ludu* (the party newspaper) and *Słowo Powszechne* (the Pax periodical) published unsigned articles on the university demonstration. Both newspapers included many of the same details and both carried a list of the "ring-leaders," with information on the background of their parents.

In *Słowo Powszechne* the word "Zyonists" appeared (difficulties with the spelling of this word were to last for quite some time). The newspaper stated that the "Zyonists in Poland" were taking political orders from West Germany. This Zionist presence was reaffirmed by *Słowo Powszechne's* list of the "ring-leaders." This list was almost identical to the one that appeared in *Trybuna Ludu* except for the addition of four names with a non-Slavic ring. According to *Słowo Powszechne,* "this kind of people [Zionists] had easily made contacts in those isolated quarters in which political blindness led to direct or indirect service to the anti-Polish policies of West Germany." At least five of those named by *Słowo Powszechne* were already in prison.

On the same day these articles appeared, a conference of Warsaw party activists was held. The term "activists," by the way, is nowhere defined by party statutes, but in March it came to mean party members who were charged with actively upholding party policy.

The information disseminated during the Warsaw conference of the activists on March 11 was almost identical (down to the lists of previously little-known people) to that contained in the *Słowo Powszechne* and *Trybuna Ludu* articles. Clearly they all shared the same source of information, which could only be the Security Service. The police was clearly not acting as an organ of the government in this instance but rather as a party organ, conducting political activities in coordination with the Warsaw Committee of PZPR, if not also with the Press Bureau of the Central Committee.

At the conference of the "activists," the first secretary of the Warsaw party committee, Józef Kępa, also took up the theme of Zionism, but introduced subtle distinctions: those combatting Zionism need not fear being accused of anti-Semitism. "We will not be blackmailed with the scarecrow of anti-Semitism. . . . We are decisively against anti-Semitism, but we will not allow Zionist propaganda and activities to be conducted here. Nor will we allow the Zionists to seek evasion by accusing others of anti-Semitism."

But who are the Zionists, and what is Zionism? Clearly party activists must have had some ideas, but the terms were vague enough to the general public that on March 15 *Trybuna Ludu* published an article entitled "What is Zionism?"

In March 1968, the word "Zionism" referred to more than an opinion.

A person who was not of "Jewish descent" but who expressed his sympathy with such people or with Israel was not called a "Zionist." At most, he was a "supporter of Zionism." Thus a "Zionist" had to be of Jewish descent. But were there Jews who were not Zionists? This was not clear. Gomułka addressed this issue on March 19, to a rapt audience of "activists" in Warsaw. The first secretary declared that not all people of "Jewish descent" were Zionist; some "honestly served People's Poland." However, the "activists" were skeptical.

For the "activists" the real issue was which people of "Jewish descent" could be thrown out of work immediately, and which could not yet be touched. In this regard, the police were providing a vital service to the activists by identifying those to go after.

Throughout March 11, in an atmosphere of heightened police activity around the university and growing crowds of spectators, meetings and rallies were taking place in different university departments and at the Polytechnic. The students were anxious to respond, at least verbally, to the rather surprising recent events. The Department of Architecture pleaded for solidarity with other universities, demanded the autonomy of the university, and condemned anti-Semitism.

The university-wide resolution, formulated by the philosophy department, contained questions as well as statements and demands. The students felt they had a right to know who had called in the goon squads before the demonstration had even begun; who was responsible for the police brutality; and who was the author of the mendacious articles in the press. They demanded "the reinstatement of full academic rights to the students expelled from the university . . . the freeing of all students and faculty members detained and arrested in connection with the recent events . . . the punishment of those responsible for calling the police and civil thugs into the university . . . compensation for the moral and physical injuries to the victims of the events . . . correction of the distorted coverage in the press, and publication of the names of those responsible for the repressions against the students." The students demanded "institutional guarantees of the principles of academic freedom and freedom of science," and "a legal guarantee of the principle of university autonomy."

Representatives of the University Senate who were present at the school-wide meeting informed the students about the creation of a Senate

Commission to consider the situation at the university and especially to document the injuries suffered by students during the police action. The first student committee of three persons was also appointed to help in the work of the Senate Commission.

Demonstrations were also taking place at other Warsaw schools. A "general meeting of students, the rector, and the Faculty of the Main School of Planning and Statistics" adopted a reolution similar to the one drafted at the university.

A resolution adopted on March 11 by the Warsaw State College of Theatrical Arts stated that its students and professors at a joint meeting agreed to "express their full solidarity with those declarations by unions and associations of intellectuals and artists who have defended our national culture." The resolution was signed by 125 students and professors.

During the afternoon of March 11, there were street confrontations between Warsaw citizens and the police. The crowd that had gathered began marching toward the Central Committee building. As with March 8, when the police actually forced students out into the streets from the enclosed university courtyard, on March 11 the police made no attempt to prevent the gathering of crowds in front of the Central Committee building. It has been suggested that the police was by no means instructed to preserve order and that those who directed the police (in the Warsaw Committee and MSW) were interested in creating an atmosphere of danger for the highest authorities, or, to be more specific, for Gomułka.

In Cracow on March 11, 1968, students from Jagiellonian University adopted a resolution demanding that the Constitutional provisions guaranteeing the rights of citizens be observed, and solidarity with the students of Warsaw was expressed. An intercollegiate resolution of Cracow students, besides reaffirming many of the demands of the Warsaw students, contained a provision concerning "support for the social and political changes which have taken place in Poland in the twenty years since the war." It stated, "we support and recognize the foreign policy of People's Poland as the only possible policy. . . . All suggestions that we are acting on behalf of forces hostile to People's Poland are false." This was in response to official accusations.

On March 11, the Znak deputies addressed the following interpellation to Prime Minister Cyrankiewicz:

1. What plans does the government have to restrain police and ORMO brutality against the students, and how does it plan to investigate who is responsible for the brutal treatment of these young people?
2. What plans does the government have to answer the substantive questions being posed by the students, questions which also concern wider segments of public opinion and address the problem of citizens' democratic rights and the government's cultural policies?

In conclusion the deputies stated: "Crushing the demonstrations will not provide a solution, the aim of which should be to preserve the possibilities of communication with society. We appeal for this manner of solving the problem."

Prime Minister Cyrankiewicz answered the interpellation a month later, On April 10.

Tuesday, March 12

On March 12, two PAP communiqués were published, one providing information on rallies taking place in factories and another on the "conference of socio-political activists" and the speech of the first secretary of the Warsaw Committee of PZPR, Józef Kępa. Kępa's speech was published under the title: "What is Hidden Behind the Street Disturbances?" However, if it is possible to speak of street disturbances at all, they took place only on March 11—that is, on the day of Kępa's speech. But Kępa spoke about the events of March 8 and 9, which were not street disturbances. The police was then simply beating the students.

The March 12 issue of *Trybuna Ludu* published a front page story about a rally in the Żerań Automobile Factory (FSO). The party newspaper wrote: "Above a crowd of more than six thousand workers, who came here directly from their individual workplaces, we read banners with such admonitions as 'Students to their studies, writers to their pens' ... or 'Purge the party of Zionists'.... Michał Kosowski, a tool metalworker and one of the oldest employees of the factory at Żerań, reads a draft of the resolution." The resolution named eight students who "are known for their political trouble making.... Among them we find the sons and daughters of highly-placed employees of the state administration."

From Kępa's speech and from the party rallies organized on March 11, it is clear that already before March 11, if not before March 8, the decision had been made by the authorities about what to publicize regarding the events at Warsaw University, which names were important, and for what purposes. From then on, workers in various places, identified by name in the newspapers, read resolutions at rallies and mass meetings in which the students mentioned on March 11 (and earlier) would be named over and over again.

The entire course of events, beginning with March 8, had no influence at all on the media "coverage." This complete disregard of real events was deeply shocking to the participants in those events, and "The Press is Lying" became a popular student slogan. To this day the symbol of tearing or burning a newspaper is alive in the poetry of the young and in student theater. The reason for the outrage, or even feelings of horror and disgust, was not so much the lies in themselves but the fact that they reflected a total dissociation from reality on the part of the press. The press simply had no contact with nor interest in reality. What the press was interested in was party politics. While students were being beaten by the police, the press was demanding the removal of "Zionist" party officials and was attacking select children of "highly placed employees of the state administration."

Departmental resolutions were being drafted on March 12 at the university that both students and faculty were adopting.

The resolution of the Council of the Faculty of Philosophy, adopted unanimously, like so many others, was singled out in the press and became the best known. The resolution states in part: "The student movement, which has developed independently of the official framework of student organizations, has in the last four days become a truly mass movement that unites an overwhelming majority of university students."

The Council of the Faculty of Philosophy also supported the students' demands for redress, both against the press and those responsible for the police brutality.

It was indeed the case that a mass movement had been created. On March 12 there were student demonstrations in Poznań, Lublin, Wrocław, and Gdańsk. All proclaimed solidarity with the Warsaw students, condemned the police brutality, anti-Semitism, expulsions of students from the university, censorship, and arrests and demanded redress.

There was an attempt by the authorities to hold an official rally on March 12 in the main auditorium of Gdańsk Polytechnic, however, the results clearly were not what was intended. Following the speech of the district committee's first secretary, the students of the Polytechnic adopted a resolution that stated in part: "We express our solidarity with Polish society, and above all with the Polish working class. We decisively support the Warsaw students. We condemn the police methods used in their handling of the Warsaw demonstrations."

The efforts of the authorities, or at least some of the authorities, in manipulating the press were evidently more successful. In the afternoon of March 12, *Kurier Polski* published an article entitled "Let's Take a Good Look at the Prophets." In the article it was stated that a small group of young people were using their university studies "as a cover for political oppositional activity, steered by people whose careers came to an end together with the Stalinist period." The morning *Słowo Powszechne* wrote, "Among the instigators we find the same people who were responsibile for the errors and illegalities of the Stalinist period." *Trybuna Ludu* spoke about "political bankrupts," while Józef Kępa, first secretary of the Warsaw Party Committee, cited names, calling the former party leaders "consummate political players," "experienced in the arcana of political struggle."

Also in the March 12 issue of *Kurier Polski* was an article by Ryszard Gontarz entitled "The Inspirers." In the article Gontarz attacked mostly writers and scientists. And his article was characteristic for two important reasons. First, the very detailed information it contained could only have been provided by the MSW (this also pointed very clearly to the MSW's contribution to the media campaign). Second, the article not only singled out students with parents in high political positions but students of Jewish origin. The article ended with the call: "Do not let yourselves be led on a leash by provocateurs." Clearly if anyone was a provocateur in this instance it was the MSW collaborating with the Warsaw Party Committee and acting with the help of some journalists, shielded by the Press Bureau of the Central Committee.

Wednesday, March 13

On March 13 PAP announced the firing of three high state functionaries by the prime minister. These were all functionaries whose children had been named in the press already on March 11.

On the same day, *Życie Warszawy* carried two front page headlines: "The Workers of the Entire Country Demand Calm in Warsaw and

Punishment for the Inspirers of the Events," and "A Peaceful Tuesday in Warsaw."

In the *Trybuna Ludu* of March 13 Kazimierz Konstański, chairman of the School Council of ZSP (Union of Polish Students) at Warsaw University, was quoted as saying, "Why do we feel cheated? Because when we attempt to conduct discussions with our colleagues, the Council of the Faculty of Philosophy adopts a resolution implicitly supporting the ringleaders of the brawls! And party members vote for this resolution!"

Konstański later declared that he had said nothing of the sort. One can easily believe him, since he was quoted as having made the statement a day before the Council of the Faculty of Philosophy adopted its resolution.

The *Trybuna Ludu* piece can be seen as preparation for the decision by the minister of higher education to relieve four professors and two associate professors of their positions at Warsaw University (three of these professors had been mentioned by Gontarz already on March 12; Gomułka named five of them on March 19).

In the meantime, new student actions were taking place in Poznań. According to an official statement issued by the senate at Adam Mickiewicz University: "On March 13, a group of students, incited by ringleaders and disregarding an appeal by the Poznań rectors, caused new excesses in front of the Rectorate building of the university. The police have detained 84 participants in the events; most have already been released and investigations continue against 14 persons (9 students and 5 non-students)."

On March 13, the Poznań students adopted a "Supplication" expressing "support for the students of Warsaw" and demanding "the return of 'Forefathers' Eve' to the stage," "the abolition of political censorship in the mass media," "the release of the arrested students," and "explanation of the true reasons for the Warsaw events." This "Supplication" also stated: "We feel solidarity with and send greetings to the courageous students of fraternal Czechoslovakia."

Solidarity of Polish students with Czechoslovak students was a consistent theme of the period, beginning with a March 8 Warsaw University handbill that stated, "We have the same rights as the Czechoslovak students, and we have the same means of defense." Czechoslovakian and Polish students indeed had much in common, though the student movement in Czechoslovakia was synchronized with a more generalized social and political movement. The solidarity between the students of both nations was quite natural all the same and found its expression when the students of Prague demonstrated in front of the Polish embassy on May 1.

In March 1968, the authorities were attempting to hinder contacts among students in various cities. At train and bus stations, the police stopped young people to check their identification cards, and students were then detained. Yet despite this, resolutions and documents continued to be transmitted between cities, copied on typewriters, distributed as photographs, or sometimes mimeographed.

The events in Cracow on March 13, for example, became widely known through this system. At 10:00 A.M. on March 13, students gathered for a demonstration in front of a university dormitory. Students from all over Cracow were present, as was the rector of Jagiellonian University and other university authorities. In an attempt to march from the dormitory to the Marketplace, the students were "brutally attacked by the police and ORMO, who were using an armored water gun, tear gas grenades, and truncheons. . . . The police then entered the Collegium Novum, breaking the promise given only the previous day by the first secretary of the Cracow Party Committee to the university rector to the effect that 'under no circumstances will the police enter the grounds of the university.'"

Putting aside all ethical considerations, the police were acting in a manner that was entirely unnecessary, and, moreover, counter-productive to the presumed intention of maintaining order.

Thursday, March 14

On March 14, while Wrocław students were expressing solidarity with "the struggle of writers for greater democratic freedom and for the limitation of censorship," official rallies were being held condemning members of the writer's union (ZLP) as "the inspirers of and participants in the street altercations in Warsaw." Paweł Jasienica, a writer and historian, came in for particular criticism as "a deserter from the Polish Army and the right hand of a band leader infamous for his numerous murders of peaceful Bialystok residents in 1944–48." At the meeting of the Polish Writers' Union on February 29, Jasienica criticized the official anti-Semitic propaganda.

On March 14, *Życie Warszawy* devoted an article to another prominent writer, Stefan Kisielewski. This text, called "The Dictatorship of Ignoramuses," and later reprinted in many provincial papers, took its title from an expression coined by Kisielewski. Though referring to "the reality of People's Poland," Kisielewski was taken to task for having the workers in mind. But due to the striking accuracy of Kisielewski's view, his interpretation won the day, and thanks to *Życie Warszawy* the term gained wide currency.

An important event on the party scene took place on March 14. Edward Gierek addressed a rally of several thousand party members in Katowice and made public his views on the March events. He was the second district party secretary, after Kępa, and the first Politburo member to do so. Gierek fully supported Kępa's standpoint, and in some respects he went even further than Kępa.

> The dirty froth that floated to the surface on the wave of the October events eleven years ago has not been fully removed from the current of our life.
>
> Today our district police stopped a car of Warsaw students coming to Silesia; they were coming here to muddy the peaceful Silesian waters. It is not difficult to imagine whose money is being used to finance the travels of these young emissaries. It is not difficult to imagine who is paying for the organization of troubles in Warsaw and in the country at large. Those are the same disappointed enemies of People's Poland who have not learned their lesson, and who expose themselves on every occasion; they are the various die-hards of the previous system, the revisionists, Zionists, and servants of imperialism.
>
> I want to assert from here that Silesian waters never did and never shall power their mills. The powerful Silesian current will break the bones of anyone who attempts to divert our course from the road chosen by the nation.

However, there was one entirely new element in Gierek's speech. On March 9 the press reported the return from Sofia of a delegation headed by Gomułka. From that time until Gierek's speech, Gomułka's name could hardly be found in the newspapers. At the Katowice rally on March 14 a large portrait of Gomułka hung over the lectern with the legend, "Long Live the Central Committee of PZPR with Władysław Gomułka at its Head." From then on, "We are with you, Comrade Wiesław," became a constant refrain of the March propaganda.

It had been a long time since such slogans were part of the regular ritual, and it was not always a sign of a party leader's strength. Indeed, it may well have given Gierek pause to hear in June 1976 the slogan, "We are with you, Comrade Gierek."

Saturday, March 16

On Saturday, other district secretaries, following in the footsteps of Kępa and Gierek, made their views known. The district secretaries uniformly held the Zionists responsible for the disturbances and demanded their removal from party and state positions.

A picture published in *Życie Warszawy* over the caption "A Rally in Ursus" shows apathetic faces in a hall decorated with banners on which were written such simple thoughts as "Zionists Go to Dayan," "Punish the Ring-leaders," and the more complex "Anti-Semitism—No; Anti-Zionism—Yes!"

For their part, the students were becoming increasingly critical of the authorities and were organizing strikes and sit-ins. At the end of a "48-hour sit-in rally" of Wrocław college students, the Committee of the Wrocław Polytechnic published the following "Communiqué Pertaining to the Observance of Order":

1. We abide by our decision to end the strike at 2:00 P.M.
2. We are leaving the school by departments and classes, in small groups, carrying our identification cards.
3. We walk only on sidewalks and do not gather at bus stops or trolley stops.
4. If there are people assembled in front of the school before our evacuation begins, we appeal to them by megaphone not to hinder our evacuation.
5. If, despite the observance of these precautionary measures, the first groups are attacked with truncheons, we suspend the evacuation.
6. We resume it only after receiving assurances of safety.
7. The guards leave last—they are responsible for the maintenance of order in the building and for the return of the building to school authorities.
8. Classes begin at 2:30 P.M.
9. The Committee of Rallies and the guards are dismissed at the end of the evacuation.
10. Every student leaves the demonstration with the text of the resolution.

Information about the Cracow and Wrocław strikes appeared in March only in the local press. Only in May were they mentioned in *Nowe Drogi*, by Minister Jabłoński. According to the minister's evaluation: "In large centers such as, for example, Wrocław, Cracow, and Łódź, where certain groups were already active, or where the leadership of the troublemakers formed quickly, the disturbances created lasting difficulties.

"The most serious—apart from Warsaw—was the situation in Wroclaw (especially at the Polytechnic) and in the Cracow colleges, where even the youth desiring to learn were subject to moral and physical terror. . . .

"In this situation, only the radical move by the rector of Wrocław Polytechnic, who expelled all those not attending classes and organized new admissions for two departments and one institute, was able to stop the disruption in the work of the school.

"In Cracow, only the threat of expelling all those who broke school regulations, accompanied by extensive educational action, produced the desired results."

A similar threat was used at Gdańsk Polytechnic.

As a sign of solidarity with the Wrocław students, a lecturer of mathematics at Wrocław Polytechnic, Professor Ryszard Krasnodębski, began a hunger strike; and on March 18 he addressed a "communiqué" to the students. He described how he understood the student voice of protest: "You expect elementary human rights to be respected; you want to see a free, substantive, and many-sided discussion of all the cultural and economic aspects of life in our country. You want to participate in this discussion. . . . You expect freedom of speech because you know that without it irresponsibility follows, and this has catastrophic economic results. Freedom of speech is irreconcilable with censorship."

The Second Week

In the March 19 issue of *Gazeta Krakowska* (*Cracow Gazette*), the same issue that reported the continuance of the Cracow student strike, there appeared a notice whether by coincidence, or as a deliberate scare tactic, or simply reflecting some serious disturbances or demonstrations in the workers' community that read: "Yesterday the surgical department of the Emergency Health Service gave first aid to 112 persons. Most of the victims had been wounded at their workplaces. Many had been bitten by dogs."

In the ZMS bulletin *Nasza Walka* there was information on the antistrike activities of the Cracow ZMS (Association of Socialist Youth), which created an "order guard." It was reported that "on March 18, the order guard, composed of 431 students, was assigned to remove pickets from the dormitories and school buildings. In the morning 80 ZMS members clashed with a group of pickets 200 strong from the dormitory of the Academy of Mining and Smelting. Fire extinguishers, pieces of glass, clubs, etc. were used against the order guard. At the request of the dean of the academy, the order guard members withdrew after several minutes." To the students this account was rather puzzling. The ZMS "order guard" stormed the dormitories, and the dormitory residents (called pickets) were, in fact, defending themselves. And only the dean restored order by asking the intruders to leave.

In the afternoon of March 19, Warsaw party activists gathered in the Congress Auditorium of the Palace of Culture in Warsaw. On the platform were members of the Politburo and of the Central Committee Secretariat, among other high party officials. As the press reported on the following morning, the audience was composed of "three thousand Warsaw activists." The banners read: "Those for Poland are for Gomułka," "One Can Only Have One Motherland," "Long Live Comrade Gomułka," and the familiar, "We Trust You, Wiesław."

The assembly was addressed by Gomułka himself, who was introduced by Józef Kępa.

Gomulka touched on "Forefathers' Eve" and the writers, Zionism, and even the Council of the Faculty of Philosophy. But he supplemented this with a strong emphasis on the necessity of an alliance with the USSR. "An alliance in politics is always based on mutual interests. Where such interests end, the alliance ends as well. Poland, without an alliance with the USSR, would never be able to defend and retain its western territories, could not resist German imperialism, and could not exist as an independent state."

One has to acknowledge that the issue of the alliance with the Soviet Union was only loosely connected with the rest of the speech. But this one fragment was the only thing in Gomułka's speech clearly identifiable as his own and reminiscent of his October 1956 position; the rest was a collage of facts and ideas supplied by the Warsaw Party Committee and by the Ministry of Internal Affairs. Gomułka joined Kępa's line, as Gierek and other district secretaries had done before.

Also in his speech, Gomułka distinguished three types of persons of "Jewish descent or nationality": those who would "sooner or later leave our country"; those "who, because of their cosmopolitan feelings, should avoid areas of work in which national affirmation is indispensable"; and those who "truly served People's Poland."

Some saw evidence of progress in Gomułka's speech compared to Kępa's speech which did not concern itself with such distinctions. However, this relative progressiveness is questionable. In practice, it was not always so easy to discern to what category a person belonged beyond the fact that he was simply "of Jewish descent" (someone had somehow provided lists of such citizens).

The "activists" in the hall became extremely lively when Gomułka discussed the problem of Zionism. Gomułka was frequently interrupted. When he mentioned the category of Jews "who will sooner or later leave our country," the "activists" demanded that they leave immediately. There were shouts not usually heard during such meetings. Only a part of the audience chanted, "Wiesław! Wiesław!" Another part chanted, "Gierek! Gierek!" Television and radio were transmitting all this directly, and the entire population could see that the activists assembled by Kępa wanted a replacement for Gomułka. They shouted, "Be bolder!" Gierek had indeed spoken more boldly in Katowice, and he did eventually replace Gomułka. Yet it was not the activists who made this decision but rather high level party functionaries, the police, and the Soviets. The "activists" were there just to chant.

As it was, in the student community, Gomułka's speech evoked a mixture of horror and derision. Later they sang, "Comrade Wiesław speaks with reason, Poland's a democratic prison." A statement by the students of Wrocław on March 20 can be treated as an answer to Gomułka's speech. Its main points were:

> The last statements of the party leadership stubbornly attempt to isolate our movement from its social roots by singling out a supposedly small "group of inspirers" and by ignoring the social background of the events. . . . We are only a barometer of social moods, and we shall not allow our endeavors to be reduced to the problems of Zionism, a factional power struggle, or hooliganism.
> The conscious misinformation of society, our absence from workers' rallies, and the disregard for our own progressive resolutions and rallies are all part of the telling campaign against the possibility of having an honest discussion. The creation of rifts in society is aimed at diverting public attention away from the difficult economic problems that today's leadership is incapable of solving.
> The example of Czechoslovakia demonstrates clearly that democratizing the internal life of society is consistent with the spirit of socialism. This is the truth, and we have made our choice: to fight staunchly for our ideals.

On March 20, the topic of the day was Gomułka's speech. A report from Warsaw Polytechnic notes under this date: "the content of Gomułka's speech was received with general indignation. A rally was held, which decided on a 48-hour protest strike."

On the morning of March 21, an appeal from the rector forbidding students to strike was posted around the Polytechnic. Nevertheless, several hundred persons gathered in the auditorium at 8:00 A.M. They elected a strike committee and began a sit-in strike.

On the same day, a rally was held at Warsaw University in the Auditorium Maximum. A sit-in strike was called for 8:00 P.M., so that classes would not be disrupted. A declaration adopted at the rally stated in part:

"We still demand the release of the arrested students and faculty members, an end to the disciplinary proceedings, and the restoration of full academic rights to the expelled students. We demand satisfaction for the professors and writers who have been slandered in the press."

The declaration also formulated more general principles and goals. Like other student statements, it attempted to counteract the official disinformation. The students said:

> We stand on the ground of socialism: we are defending social control of economic decisions. We stand on the ground of patriotism. As citizens we are acting on the basis of the Constitution of the Polish People's Republic. We demand respect for inalienable civil rights: the right of free speech, print, assembly, manifestations, the right of free cultural creation, and academic freedom.
>
> We demand institutional and legal guarantees of constitutional freedoms, the abolition of preventive censorship, the abolition of the information monopoly, and the assurance of citizens' control over the actions of administrative authorities.
>
> All racial, national, and religious discrimination is alien to us.
>
> Nationalism is alien to us. Ascribing anti-Soviet slogans to the student movement is baseless.
>
> Treating some professors, writers, or a small group of students as responsible for the recent events is unjustified and cannot turn anyone's attention away from those who are guilty of serious mistakes and abuses of power committed because of the lack of self-government, because of administration from the top and the suppression of criticism.

Once again, the students addressed the authorities hoping (as it happened, mistakenly) that there was still a chance they would understand what was being said to them:

"We appeal to the state authorities not to accept false information and tendentious interpretations of recent events."

The strike was meant to serve as a defense for student demands; it was supposed to help project to the population a true picture of the events.

Student occupation of the university began on the evening of March 21 and continued through the following two nights. The students were accompanied by faculty members. Deliberations took place in the Auditorium Maximum; resolutions and appeals were copied by hand. The student police under the Committee of Department Delegates maintained order. Throughout the strike, the delegates remained in constant touch by telephone with professors ready to intervene in case the police entered the university.

On March 21, an important voice rose in defense of the students. During the 107th Conference of the Polish Episcopate, cardinals, archbishops, and bishops directed a memorial to the government, addressed to Prime Minister Cyrankiewicz. The memorial stated in part:

> Serious objections can be made against violent police methods of repression, especially in the streets of Warsaw, Poznań, Katowice, Gliwice, Cracow, Gdańsk, etc. . . . The problem of freedom of opinion, raised by society, the writers, and the episcopate, was made especially apparent during the academic manifestations. The right to honest information guaranteed by the PRL Constitution and by the UN Declaration requires a free press, limitation of the activities of the censorship, and objectivity in information. . . . The most important single cause of student indignation was the obvious lies in the press. . . . The episcopate, which for many years has suffered just such dishonesty of the press, well understands the indignation of the students.

The bishops formulated four demands in their letter to the government:

> 1. Release of the youth arrested or detained in prison.
> 2. Limitation of the drastic methods of punishment and interrogation, news about which is reaching society.
> 3. Influencing the press to inform public opinion accurately, or at least in such a way as to stop provoking youth and society by tendentious interpretations.
> 4. Effectively influencing the security organs to cease using anachronistic methods of repression, so very compromised in the memory of our nation.

Prime Minister Cyrankiewicz never publicly answered the episcopate. Student strikes continued in Wrocław and Warsaw from March 21–23. A report from Warsaw University states: "On Saturday morning, March 23, the strike ends with a rally in the Auditorium Maximum. A declaration about youth organizations is drafted and adopted, along with a letter to Gomułka demanding once again that the student demands be met."

The declaration read in part:

We demand:
1. The creation of a new political youth organization.
2. The creation of an independent student press and the reactivation of a national periodical for students and young intelligentsia.
3. The creation of clubs and discussion centers in which issues of concern to the academic community can be raised and discussed.

The Third Week

The decision to expel six faculty members of Warsaw University was signed on March 25 by Minister Jabłonski. Fired were three full professors of the Faculty of Philosophy—Bronisław Baczko, Leszek Kołakowski, and Stefan Morawski—two associate sociology professors—Zygmunt Bauman and Maria Hirszowicz—and also a professor of the Faculty of Political Ecomony, Włodzimierz Brus. The decision was announced in a PAP communiqué, which appeared in the papers on the morning of March 26, and was where those fired learned of their expulsion, as did the deans and the Councils of the Faculties of Philosophy and Political Economy.

The decision of the minister, like many other personnel decisions made public, was meant as a warning to other faculty members.

On March 28, despite a threatening article in *Trybuna Ludu* entitled "There Will Be No Tolerance for Trouble-Makers," a rally was held in the Auditorium Maximum. The rally adopted a "Declaration of the Student Movement"—the longest text adopted during the student meetings in March.

This declaration contained an analysis of the situation and listed four groups of demands, concerning the youth movement, economic life, the organization of society and the circulation of information, and the legal system and the rule of law. Throughout, the importance of democrary and the need for legal guarantees to ensure citizens' rights to organize and to express their needs and opinions, if society is to function properly, was stressed. Along with this, public access to information concerning the activities of state organs and freedom for the public to evaluate these activities were also considered essential. As a result, the activities of the censorship were seen as socially harmful. The declaration demanded "the abolition of censorship" and called for "punishing authors in a legally predictable manner only when they publish texts infringing on the interest of citizens or of society."

In the economic realm, it was demanded that "society exercise full and constant control over the entirety of the economic process" and that all social groups have their say in economic policy making. It was also asserted that the workers must be guaranteed the right to defend their interests, "especially by means of self-government and independent labor unions."

The declaration did not mention any changes concerning the recognized ownership of the means of production. But it did postulate social control of state property and suggested some forms such control might take. In this regard, "self-government of the employees" became a key expression and replaced the October 1956 term "workers' councils." But employees' self-government, which included workers' councils, was not considered the only method by which society could control the national economy: in asking for "full and constant control over the entirety of the economic process," the declaration mentioned the role of local self-government and political and social organizations, and also that of the Diet. As the declaration recognized, these issues required further discussion.

The fourth group of postulates in the declaration dealt with the law and the rule of law. In many countries, it is more common to speak of the law than of the rule of law. When the expression "law and the rule of law" is used in Poland, what is at issue is not only written law but also how this law is applied, how it is fulfilled by the party and state powers.

In March 1968, in the face of the lawless behavior of the authorities, the students discovered that laws existed, and, much to their surprise, that these written laws were not without relevance.

"Bread and Freedom" was the slogan of the Poznań workers in 1956. It was later understood that this widening of freedom should be accompanied by legal and institutional guarantees. Such guarantees are necessary, if only to make any breaches of the law by the authorities visible. Even if the actions of the authorities cannot be corrected at once, at least they can be named (in such cases, the naming of an act does have its significance). The demand for legal guarantees opposes the official disregard for the law, which the authorities managed to spread throughout

Polish society. It was not uncommon to hear, "What the law says is irrelevant, the authorities will do what they want anyway."

Beyond this, there was also the question of the clarity and constitutionality of the laws themselves. As there was no institution responsible for ensuring that laws were consistent with the Constitution, the declaration demanded the creation of a constitutional court.

The following demands of the declaration concerned the legal system:

1. We support the tendency to widen the actual role of the Diet. We demand honest and unbiased information about the work of the Diet.

2. We believe that a public discussion of the legal system in Poland is in order. We demand widening the discussion of proposed laws before they are introduced in the Diet.

3. We demand agreement between specific laws and the Constitution, so that these laws also guarantee basic civil rights: the right of free speech, the freedom of science and art, the right to assembly, rallies, marches, manifestations (Articles 71 and 72 of the Constitution), the observance of the inviolability of citizens and their homes, and the privacy of correspondence and telephone conversations (Article 74 of the Constitution).

4. We demand the creation of a constitutional court, which would monitor the accord between the orders and acts of the authorities with the Constitution and the law.

5. The Small Criminal Code should be [repealed]. . . . We demand the repeal of the decrees on assemblies and on censorship, which are in conflict with the Constitution.

6. We demand that the principle of the independence of the courts be respected and that secret trials, summary convictions, and accelerated procedure in political trials be disallowed.

7. The Polish Criminal Code does not include expulsion from work, the refusal of a passport for travel abroad, and military conscription as punishments. The use of such practices as punishment should be prohibited by law.

8. The law must state unequivocally what is and is not a crime; it must do so in accordance with the Constitution and with the moral code of society. Unclear legal principles, pressure exerted on the courts, and repression used against counsels for the defense make the law and the legal process devoid of justice and turn it into a means of revenge and political repression.

These issues were rather broad, and no one expected that they would be realized immediately. The conclusion stated: "The realization of our postulates will not be easy, but [unless something is done toward their realization] our country will be threatened with a further deepening of the existing conflicts. The consequences of a policy that does not take public opinion into account will weigh not only upon the present administration but on the entire society."

This warning acted, as it happened, as a farewell with which the March student movement was leaving the stage, at least as a mass movement.

In April, *Walka Młodych,* the organ of the ZMS, published an article entitled "Expose the Prompters," which ended with a metaphorical warning: "Polish students will not go to the stake for those who have neither Polish nor socialist interests in mind." It is difficult to understand what the authors meant by "socialist interests." The course of the March events was making it increasingly apparent that it was not Polish but international (that is, Soviet) interests that were important for the organizers of the propaganda campaign.

On March 30, PAP published a communiqué stating that in connection with the March 28 rally, described as an "illegal gathering," "the rector of Warsaw University decided on March 29 to expel 34 students, and suspend 11, of those who organized and participated in the March 28 rally. . . . The rector of Warsaw University, with the permission of the minister of higher education, decided to do away with the following institutes at Warsaw University: theory of economy, economics, and econometrics in the Faculty of Economics; philosophy and sociology in the Faculty of Philosophy; and psychology in the Faculty of Pedagogy, as well as the third year of studies in mathematics and physics in the Faculty of Physics and Mathematics. New registration for these institutes has been ordered by the rector."

According to information that became available only later, this decision resulted in the expulsion of 1600 students. This decision, announced on March 30, ended the March events in the calendar sense of the term.

The student movement was slowly being taken off to prison. The movement's leaders (members of the student committees, above all) were particular targets, together with persons chosen early for political and propaganda reasons, as well as those whose friends and colleagues were not sufficiently discreet. Some were arrested on the morning of March 8; others not until June. Some left prison after several years, while others could tell their tales of prison interrogation as early as May 1968. Yet it was the students who were acting in accordance with the law and not their prosecutors and judges.

The student movement was sufficiently widespread to continue in part even after the arrests. It is true that the demonstrations and rallies at the universities ended in late March. But the propaganda campaign continued, and many important precedents were established that were to come in handy later. In March, students learned to use computer printers to duplicate texts; they learned how to make a mimeograph machine from a clothes-wringer. They discovered that fliers could best be thrown from tall buildings or from the roof-windows of buses, which came in handy as early as August 1968, after the invasion of Czechoslovakia. One could, however, encounter the opinion that all of this testified only to the students' naïveté: what good were all these resolutions, fliers, and statements which only repeated truths known to everybody? But for the students, the mere fact that they were asserting the truth was what was important. They were probably too young and inexperienced to know that in public matters it may be better to lie. So the students proclaimed the truth, while the "responsible" members of the older generation chose silence, at best. The struggle for truth in public life—sometimes even for very simple truths—is an achievement which these students, criticized in 1968 for their lack of common sense, have passed on to their successors. It was also in March that attempts were made to establish contact between the academic community and other social groups, particularly the workers. Such attempts continued.

The March protests were from the very beginning directed against specific actions of the authorities: the ban on "Forefathers' Eve" and the party and police action in the Warsaw University courtyard on March 8. The students were responding to provocations by the authorities and were concerned with rectifying these specific abuses. Later the scope of the protests broadened.

The role of the party in the political system generally went unchallenged. Resolutions questioned the right of the Ministry of Internal Affairs to interfere in academic life, but no one questioned the right of the party, and especially the Warsaw Party Committee, in this matter. This was, perhaps, done not only for tactical reasons. Both the memory of 1956 and the events occuring in Czechoslovakia tended to make the students believe the party could be induced to make changes. Also, in a centralized system, and one where outside intervention is always possible, much depends on the behavior of the authorities.

Almost the entire student movement attempted to act in accordance with the law. The students demanded that the authorities obey the law, and they did all they could to uphold it themselves. The Office of the Rector of Warsaw University had approved the intrusion of party and police thugs into the university. The minister of higher education illegally expelled students. But the students of Warsaw University organized their sit-in strike at night, so that they could not be accused of violating university rules. The students of Warsaw Polytechnic may have used mimeograph machines during the strike without the permission of school authorities, but this was an exception: Warsaw University students in fact decided against using university mimeograph machines, and copied their texts by hand instead. After reports in the press concerning traffic disturbances supposedly caused by the students, Gdańsk students tried to use only the sidewalks in a demonstration, so as to avoid disturbing traffic. Two months later, French students built barricades and burned cars in the streets of Paris.

Even "loyalty to the socialist idea" was affirmed. The reigning student view at the time was basically: call the reality whatever is necessary, let it be called socialism, but let it be at least a little better. "Socialism does not equal truncheons," proclaimed the graffiti on the walls of Warsaw University.

Behind the students' postulates was the belief that the authorities must be held accountable for their actions, that one has to know what the authorities are doing and to pose demands. Such concern is an expression of a civic attitude. Their adversaries, in contrast, popularized slogans such as, "We are with the party," "We are with Comrade Wiesław," "The whole nation supports the party line" (even if it was not always clear what this line was or where it might lead). This was the propaganda of an uncivic attitude, of an attitude directed by fear or self-interest. The March dispute came down to whether the authorities had unlimited rights, or whether, on the contrary, the citizens had both the right and the responsibility to demand explanations from the authorities and to insist that the authorities consider public opinion in their actions.

Conclusion

March ended, but the March activities of the authorities continued, particularly regarding personnel changes at middle and even high levels and the crackdown in the universities.

In December of 1968, new legislation legalized party intervention in academic life and abolished the elective nature of the more important university positions. This is just one example of the overall changes taking place in the government's cultural policy, enforced by the censorship office and mass media.

March remained as a partially unfinished episode in the party. Slowly, there was a retreat from the more drastic measures (such as the anti-Zionist campaign). Some publicists who were very vocal at the time returned to their previous non-existence. Nevertheless, many others still hold important positions today that were opportunistically obtained around March 1968.

The March actions of the authorities began in the Warsaw Party Committee and in the Ministry of Internal Affairs, with probable assistance from outside—i.e., Soviet—agencies. But without at least the tacit support of those occupying the highest positions in the party, the actions would not have been possible. (The party leaders were those who had been ousted from their positions in 1948 as members of the "rightist-nationalist deviation" and had returned in 1956, and those who supported their return.) Nevertheless, already in April 1968 some of them were dismissed (Ochab from the Politburo and Spychalski from his position as minister of national defense). Shortly afterwards, Rapacki ceased to be minister of foreign affairs. Gomułka, Kliszko, and Cyrankiewicz survived, only to leave two years later. A political grave was dug for them in 1968, and they helped in the digging. Ironically, this rightist-nationalist deviation was vanquished once and for all in an atmosphere of officially heightened "nationalism." Yet if by August 1968 anyone was left without real doubts as to the true nature of this "nationalism" the Soviet invasion of Czechoslovakia made things crystal clear. This "nationalism" culminated in the February 1976 amendments to the Polish Constitution, in which the Polish People's Republic affirmed its commitment to strengthen "friendship and cooperation with the Union of Soviet Socialist Republics."

The year 1968 marked a turning point in party policy and the reversion to a period of intellectual darkness, though not as black as in the days of Stalinism. In inaugurating this repressive atmosphere, the authorities were to lose the few points of contact they had with economic and social realities. The result would be December 1970 and June 1976 —these are the fires that were set against the darkness.

CHAPTER 4

INTERLUDE

The Intervention in Czechoslovakia

Before May 1968, information in the Polish press on Czechoslovakia was not very extensive. But if there was little in the Polish press on what was going on beyond the southern Polish border, there was always the foreign radio stations, and above all Radio Free Europe. From the foreign broadcasts, people learned about the student demonstrations in Prague of late October 1967 and about the turnover of functionaries that began at the January Plenary Meeting of the Czechoslovak Central Committee. (On the evening of January 5 it was announced that the first secretary, Antonín Novotný, had been replaced by Aleksander Dubček.) Some information appeared about the freer tone of the Czechoslovak press, and there was much interest in the new grass-roots organizations. Such groups as the Club of Concerned Non-Party Members (KAN), begun in March, and the Club of "K231," a gathering of former political prisoners begun in April, did not look to the government for permission to exist or for guidance.

On June 27, four Czechoslovak periodicals (*Literarni Listy, Mlada Fronta, Prace,* and *Zemledelske Noviny*) published an appeal, "2000 Words to Workers, Farmers, Officials, Scientists, Artists, and to Everyone."

The authors of the manifesto stated that Czechoslovakia was undergoing "a process of democratization.... This process could not have started anywhere else [but in the party], because for the past twenty years only the communists could engage in political life, only a communist critique could have any influence on the course of events, and only opposition from within the communist party had the priviledge of meeting its opponent. The effort and the initiative of the communists is only repayment of the debt owed by the party to the non-communists, who were continuously persecuted."

The appeal of "2000 Words" stated further: "Most recently, people have become worried that the process of democratization has stopped. This feeling is partially a result of their fatigue after the excitement of recent events, but in part it corresponds to the truth. The period of high-level dismissals and sensational revelations . . . may be over, but the struggle between conflicting forces is continuing, only it is less public. This struggle now concerns the form and content of laws. . . ."

As a political program "2000 Words" also concerned personnel policies. It appealed: "We demand the dismissal of those who have abused power, wasted the public wealth, or acted dishonestly or brutally. . . . Let us form our own citizens' councils and commissions for dealing with embarrassing and concealed facts. . . . The provincial and local press, which has degenerated to the extent of becoming only an official megaphone, should be transformed into a tribune for all positive political forces. We demand the creation of editorial councils from the delegates of the national front, or let us form our own newspapers. Let us create committees to defend freedom of speech. Let us organize our own order guard for our meetings. When we come across some suspicious occurrences, let us investigate them, let us send a delegation to the appropriate organs, and let us publish their answers—even if only on walls."

The text of "2000 Words" proclaimed confidence in the government, but it was a conditional confidence: "We can show our government, should the need arise, that we will defend it with arms, if only it will act in accordance with its mandate."

The appeal provoked controversy in Czechoslovakia and concern among the leaders of fraternal parties. On July 4, five parties (without Rumania's) sent protest letters to the Czechoslovak Central Committee. In July the Soviet press published several articles strongly attacking the text of "2000 Words," while on July 14 and 15 leaders of five Warsaw Pact countries (excluding Rumania and Czechoslovakia) met in Warsaw. They asserted that socialism was being threatened in Czechoslovakia, and they accused the Czechoslovak Central Committee of allowing counter-revolutionary forces to speak. According to the leaders of the five countries, antisocialist and revisionist forces both inside and outside the Czechoslovak party were creating a situation unacceptable in a socialist country.

In response, the Czechoslovak Central Committee referred to the declaration of the Soviet government of October 30, 1956, which defended the principles of "full equality, respect for territorial integrity, state independence and sovereignty, and mutual non-interference in internal affairs" in relations among socialist countries. As we know, the Soviet declaration of October 30, 1956 directly preceded the Soviet intervention in Hungary.

Officially, the intervention of troops in Czechoslovakia took place at the request of "party and state activists of the Czechoslovak Socialist Republic" (though their names have never been made public). This request, according to an official Polish government statement on August 21, 1968, was caused by a "threat to the socialist system in Czechoslovakia and to the state as defined by the Constitution from counter-revolutionary forces, which are in cahoots with external forces hostile to socialism." This statement asserted that the "support, strengthening, and defense of the nations' socialist achievements are the common international responsibility of all socialist states. . . . We will never allow anyone to remove a link from the chain of the community of socialist countries." This was a far-reaching proclamation of the doctrine of limited sovereignty of Soviet bloc countries, and it was further exemplified in the Moscow protocol, signed by Soviet and Czechoslovak party leaders on August 26 and dealing with many issues of internal Czechoslovak policy.

The invasion of Czechoslovakia by Warsaw Pact troops was presented not only as an action to defend socialism, but also as a triumph of the reasons of state, and not only concerning the Soviet state. One could learn that the intervention not only protected Czechs and Slovaks from counter-revolution, and especially from the abolition of censorship, but saved all Warsaw Pact members from the immediate danger of West German revanchism, for example.

On September 19, Soviet Premier Alexei Kosygin declared that the intervention in Czechoslovakia was necessary "because the security of the Soviet Union was threatened." On Novermber 12, Leonid Brezhnev stated in Warsaw that the threat to socialism was not exclusively an internal affair of the country in which this was taking place, but constituted a matter of common concern for all socialist states. These kinds of declarations were regarded in the West as proclamations of the "Brezhnev doctrine," the existence of which was officially denied in the

Soviet Union, though it was not the first time such an outlook was expressed.

After the August invasion there were no disturbances or collective protests in Poland. The March settling of accounts with the intellectual and academic communities—which, it should be remembered, was preceded by the inauguaration of the Prague Spring in January—certainly helped achieve this result. If we compare the reaction of Polish society to the Soviet intervention in Hungary in 1956, when money for help was collected in Poland, blood was given, and medicine was sent, with its reaction to the intervention in Czechoslovakia in 1968, we can see that basic changes had taken place in Poland during these twelve years. (Clearly the March events contributed to these changes, and there is good reason to suspect that the Soviets had a hand in them.) Yet, despite police pressure, there were those Poles who spoke out against the 1968 invasion. Jerzy Andrzejewski, Zygmunt Mycielski, Sławomir Mrożek, and Jan Lebenstein publicly protested against the participation of the Polish government in the armed aggression in Czechoslovakia.

Fliers protesting against the aggression appeared in Warsaw, thrown from buses or mailed to private addresses.

The motives underlying the Soviet intervention in Czechoslovakia were analyzed not only in Czechoslovakia but also in Poland. The Hungarian government in 1956 had announced its intention of withdrawing from the Warsaw Pact; the Czechoslovak government had done nothing of the sort. Where was the point at which Czechoslovakia had gone beyond the Soviet measure of allowed freedom? What were the decisive factors: the danger of eliminating pro-Soviet Communists from the party leadership at the imminent Fourteenth Party Congress, the curtailment of the Czechoslovak political police, or the threat of introducing a truly multiparty system? Or perhaps it was the elimination of censorship and too much freedom in the mass media? In the Moscow protocol of August 26 one can find evidence in support of all these hypotheses. It is difficult to predict future Soviet reactions, but, in spite of this, events in Czechoslovakia were not without influence on the demands made in Poland many years later. Thus the demand for a truly multiparty system was for some time considered unrealistic (whereas in the forties these demands were advocated as consistent with the Yalta agreements). It was also deemed unrealistic to demand the elimination of censorship. It was occasionally noted that the Czechoslovak government had committed a mistake in making the price of intervention, from the very beginning, relatively small for the USSR: with the lack of preparedness of Czechoslovak defenses, Soviet politicians might have considered the political costs of the presence of Warsaw Pact troops in Czechoslovakia, but they did not need to consider the political costs of an armed struggle.

International Affairs: The Treaty with West Germany

West Germany was almost continuously present in the propaganda and official ideology of the Polish People's Republic. It was known that there was a good Germany (the GDR) and a bad Germany (the FRG). This bad Germany was portrayed as the successor to the Nazi regime and the home of militarism, retaliatory groups, and associations of expatriates. The good Germany was a peaceful country. West Germany, in fact, did not have diplomatic relations with Poland and officially questioned the western Polish border, but this just made it more convenient as a reminder of World War II, enabling the government to enlist some support against a common enemy.

In 1955, the West German chancellor, Konrad Adenauer, went to Moscow, where it was decided that diplomatic relations would be established between the USSR and West Germany. However, in December of the same year the West German government announced that it would break diplomatic relations with any country that recognized the GDR —this resolution was known as the Hallstein doctrine and was observed by West Germany until the end of the sixties; the Soviet Union was to be the only exception to the doctrine.

In December 1965, Polish bishops wrote a letter to their German counterparts expressing regret over animosity between Poland and Germany and seeking to achieve reconciliation. This letter provoked a bitter and denunciatory propaganda campaign by the authorities, and it seemed that West Germany would remain at the top of Poland's enemy list for some time.

In the meantime, the government of West Germany offered proposals aimed at reducing tension in Europe. On March 25, 1966, the West German government drafted a note that included Poland and the other East European countries among its addressees. The note contained a proposal for exchanging pledges with the Soviet Union, Poland, Czechoslovakia, or any other country of Eastern Europe, concerning the exclusion of the use of force as a means of solving international problems. The note recalled that regarding the solution of border issues no final agreement could be made until the time of a peace treaty with a united German state, as specified by the Allied agreements of 1945. But it stressed that this would not stop Poles and Germans from reaching agreement.

In late April and early May, Poland, Czechoslovakia, and the Soviet Union responded by reiterating their attacks on West Germany for agressive and militaristic policies. Their replies also asserted that the Oder-Neisse border had been established at Postdam and finally fixed in the treaty between Poland and the GDR signed in Zgorzelec in 1950. This border was final.

As the West Germans softened their application of the Hallstein doctrine—following the replacement of the liberals (FDP) by the Social Democrats (SPD) in the Christian Democrat coalition (CDU-CSU)—and inaugurated a trade agreement with East Germany in December 1968, the PZPR added a new enemy to their list—Israel—and, as a consolation prize, new friends—the "progressive" Arab states. All the Soviet bloc countries (with the exception of Rumania) broke diplomatic relations with Israel. Immediately before March 1968, one could learn that both enemies, Israel and West Germany, had joined forces to threaten world peace and act in an anti-Polish manner. In March 1968, the Polish press produced many proofs of collaboration between Jews and Germans. It was difficult to assess on whom, either the Germans or the Jews, this traditional collaboration brought more discredit. In any event, after the anti-Zionist excitement helped vacate some party positions and compelled many people to emigrate, the dangers, as portrayed in the press, soon faded.

The intervention in Czechoslovakia revived some of the anti-German propaganda, while anti-Zionism was recalled only occasionally. But this West German threat was again short-lived.

In a public speech delivered on May 17, 1969, Władysław Gomułka addressed a proposal to West Germany suggesting talks about the normalization of relations. On October 28, 1969, a month after a new coalition government was formed of Social Democrats and Liberals (forcing the Christian Democrats into opposition), the new German chancellor, Willy Brandt, delivered a speech in the Bundestag in which he stated that the federal government was ready to open talks with East European countries. Such talks were to concern the adoption of nonaggression pacts or of treaties disavowing the use of force. The treaties would also contain an acknowledgment of the territorial integrity of the states party to the agreements. Talks between West Germany and Poland began in February 1970.

On August 12, 1970, the USSR and West Germany signed a treaty obligating them to "unconditional respect for the territorial integrity in their present borders of all the countries of Europe," and they declared "that they have no territorial claims toward anyone and will not raise such claims in the future. They consider the borders of all the countries of Europe, as they are presently drawn, to be inviolable both now and in the future, including the Oder-Neisse line, which constitutes the western border of the Polish People's Republic, and the border between the Federal Republic of Germany and the German Democratic Republic" (Article 3).

Thus, in the USSR-FRG treaty, the border between Poland and East Germany was considered "inviolable." Talks between Poland and West Germany were held on the ministerial level from Novermber 3–14, 1970. On November 18, the ministers of foreign affairs of both countries initialed "a treaty between the Polish People's Republic and the Federal Republic of Germany concerning the basis for normalization of mutual relations." This treaty was signed in Warsaw on December 7, 1970, by Premier Cyrankiewicz and Foreign Minister Stefan Jędrychowski representing Poland, and by Chancellor Willy Brandt and Minister of Foreign Affairs Walter Scheel representing West Germany.

The parties to the treaty confirmed "the inviolability of their existing borders now and for the future," and they agreed to respect unconditionally their territorial integrity (Article I, 2). Both countries stated that "they have no territorial claims toward each other, and they will not raise such claims in the future" (Article I, 3).

The PRL and the FRG also declared that "they will settle all disagreements exclusively by political means, and they will refrain from the threat or use of force in all issues concerning European or international security as well as in their mutual relations" (Article II, 2).

The ratification of the West German treaties with Poland and the USSR was debated for some time in West Germany. Final ratification was facilitated by a common resolution of all West German political parties, which claimed that the treaties did not prejudge the contents of a peace treaty with East Germany and did not constitute a legal justification for the present borders.

When it came to ratification, only half of the deputies (248) voted for the treaties with the Soviet Union and Poland; the other half mostly abstained. On May 23, President Heinemann signed the bill ratifying the treaty. On May 25 the ratification became law. In Poland and the Soviet Union, the ratification process was simpler.

The exchange of both documents took place in Bonn on June 3, 1972, and the treaties became binding as of this date.

The treaty between Poland and West Germany concerned the basis of normalization. Further talks dealt mainly with economic issues (German loans to Poland) and the issue of the repatriation of "ethnic Germans" living in Poland. On August 1, 1975, during a meeting between First Secretary Edward Gierek and West German Chancellor Schmidt in Helsinki, it was agreed that over the following four years 125,000 "ethnic Germans" would leave Poland. It was also agreed that West Germany would pay 520 million dollars in reparations to Poland and that it would grant an additional 400 million dollars to Poland in the form of a long-term low-interest loan.

The Economy

In the late sixties, a quarter of a century of party rule was taking its toll on the Polish economy. The economy was burdened by doctrinaire commands and by obligations to its eastern neighbor (involving the development of antiquated heavy industries) as well as by the nineteenth-century vision of modernity as the building of steel mills and iron works. The disregard of education, scientific research, agriculture, health services, and housing needs, and the disdain for modern branches of industry based on skilled labor and complicated technologies (for example, the development of computer technologies) further undermined the Polish economy. The economy suffered from the inertia characteristic of highly centralized bureaucratized organisms, which were directed by party politicians in accordance with ideological economic dogma. Prices were set by the planners, while economic mechanisms and consumer needs played a very minor role.

Discussions were conducted in 1956 and 1957 about changes in the economic system—the need for decentralization, increasing the role of the market, rationalizing the price system, and about increasing the autonomy of enterprises—but their conclusions were never implemented. The party leadership considered any change dangerous; there was probably concern that emancipating one area might lead to the loss of party control over another.

Little was heard in the sixties about changing the economic model. Instead, much official attention was devoted to economic crimes, called "affairs." The press reported on such "affairs" in the leather industry (for example, in Radom) and the meat industry (for example, in Warsaw). There were trials at which defendants were sentenced to life imprisonment and even, at least on two occasions, to death, one of which was actually carried out.

Oftentimes, the so-called economic crime was a socially useful activity necessary for the functioning of the system; however, sometimes it was simply theft, often regarded with approval by the middle ranks of the political and economic hierarchy.

In November 1967, an increase in the price of meat and meat products was announced, averaging about 17 percent. Consumers had no reason to rejoice, and at factory meetings set up to justify the price increases workers complained and protested. On this occasion, as on previous such occasions, there were no violent demonstrations. At first, the Polish government considered any discussion of economic reform, which was in the air in 1968, tantamount to revisionism. They then categorized such discussions as "diversion," which was reminiscent of the Ministry of Internal Affairs calling for a struggle against informational diversion (i.e., of publishing Polish books abroad and speaking in Polish on foreign radio broadcasts). In party jargon, "diversion" meant competition, in any area.

Even during the darkest of times, there were some who tried to introduce elements of common sense into the nationalized economy and who attempted to conduct public discussions on the possibility of partial improvements. The weekly *Polityka* occasionally initiated such discussions, and there was also the weekly section of *Życie Warszawy* entitled "Życie i Nowoczesność" ("Life and Modernity"), which began publication in 1968. "Życie i Nowoczesność" devoted attention to the modern branches of industry developed in other countries and insisted on the need for creativity and initiative in the economy. Sometimes it popularized local economic initiatives and achievements of a somewhat unusual character. After December 1970, "Życie i Nowoczesność" singled out the contributions of a farmer named Jan Stach, who used an extremely archaic technology to build an archless stone bridge across a ravine by filling the ravine with boulders.

The need to introduce "material incentives" into the Polish economy began to be officially voiced at the end of the sixties. It was not altogether clear on how these incentives were to be implemented, only that they were to serve as an encouragement for workers' efforts. These efforts were supposed to compensate for the absence of organizational changes, which were rejected by the economic leadership.

Cultural Life at the
End of Gomułka's Reign

Histories of Polish culture will not refer to the late sixties as years of enlightenment; on the contrary. The early fifties, at least when judged by what was being published in Poland at the time, was also a period of cultural decline. There was a revival around 1956, but it was slowly extinguished in the course of the sixties.

In the sixties, explicit challenges to official policy were often met by propaganda campaigns against "anti-Polish activity." "The letter of the 34," addressed to Prime Minister Cyrankiewicz and signed by thirty-four prominent writers and scientists to protest the censorship (and paper shortages), precipitated a campaign against Radio Free Europe for reading and commenting on the letter. The authorities were consequently able to marshal support from several hundred writers who, although not particularly well-disposed towards censorship, were nevertheless willing to condemn Radio Free Europe and other Western mass media. Even some signatories of "the letter of the 34" wrote to the London *Times* stating that they had no intention of publicizing Polish internal affairs. Clearly, making cultural issues a question of the PRL against foreigners (or Radio Free Europe)—"us" against "them"—was an effective means for the authorities to enlist domestic support and to distract attention from any embarrassing issues.

This tactic was also used in response to a letter sent by Polish bishops to German bishops in late 1965 at the end of the Second Vatican Council. This effort to reach an understanding between Poland and Germany was condemned in the press as negotiations with strangers, with "them." Rallies against the Polish bishops were organized, and the press declaimed constantly about the German threat and about Polish bishops allied with "retaliatory forces."

References to Polish history were generally prohibited by the censorship (mainly when it concerned Russian/Polish relations). Occasionally, however, the censorship office exercised some leniency. On the fiftieth anniversary of Polish independence, for example, the monthly *Znak* published a special issue containing excerpts from the writings of those who had distinguished themselves in the struggle for independence. It was a rare occasion that names such as Piłsudski, Grabski, and Dmowski could be found in the press, especially in a positive or neutral context. The same *Znak* issue carried an article by Bohdan Cywiński on the educational movement under the Russian partition and the secret libraries of high-school and university students. Published shortly after March 1968 (and later incorporated into Cywiński's book, *A Genealogy of the Insubordinate*), this article was not without contemporary relevance: obtaining access to uncensored books and publications was an important issue at the time.

Writers who wanted to speak about current issues traveled into the past or the future, sometimes into the world of fairy tales. Jacek Bocheński wrote about ancient Rome (*Nazo the Poet,* 1969). A fairy-tale reconstruction of history was presented in numerous novels by Teodor Parnicki. *The Skull inside a Skull* (1970), by Piotr Wojciechowski, displayed an even more fantastic character. Sometimes recent history was also treated, but only as seen through the eyes of a youth or a child (for example, *Memoirs of the Warsaw Uprising,* by Miron Białoszewski). Stanisław Lem's futuristic novels, stories, and tales were also published, despite the fact that he was often fascinated by the idea of centralized and despotic regimes on other planets where the control of information would be often quite advanced.

The world of the fringes of society was portrayed in the stories of Marek Nowakowski and Jan Himilsbach. The new class of semi-intelligentsia, con-men, and upstarts living under socialism was described by Janusz Głowacki.

A 1970 movie by Marek Piwowski, *The Cruise,* barely squeezed through the censorship; as it was, the censor made many changes. Scenes from a boat trip on the Vistula showed Polish society in miniature: official meetings, nervous private conversations, the removal of people from the "Cruise Council," and unofficial denunciations and intrigues. The film originally ended with a scene of the ship running aground, but this last scene did not survive the censor's scissors, for perhaps obvious reasons.

During the sixties the press revived their attacks against the emigration, especially against the Paris journal *Kultura* (published by the Literary Institute) and Radio Free Europe. Contacts with these institutions served as the basis for accusations in political trials.

In the meantime, it was precisely the Literary Institute in Paris, in its series *Kultura's Library,* where valuable testaments of these years were being published and where Tomasz Staliński made his debut in 1967. Since then, he has written five novels on Polish life. (In 1980, Stefan Kisielewski announced that Tomasz Staliński was his pseudonym.) Staliński's first novel, *Seen From Above* (1967), dealt with the party power elite and its Communist inheritance, with prewar and wartime factions, the rulers' contemporary problems, their quarrels, and the shifting of positions that occurs within the internal hierarchy (which is often inscrutable). In the last regard, the author defended a theory of air currents, which took the following form: not all are equal within the party elite. Some hold superior positions (for formal or informal reasons), while others support those who occupy this or that important position. If someone in the leading group gets on the wrong side of several persons occupying the most important positions, the effect is immediate and dramatic: this person (together with his problems) finds himself in a drafty place and is quickly blown away. This is a normal, daily occurrence in the party. Periods of violent change are different. In *Seen From Above,* Staliński describes the daily life of the party official. His novel is not a document, but it certainly helps to show how Poland is seen from above.

Towards the end of his second reign in the party (1956–70), Gomułka himself appeared in several novels. In his rhymed opera *The Taciturn and the Geese,* Janusz Szpotański recorded the economic and ideological views of the then first secretary, who is called Gnome. Gnome makes plans for a crematorium to be named after the Millennium, suggests a reconciliation to the intellectuals—the geese—(which, however, they reject), and battles the Church, the primate, and Professor Halecki. As a result, Szpotański was sentenced to three years in prison and was publicly reviled by the ungrateful leader in a speech broadcast across the entire country from the Congress Auditorium in Warsaw (on March 19, 1968). Nevertheless, Szpotański continued his efforts to preserve the memory of Gomułka for posterity. Himself in prison, he writes about Gnome having a conversation with the progressive Ukrainian poet Taras while peeling potatoes in a prewar Polish prison. The two discuss the future prisons that will be built in Poland: "The street of Polish Socialism leads through prisons of concrete," declares Gnome.

Shortly after Gomułka's fall from power, the political scientist Adam

Bromke drew a parallel between the former first secretary and Marshal Piłsudski: both had a tendency toward informal autocracy, both were in power twice, and both ended their second term unhappily. One can gain further insight by extending the parallel to whom they chose to imprison. At the end of his second, though unofficial, term, Piłsudski contributed to the imprisonment of leaders of the great parliamentary and extra-parliamentary opposition. Two years before his departure, Gomułka imprisoned a satirist who wrote ironical poems about him and students who shouted that the press was lying.

Two years later, Gomułka officially ceased to exist in Poland. He joined the ranks of those who first enjoyed the absolute power of the censor, and whose names were later entirely erased from official publications.

In August 1970, Paweł Jasienica died, a man whom Gomułka had attacked, together with Szpotański, in his March 1968 speech. Jerzy Andrzejewski spoke over Jasienica's grave: "He was accused of actions he never performed and of crimes he never committed. Publicly abused and insulted, he had no possibility of defending himself. The right to publish was taken away from him; his old books were removed from bookstores, and his new ones were not allowed to appear. This is something that one would think would be inconceivable after all the experiences of totalitarian governments, but—sadly—it is true. An eminent Polish writer, a creator of permanent cultural values, enjoying the great trust and respect of thousands of readers, in the prime of his literary life, was in one day pushed to the margin of public life and condemned to civil death."

Those who gathered for Jasienica's funeral heard words of truth. The church, the cemetery, and the courtroom became the only public places in Poland where free words could be heard.

In the area of analytic and programmatic pronouncements, these did not end as a result of the March arrests. Of the political programs and diagnoses written after March 1968, one can mention that of the "Ruch" ("Movement") group, "As Time Goes By."

The Ruch group declared that it was not a direct continuation of any of the known postwar political movements in Poland, but it attempted to draw positive elements from all the movements. These elements are represented in the following demands:

- independence as the basic factor of social and economic development
- respect for the individual and his inalienable rights

- effective economic development
- state planning regarding the general outlines of economic development
- effectiveness in social action
- intellectual development
- social equality and equal opportunities for all
- the elimination of unjustified privileges and social exploitation
- freedom of the press and of assembly
- an effective, competent, responsible, and stable legal system
- institutional guarantees of free elections of the representatives of society
- an ordered social and political life
- constructive participation in world affairs
- the elimination of doctrinaire economic and political myths

The program presented here was clearly anti-Communist and without any Marxist influence. The authors explicitly formulated both the postulate of independence and of defending human rights; they spoke about the freedom and equality of citizens and about the rights of the state, although they saw these as limited by guarantees of freedom and respect for the law.

In an unsigned document, "Attempt at a Diagnosis," the contemporary social mood is analyzed and how it was affected by March 1968. The article noted that the system had encouraged aspirations which it could not satisfy, but it also observed that ideology and fear continued to guide much of people's behavior. As to "why the system no longer needed to rely on open terror?" the authors answered, "it appears that people are afraid even without any objective threat."

The authors acknowledged that socialism was derived from "an involved struggle for justice and for better forms of human life," but they voiced their opposition to its manifest properties. They expressed their support for both "a positivism based on ideals" (i.e., social activity based on moral principles) and for "active protest" in extreme circumstances, in order to defend threatened values.

The year 1970 was celebrated by the authorities as the Year of Lenin. This emphasized even more strongly Poland's dependence on the Soviet Union, which was clearly resented by the Ruch group, which planned to set fire to the Lenin Museum in Poronin.

The problems of Polish dependence on the USSR were much discussed in independent journals, and for some time in 1970 the Paris *Kultura* ran an ongoing debate on the nature of the Soviet system and its connection to Russian traditions.

The revival of publicistic and programmatic thought in Poland in 1968 was to a degree connected with the academic movement. Some authors sought escape in historical topics, where they were occasionally able to raise important issues, drawing analogies with the present, at least implicitly. Literature, despite everything, attempted to confront the issues of contemporary life; but publishing such texts in Poland was not easy. They appeared in émigré publishing houses, especially in the Paris *Kultura.* Typescripts still circulated among the people, and were later published abroad. Despite the official policy, cultural and political thought in Poland was not completely suppressed.

Political Trials

Officially there are no political crimes in Poland. There are also no political prisoners. But there are crimes defined by the Criminal Code as against the interests of the state or against public order. They consist of such actions as talking to someone, writing something, having a certain book at home, or lending it to a friend. As the law against secret organizations stands, any unauthorized alliance between people can be considered a crime. In the Communist system, safeguarding the state monopoly over information and organization is a duty of the law, and those suspected of infringing the state monopoly of information or organization are dealt with according to criminal law.

In postwar Polish history, the penal policies regarding political cases have gone through numerous changes and constitute an important indicator to the citizens of permissible action. During the initial period of the people's democracy, political trials were used to condemn actual political opponents as well as various potential enemies, such as the resistance activists during the occupation or even ordinary people guilty of careless statements or those who were denounced to the police. Peasants who did not want to "join a kolkhoz" were arrested, along with priests who "abused the freedom of religion" and workers who "violated work discipline." In April 1956 there was an amnesty and numerous rehabilitations, but this did not stop the authorities from prosecuting the participants in the Poznań workers' disturbances.

In the sixties, the security organs focused their attention on the literary milieu, because of its relative independence. Private letters were intercepted, and authors who published in the émigré press were persecuted (for example, the case of Jan Nepomucen Miller and Stanisław Cat-Mackiewicz). The conflict between intellectuals and the security service was described in *The Taciturn and the Geese,* by Janusz Szpotański.

On February 19, 1968, the court sentenced Szpotański to three years' imprisonment on the basis of Article 23 of the Small Criminal Code. This article, often used in such cases, concerned the distribution of texts that "contain false information which could inflict substantial harm on the interests of the Polish state or lessen the estime of its leading organs" (assuming this estime could be lessened any further). It was difficult not to write satire at this time, although writing it was dangerous.

In the fall of 1968, after the rallies, demonstrations, and student strikes had ended and after the fervor of the propaganda campaign had died down, a series of trials concerning a group of thirteen people began. This group was defined in the indictment as members of a secret association of "commandos." The last trial in this series took place in April 1969.

According to the prosecutors and the court, these "commandos" had in some cases met with acquaintances and discussed political and social problems, not to mention editing one-page typewritten texts, which were distributed and posted at Warsaw University. The defendants were also accused of initiating a petition to the Diet protesting against the ban on "Forefathers' Eve" and of contributing to the call for the March 8 rally at Warsaw University. All of this was attributed to the secret association of "commandos." Altogether, five trials were held, with two to four persons sentenced in each. The sentences ranged from a year and a half to three years and a half imprisonment. The events of March 8 also concerned several less well-known trials in Warsaw, Cracow, Wrocław, Łódź, and other cities.

In the summer and fall of 1969 there were several trials of persons accused of having produced fliers between March and October 1968. Some of these fliers protested against the invasion of Czechoslovakia by Warsaw Pact troops. The highest sentence in these trials was a three-year sentence (given to Bogusława Blajfer, who was tried in September 1969); it was reduced to a year and a half as a result of a July 1969 amnesty. Blajfer's crime consisted of "writing, preparing, and distributing fliers calling for opposition to the state authorities and containing false information, mostly of a social and political nature, which could inflict substantial harm on the interests of the Polish state or lessen the estime of its leading organs" (Article 23, Section 1).

A trial of five people accused of contacts with the Literary Institute in Paris took place at the beginning of 1970. According to the indictments and the verdicts, these contacts consisted of transporting books into Poland (through the Tatra mountains) as well as taking texts to

France to be published by the Literary Institute. One person was also accused of distributing these texts in Poland. The sentences ranged from a year and a half to four years imprisonment. On the basis of the July 1969 amnesty they were reduced to from a year and a half to three years (the highest sentence was given to Maciej Kozłowski).

Changes in the party leadership in December 1970, when Edward Gierek replaced Gomułka as first party secretary, did not alter the severity of legal practices. The punishments meted out in 1971 and 1972 were as draconian, and even more so, than in 1968-70. There was one difference, however: both known and less well-known citizens began to appeal on behalf of the accused. People wrote letters regarding the Kowalczyk brothers, one of whom was sentenced to death and the other to 25 years for destroying the auditorium of the Opole Higher School of Education. And later people wrote regarding the case of Ruch members sentenced to 7-year prison terms, for "preparing to overthrow the government by force" presumably by duplicating bulletins, stealing state typewriters, and planning, but never executing, a fire in the Lenin Museum in Poronin. These actions enjoyed a measure of success and probably contributed to the fact that the death sentence of Jerzy Kowalczyk was never carried out. In 1974, in honor of the thirtieth anniversary of the PKWN (Lublin) Manifesto, there was another amnesty, which resulted in the release of the Ruch members after four years imprisonment. Like previous amnesties, the amnesty of 1974 did not include crimes from the Nineteenth Chapter of the Criminal Code (crimes against the basic political and economic interests of the PRL), with the exception of two articles, those according to which Ruch members had been sentenced.

There were no public protests or appeals for sentence reductions for those tried in 1968-70 for typing texts or carrying books across the mountains. It was only in 1972-74, when heavy sentences were handed down for the destruction of a public building, for a supposed attempt on the lives of "public functionaries or state activists," and for preparing to overthrow the system by force and to set fire to the Lenin Museum, that voices of concern could be heard. The authorities began to feel pressure, and, moreover, this pressure had an effect. Such pressure on the authorities was also used later in 1976-77 in defense of the workers of Ursus and Radom.

CHAPTER 5

RECKONING

December 1970

Price increases were usually announced in Poland on Saturday afternoons, so the stores would have time on Sunday to change price-tags and so the people would have until Monday to get used to the changes.

On Saturday, December 12, 1970, two weeks before Christmas and thus at a time of heavy shopping, there was an announcement of "changes in the retail prices of a wide range of products." The communiqué stated that "the changes are of a dual character. . . ." Indeed, the prices of certain goods were lowered.

One could read in the newspapers that the prices of 40 categories of goods decreased. Their list began with pharmaceutical products and ended with roofing paper, including along the way such items as television sets, vacuum cleaners, blankets, "certain kinds of boots from synthetic materials," and "certain kinds of toothpaste." The lowering of prices generally affected those goods that state commerce was unable to sell at the previous prices.

Much more important than the price decreases were the price increases. The prices of meat and meat products, flour, milk and dairy products, fish, noodles, building materials, coal, cotton fabrics, wool, leather shoes, hygienic products, metal products, "certain paper products," and "certain furniture and wood products," and of many other goods (46 categories of goods in all) went up. The press published articles justifying the correctness of the decisions.

At the Sixth Plenary Meeting of the Central Committee on Monday, December 14, Gomułka stated:

> Today's meeting is taking place immediately after the change in retail prices ordered by the state. The necessity of this decision was explained in a letter from the Politburo

to the party organizations and in the documents of today's meeting. While the lowering of prices is welcomed by society, price increases are unpopular and always encounter criticism, whether justified or not. These changes in retail prices are thoroughly justified. However, they will not bring about radical transformations in consumption.

The average citizen was of a different mind regarding the effect that the price changes would have on consumption. On the very morning Gomułka was speaking at the plenary meeting, several thousand workers at the Gdańsk shipyards gathered in front of the shipyards to protest the price hikes and then marched to the District Party Committee building, where they split into several groups: some reached the northern shipyards, others the Polytechnic, and still others the radio station in Wrzeszcz. At three in the afternoon, a crowd broke through the police line and gathered again in front of the District Party Committee building, shouting "Bread!" and "The press is lying!" Later in the day there was an unsuccessful attempt to set the committee building on fire, and rioting lasted until late in the evening.

On Tuesday, December 15, shipyard, dock, and other workers in Gdańsk did not report for work, and there were demonstrators in front of the Regional Party Headquarters, the district police headquarters, and the city government building. The crowd attacked the police headquarters and the prison, but was driven back by the police. After several attempts to set fire to the party headquarters, it finally ignited before ten in the morning. By then, only soldiers had been left in the building; according to the local newspaper the soldiers had been allowed the use of their firearms and had fired into the crowd.

In the afternoon armored military vehicles were used against a crowd in front of the train station. There were both killed and wounded.

On the same day, there were rallies in Gdynia in the shipyards and other factories. People marched to the city government building to demonstrate.

A police curfew was introduced in both Gdynia and Gdańsk for 6:00 P.M. This was a prohibition against leaving one's house, and was published in the local press on the morning of December 16. (The rest of the country was still not officially informed about the events.)

On Tuesday evening, Vice-Premier Kociołek spoke on Gdańsk television, justifying the use of the police and the army. He claimed that 5 persons had been killed and 33 seriously wounded, and he called on the inhabitants to return to work.

Armored vehicles were brought in on Tuesday, and on Wednesday

there were tanks in the streets of Gdańsk and Gdynia and army detachments were positioned at the gates of the Gdańsk shipyard, where workers had been demonstrating since early morning. When, around 8:00
A.M., the workers wanted to leave the shipyard for the city, the army
began shooting and forced them to retreat. *Głos Wybrzeża* (December
28) wrote of these events: "A group of young people who did not heed
the warnings. . . decided to march straight toward the tanks and test the
reaction of the soldiers to the workers' attempt to leave the shipyard.
This ended in tragedy. Shots were fired. Two persons were killed, 11
workers were wounded, and the demonstrators withdrew back into the
shipyard."

At 9:00 A.M., the shipyard workers announced a sit-down strike and
were joined by the Gdańsk dock workers.

In Gdynia on Wednesday morning, army and police detachments also
were stationed at the entrance of the shipyard. Inside the shipyard, the
workers demanded that their colleagues arrested the previous day be
released. In the afternoon they were informed that their demand had
been rejected. On Wednesday afternoon, work was suspended in the
shipyards of Gdańsk and Gdynia. In the evening, Vice-Premier Kociołek again spoke on television and appealed to the workers to return to
normal work.

On Thursday, December 17, the first PAP communiqué on the events,
giving them national exposure, stated: "On December 14 and 15, serious
street disturbances occurred in Gdańsk among the workers of the shipyards. Exploiting the situation, hooligans and other criminal elements
that have nothing to do with the working class demolished and burned
several public buildings and looted dozens of stores. Murders were committed against the intervening forces of public order. Many were seriously wounded and are now in hospitals. As a result of these
confrontations caused by hooligans, six persons were killed [one more
than had been mentioned by Kociołek on Tuesday] and dozens
wounded. Decisive steps by the authorities, which were necessary in this
situation, have led to the dispersal of the hooligan elements and to the
restoration of order in the city. At the same time, the authorities have
warned that they will react most decisively against all disturbances of
public order and against all anti-state actions."

The "decisive steps" of the authorities had supposedly already led to
"the restoration of order in the city." In spite of this, on Thursday
morning, December 17, troops stationed at the entrance to the Gdynia

shipyards fired on workers going to work and prevented them from reaching the gate of the yards. This action seemed to directly contradict Kociołek's appeal to return to work. On the previous day, the army had fired on workers attempting to leave the Gdańsk shipyard.

On December 17, the workers of the Szczecin shipyards also took to the streets. The District Party Committee building was set on fire there also. In Szczecin, as in Gdańsk and Gdynia, army detachments fired on shipyard workers.

On Thursday, December 17, at 8:00 P.M., already after the shootings in Gdańsk, Gdynia, and Szczecin, it was announced that the Council of Ministers had adopted a resolution which enjoined "the organs of the People's Militia, the security services, and other cooperating organs to employ all legally available means of coercion, including the use of firearms, against persons engaging in violent attacks on the life and health of citizens, or in the looting or destruction of public property."

This was an attempt to legalize the use of violence that had already taken place in the Gdańsk-Gdynia area on Tuesday. Even so, it did not mention anyone's right to kill people as a preventive measure—people leaving work (Wednesday in Gdańsk) or going to work (Thursday in Gdynia). There has yet to be a proper explanation of who was responsible for these murders, and this responsibility still rests with the governing institutions in Poland.

On Friday, December 18, for the third day in a row, there were disturbances in Elbląg. Every day, a crowd had gathered in front of the Party Committee building, and there were attempts to set it on fire. As previously in Gdańsk, Gdynia, and Szczecin, on December 18 the army fired on the crowds in Elbląg.

At the end of the week in some factories strikes were only just beginning, or threatened to erupt. Anyone who believed that shooting at workers would pacify them was wrong.

At the Eighth Plenary Meeting (February 6–7, 1971), a text was circulated entitled "An Evaluation of the December Events and the Conclusions To Be Drawn." In this text, it was charged that the propaganda used to justify the price increases and the actions against protesting workers had been incorrect. For example, according to the authors, the decision to use the army was premature. The price increases themselves, however, were not criticized. Responsibility for the erroneous policy was ascribed mainly to Gomułka, Jaszczuk, and Kliszko, who had all been removed from the Politburo on December 20, 1970. The Eighth

Plenary Meeting also criticized the fact that the highest party authorities had not been consulted. On the other hand, this lack of internal consultation was used to limit the responsibility of the authorities.

The report also stated: "From the very beginning, the First Secretary of the Central Committee, making individual decisions, adopted an incorrect attitude toward the events on the coast. No meeting of the Politburo was called in order to evaluate these events. Until December 19, the direction of the propaganda action was decided by the First Secretary and by Comrades Jaszczuk and Kliszko. . . . Even when the crews of the Gdańsk shipyards took to the streets, when the course of events indicated the possibility of conflict in its sharpest and most dangerous form for the country, even then, the First Secretary of the Central Committee did not deem it appropriate to inform the Central Committee, then in session, about the situation."

Could it be true that on December 14 not a single member of the Central Committee apart from Gomułka knew about the events on the coast? After all, if Gomułka knew, he knew through the party and police organs. According to some accounts, the Gdańsk events were discussed in the corridors during the December 14 plenary meeting. It was as if two meetings were taking place at the same time. More importantly, it was not only Gomułka who omitted to discuss the Monday events: no other Politburo member moved to include them in the official agenda either. The party group as a whole adopted a wait-and-see attitude.

In the document distributed at the Eighth Plenary Meeting, it was asserted that the prime source of Gomułka's erroneous response to the workers' protests followed from his misreading of criticism directed against him personally as criticism directed against the party (i.e., as counter-revolution). "The direct and basic manifestation of this attitude was the pressure to use force, including firearms. From the very first day, army detachments were used to help the People's Militia. The fact of the rapid and widespread use of troops and the order to use firearms from the very beginning of the December events followed from these evaluations. The situation was made even more complicated by the existence of many centers of command on the coast. . . ." Gomułka's misjudgment was said to be possible because it was not subject to collective analysis.

This document seemed to suggest that had the workers in fact been acting in a counter-revolutionary manner (i.e., if they were to be construed as directed against the rule of PZPR), then the suppression of the revolt by the army would have been justified. And, given the opposition to Gomułka within the party, the true test of the counter-revolutionary nature of the workers' protests was, in fact, Gomułka's ability to suppress them. In other words, using the army was justified if it worked; if it didn't work it was a reflection on the party leader and not the party.

Concerning the Central Committee approval of price increases in the first place and his role in it, Gierek defended himself by saying (in January 1971, in a speech to Szczecin shipyard workers). "In this situation, comrades, I had only one other alternative: in the Politburo or at the Plenary Meeting I could have simply, you understand, taken a public stand, that is, resign from the Politburo. I could have said, 'Comrades, in this situation I cannot be a member of the Politburo.' I could have done it, I even wondered whether I should do it. Except that other comrades explained to me, my friends explained to me: 'Don't do this, for if some scandal will pop up, they'll say you provoked it. They'll say you were the cause of this scandal.' And because of this, comrades, our speech, the speech of Comrade Grudzień, was wishy-washy, wishy-washy. That is, he spoke of difficulties, right, and so on, but this speech was wishy-washy only because we did not want anyone to say that we provoked. . . ."

The view that "scandals" can be provoked was not foreign to his comrades and friends. Fearful of being accused of a provocation, Gierek claimed, he had abstained from action. He waited to see what Gomułka would do. And, as we already know, he could afford to wait: in the event of any problem, Gomułka and his closest associates could always be blamed without compromising any other party leaders.

Gierek asserted that actions of fundamental importance for the state were ordered by small party groups. This is according to the principle of lateral subordination, according to which the army is not subordinate to the premier and the minister of national defense, but constitutes a military arm of the party leadership and can be used to defend this leadership from society. At the same time, within the party leadership itself decisions are made by small closed groups, and these decisions are not opposed by other comrades, since they do not want to be accused of "provocations." Despite this implicit criticism of party-state relations, it was precisely Edward Gierek who attempted several years later to sanction the special role of the Communist party in the state and society.

Edward Gierek was announced as the new first secretary at an extraordinary Seventh Plenary Meeting held on Sunday, December 20, less than a week after the Sixth Plenary Meeting had approved the price increases. Gomułka, who was not present at the meeting (due to reportedly bad health), resigned from his position. The membership of the Politburo and of the Central Committee Secretariat had also changed.

In addition to Gomułka, Bolesław Jaszczuk, Zenon Kliszko, Marian Spychalski, and Ryszard Strzelecki were removed from the Politburo. Edward Babiuch, Stefan Olszowski, and Jan Szydlak became new members of the Politburo, while Piotr Jaroszewicz, Władysław Kruczek, and Mieczysław Moczar advanced from the position of alternate to full members of the Politburo. Henryk Jabłoński, Wojciech Jaruzelski, and Józef Kępa became alternate members.

The "new people" were actually old hands. Babiuch had previously served as director of the Organizational Department of the Central Committee; Olszowski headed the Central Committee's Press Bureau and, along with Szydlak, was a secretary of the Central Committee; Jabłonski and Jaruzelski had been members of the government (as ministers of Public and Higher Education and of National Defense, respectively); and Kępa was the first secretary of the Warsaw Party Committee. Of the new members, Olszowski and Kępa had been in the center of the March 1968 events (as leaders of the press bureau and the Warsaw Committee). Mieczysław Moczar, who was promoted, had also played a prominent role in March, as minister of internal affairs. Wojciech Jaruzelski became minister of national defense four months before the invasion of Czechoslovakia.

On December 20, following the announcement of major personnel changes in the party leadership, radio and television broadcast a speech by the new first secretary. Gierek addressed his audience with the words: "Comrades and citizens! Compatriots!" He stated that he was speaking "in the name of the party," but that he was speaking not only to his party comrades. According to Gierek, "the coastal cities—Gdańsk, Gdynia, Szczecin, and Elbląg—became an arena of workers' demonstrations, disturbances, and street riots. Lives were lost. We all share this tragedy." He stated that "the recent events have been a painful reminder that the party must never lose contact with the working class and with the entire nation. . . ." He spoke about problems "that trouble the working people and have to be resolved. Among them is the situation of working women, the housing problem, and issues concerning our youth. . . . These problems concern everyone in the nation, both those inside and outside the party, both religious believers and non-believers, and there is a place for every citizen to resolve these problems!"

Some concessions could be read in Gierek's speech. He mentioned the workers' demonstrations and even admitted that there were people in Poland who were religious or did not belong to the party.

However, in January 1971, in response to a statement in *Głos Szczecinski* (*The Voice of Szczecin*), shipyard workers in Szczecin went on strike again. The January 20 issue of *Głos Szczeciński* stated that the pipe department of the Adolf Warski Shipyard in Szczecin had pledged to exceed its production quotas and that the machine hall had been decorated with a sign reading, "With Extra Production We Support the New Leadership of the Party." According to the paper, the workers also agreed to work on Sunday, January 24. (*Głos Szczeciński* later printed an explanation that the pledges were made on the initiative of the department director, the supervisors, and the foremen and were not intended for publication. Also, the paper retracted the statement about workers agreeing to work on Sunday, January 24, 1971.)

The information on the pledges was understood by the workers as an attempt to break their solidarity. On Friday, January 22, the strike spread throughout the shipyard and to other factories in the city. By Saturday, almost the entire city of Szczecin was on strike. The shipyard workers presented their demands in twelve points:

1. We demand the return of food prices to the level prior to December 12, 1970.

2. In accordance with the will of the workers expressed during all open departmental meetings, we demand the immediate and legal election of union authorities and workers' councils; and according to the will of a majority of party members, we demand democratic elections to the party and youth organizations at the shipyard level.

We demand a guarantee of the acceptance of this point from the district authorities within a strictly defined period of time.

3. We demand compensation to the strikers for the period of the strike.

4. We demand that the shipyard management and state authorities guarantee that strike participants and strike committee members will not be punished and that their full personal safety in the shipyard and in the city be assured.

5. We demand that the First Secretary of PZPR, Comrade Edward Gierek, and Premier Piotr Jaroszewicz come to the Adolf Warski Shipyard in order to engage in direct dialogue with representatives of the workers, that is, with the strike committees.

6. We demand honest information about the political and economic situation of the shipyard and of the country and rectification of the information on pledges accepted by the pipe works department on January 19, 1971.

7. This rectification should appear in the same media that published the information initially. This should occur before January 25.

8. We demand punishment of those responsible for the transmission of information to the media about the pipe works department's pledges.

9. We demand that our demands be published in the local mass media before January 25, 1971.

10. We demand that district party and union authorities and the shipyard management guarantee to the Workers' Commission elected from the Strike Committee the possibility of participating in the Shipyard Union Council and the Workers' Council until the legal election of authorities, as mentioned in point 2.

11. The viability of the Workers' Commission requires the following:

a) a guarantee of personal safety in the shipyard and the city;

b) exclusive control over the shipyard broadcasting system and its technical and safety personnel;

c) release of Workers' Commission members from their work so that they can oversee the realization of the above Point 2.

12. We demand that the security organs immediately cease their persecution, threats, and arrests of workers participating in the strike. Striking is not a crime and is nowhere prohibited.

Strike Committee

On Sunday, January 24, in accordance with Point 5 in the above strike demands, Gierek and Jaroszewicz visited the Szczecin shipyard, as well as the minister of national defense, Wojciech Jaruzelski, the new (as of January 24) minister of internal affairs, Franciszek Szlachcic, the secretary of the Central Committee, Kazimierz Barcikowski, Vice-Premier Franciszek Kaim, and the new first secretary of the District Party Committee in Szczecin, Eugeniusz Ołubek. A stormy meeting followed between the visitors and the workers' representatives, which was broadcast throughout the shipyard.

In the end the gathering agreed to terminate the strike without resolving the basic issue of food prices. The chairman of the Strike Committee, Edward Bałuka, commented that "this point is left open as a vote of confidence in the new leadership, and I think I speak for everyone when I express the hope that the new leadership . . . will attempt simply to fulfill this demand as soon as possible."

Strikes continued, and the demand for a return to pre-December 12, 1970 food prices was a constant theme. In mid-February, following strikes in Łódź, the authorities finally acceded to this demand. According to a PAP communiqué published on the evening of February 15: "A joint meeting of the Politburo and of the Presidium of the government was held on February 15, 1971. . . . It was decided that, thanks to credits from the Soviet Union during the past several days and in consideration of projected national meat production in the second half of this year and during the next year, it is now possible to lower food prices as of March 1—including the prices of meat and meat products—to the level of before December 13, 1970. This has been done in consultation with the Central Council of Trade Unions. At the same time, it was decided that the price changes for industrial goods should remain in effect."

A Slight Thaw

By 1970, fourteen years had elapsed since October 1956, and much can be gained from comparing the events of December 1970 to those of October 1956.

October 1956 was the culmination of a fairly slow evolutionary process. The party's structure and personnel had been changing throughout the three years following Stalin's death. And this included the relaxation of censorship and police repression and the releasing and rehabilitation of political prisoners. The December events and the leadership changes, in contrast, occurred after a period of gathering darkness in social life, following March 1968. Gierek's speech of December 20, 1970 was not preceded by a period of rationing freedom. Liberalization in 1956, though limited and brief, had been propagated by the party and its leaders both in the USSR and in Poland. The party authorities in 1971 were much less inclined toward liberalization. Gierek had been a firm supporter of the 1968 crackdown. It is enough to recall the clumsy though threatening metaphors in his speech at a Katowice rally on March 15, 1968. At that time, Gierek had spoken about "the dirty froth that floated to the surface on the wave of the October events eleven years ago," and about the fact that "if some people attempt to divert the course . . . chosen by the nation, the powerful Silesian current will break their bones."

From December 1970 until February 1971, the party was under pressure to change, and it was the workers who were exerting the pressure. Through strike actions, the workers were expressing themselves and exercising their independence, practically for the first time since World War II. They were demanding changes that included the legalization of the strike committees, the independence of trade unions, and honest information in the media. But, despite the general opinion, they were not the only social group formulating demands and postulates, as witnessed, for example, by the letters to the editors of *Polityka* (only a small number of which were ever published). Gierek's speech on becoming first secretary was directed not only to "comrades" but also to "compatriots," and he included mention of the existence of "religious believers." Also the authorities attempted to gain the approval of farmers. The government purchase prices of milk and meat were raised (in March 1971); it was announced that compulsory deliveries would be abolished, the titles to land ownership would be regulated, and that there would be changes in the tax system (in April 1971). Compulsory deliveries were finally eliminated in 1972. In 1970 and 1971, the party authorities were responding to pressure exerted by striking workers and the general public.

Gierek's Reforms

To the West, Poland was portrayed as a sternly and rationally governed country. Western political commentators and scientists wrote about "Gierek's Poland," though they often overlooked "the Poles' Poland," and Gierek was seen to be developing the economy and pampering the workers. Banking consortia and stock companies were not sparing with loans, goods, and licenses to the Polish government. The wastefulness, chaos, and lack of planning of the economy in "Gierek's Poland" were to become apparent only in the latter half of the 1970s.

The ruling economic principle of Gomułka's reign was financial self-reliance: one should borrow from abroad as little as possible. This changed after December 1970. Modernization of the economy became a primary goal, and for this licenses and capital were needed. After 1970, the value of Polish exports and imports increased (though with imports at a faster rate). Trade contacts with the West became bolder, and the share of Western countries in Polish foreign trade increased (with the share of imports greater than that of exports but not exceeding the magic 50 percent mark of all transactions). The planners' idea was that the West would finance economic development in Poland, and the repayment of credits would be financed by the increase in export goods that the credits produced. In the beginning, much attention was devoted to production of consumer goods, and salaries and wages rose quickly, even in real terms. But the abundance of Western credits was spent in a disorganized way, which only further increased Poland's debt to the West. Despite initial hopes, the Polish trade deficit with the West only grew.

In the area of agriculture, the post-December policy was inaugurated with increases in the government's purchase prices of milk and meat (announced on March 20, 1971). On April 18, 1971, the Politburo and the Presidium of the United Peasants' Party (ZSL) jointly announced the elimination of compulsory deliveries, regulation of the property of private farmers, whose ownership had not been legally clear (this involved over a million farms), and the inclusion of farming families in free health services. Changes in the tax system were also announced. These changes were introduced on January 1, 1972.

A major problem of the investment program was that it was designed to be wide-ranging while, at the same time, giving priority to the construction of the northern port in Gdańsk and of the "Katowice" Steel Mills both in terms of the supply of raw materials and in wage policies. This policy resulted in raw material and skilled labor shortages elsewhere, thus jeopardizing balanced economic development. It also led to a shortage of goods in a market saturated with money.

Changes in the educational system were announced shortly after Edward Gierek assumed his new position. In 1971 the Ministry of Public and Higher Education was divided into a Ministry of Public Education and Upbringing and a Ministry of Science, Higher Education, and Technology. This suggested a serious preoccupation with education on the part of the authorities. The name of the first-mentioned new ministry indicated also that the state did not intend to leave the task of upbringing solely to the family and the Church. The Ministry of Public Education and Upbringing prepared a new program of compulsory high-school education, ratified by the Diet in October 1973, and in a later, more detailed ten-year plan for public school, the teaching of humanities was to be limited largely to the history of the Communist party, and Russian was to remain a compulsory subject.

In the fall of 1972, the chairman of the Main Council of the Union of Polish Students, Stanisław Ciosek, announced plans to unify the three youth organizations: the Union of Polish Students (ZSP)—which was a nonpolitical organization concerned with the material, recreational, cultural, and, to some extent, scientific affairs of students—and two political organizations active in the academic community—the Union of Socialist Youth (ZMS) and the Union of Rural Youth (ZMW). This move was perceived as an attempt to do away with the relative independence of ZSP, and protest could be heard at Warsaw University, especially in the Department of Mathematics. In the spring of 1973, the congresses of the three organizations announced the creation of the Socialist Union of Polish Students.

Gierek's reforms also included a proposed law on parasitism. This was an attempt to make certain vaguely defined crimes of parasitism punishable. It sanctioned not only the right to work (mentioned in the Constitution) but also the duty to work (as exists, for example, in the Soviet Union). However, the proposal encountered rather sharp criticism, mainly among lawyers and sociologists, and was never adopted.

In October 1972, the Politburo adopted a directive concerning the so-called "nomenclature" of the leading cadres. In it, the Politburo specified which party organs were responsible for filling positions in the party as well as in the highest state organs, the state administration, judicial system, economic institutions, army, social organizations, media, and scientific institutions. Detailed lists of positions contained not only appointed positions but also those officially designated as elective. The October directive of the Politburo was one of the clearest testimonies to the party character of the state and to the fiction of state and "social" positions and institutions.

A series of changes in the territorial division and administration of the country were among the reforms introduced in the mid-seventies. They began with a law of November 29, 1972, which designated communes as the smallest units of territorial division, replacing settlements and villages which were, on average, half the size of communes. A new office of Commune Manager was created as a one-person executive of the state administration. Commune Managers were, according to the law, "managing and executive organs."

In 1973, the commune principle of one-person administrative offices was introduced in regional governments: in cities, counties, and districts. National councils, which had previously administered the regions and had not been subordinate to the government, continued to exist, but they were no longer administrative organs: they became simply organs of self-government whose functions were vaguely defined as "directing," "affecting," "inspiring," and "controlling." The new administrative organs constituted an administrative network subordinate to the government (i.e., the party).

In agriculture, following the concessions of 1970 and 1971 the policy returned to the old practice of attempting to limit the private ownership of land. Consistency toward agriculture was never a strong suit of the Polish authorities, who were always inclined toward the "socialization" of agriculture. The authorities wanted to feed the population, but they were also stubbornly attached to state or collective agriculture. The economic harassment of private farms, with talk of their collectivization or replacement with state farms, raised uncertainty in the countryside and only resulted in more and more grain and meat having to be imported from abroad.

The purpose of administrative reforms was undoubtedly to increase the efficiency of government and strengthen centralism. Lines of administrative subordination were shortened, and the power of the central authorities was enhanced at the expense of local advocacy. At the same time, there were attempts to subordinate all social life to the party, reflected in the refinement of the "nomenclature" and the unification of youth organizations, in accordance with the Soviet model. This tendency was also reinforced by propaganda. Red flags, previously avoided as everyday decorations, now appeared as permanent fixtures on party buildings and in the vignettes of party periodicals. The Soviet state sign was displayed everywhere on the occasion of the anniversary of the October revolution. School programs emphasized "internationalist" upbringing, understood as the identification of Polish interests with those of the Soviet Union.

The reforms of the seventies can be seen as an attempt to introduce enlightened autocracy. The economic changes were intended to modernize Poland and build "a socialist industrial society." The power elite saw themselves as benefactors and saw the development of industry as the building of their own monuments and mausoleums. The "Katowice" Steel Mills were to be the great monument of Edward Gierek. As a result, the modernization of the economy was conducted according to the whims of politicians and without economic mechanisms (e.g., an accounting of cost, prices, and profitability with the availability of raw materials, machines, and energy).

The economy was to be modernized in a Western manner without changing the Communist mode of organization. An Eastern superstructure was to reign supreme over a Western base.

One might well suspect that the authorities were concerned with lessening the standard of living gap between Poland and the industrialized countries of the West and thus eliminate the causes of the social revolts they had encountered in late 1970 and early 1971. Later events demonstrated that they failed to achieve their objectives.

The Church

Throughout the entire postwar history of Poland, the Catholic Church has expressed its views on the basic issues of concern to society. It did so in pastoral letters from the episcopate and the primate, as well as in a number of letters addressed to the state authorities, which were not always made public. This was also the case after the events of December 1970.

On December 29, the Main Council of the Polish Episcopate addressed a letter "To all compatriots of our common Motherland." The letter quoted a telegram from Pope Paul VI to the Primate of Poland expressing his concern for the Polish nation and assuring it of his prayers for its peaceful development.

The Main Council of the Episcopate recalled the recent signing of the treaty normalizing relations with the Federal Republic of Germany and stated that "we have greeted with joy these steps aimed at the recognition of our nation's rights by our Western neighbors."

The Main Council also spoke about the events "which have recently, shortly before Christmas, painfully affected our country, especially the cities of the coast." The letter stated:

When in international relations we succeed in confirming our just rights, we must consolidate our rights to existence and self-determination internally. The leading organs of our state are primarily responsible for this.

The recent events have made it amply apparent that the nation's right to existence and independence must include:

- the right to freedom of conscience and freedom of religious life, with full normalization of relations between the Church and the state;
- the right of our nation to free cultural activity, consistent with the spirit of the Christian principles of social cooperation;
- the right to social justice, expressing itself in the fulfillment of justified demands;
- the right to truth in social life, to truthful information, and to freedom of expression regarding opinions and demands;
- the right to material conditions that assure a dignified existence for every family and citizen;
- the right of citizens to be treated without abuse, unfair injury, or persecution.

Both the central authorities and the entire state administration, and especially those charged with the maintenance of order in society, are responsible for the assurance of these rights. All citizens of the state are to share in this responsibility.

The respect for these rights is—as taught by the encyclical [of Pope John XXIII] *Pacem in terris*—a condition of peace in social life. We emphasized this already in March 1968. The use of coercion does not contribute to the maintenance of peace in social life, especially when the innocent, or even women and children, are not spared. The life of the nation cannot develop in an atmosphere of fear; it must be led to peace in the spirit of justice and social love.

On January 27, the bishops called for prayers for the motherland, stating that "In the painful December events, firearms were used imprudently. This had tragic consequences! The streets of the coast were stained with blood, and the whole nation suffered a profound shock. . . . During the last years we have suffered a sea of troubles and humiliations. We have witnessed conceit and indifference to every free thought, to every postulate—even the most just—and to every presented demand. Our tragedy is a consequence of these humiliations suffered by the entire nation and society; they have also affected the Church in Poland."

The bishops stated: "We can do much to promote the victory of good and reason, to introduce a reign of social justice and respect for man, and, as a consequence, to promote internal order and peace, which insures the existence and freedom of our Motherland. For where there is no social peace, independence is threatened! Only within the limits of peace, order, and internal freedom can we speak about the independence of the Motherland. The search for ways of introducing peace and order is everyone's responsibility."

The bishops called for prayer:

- above all, for those who fell on the coast;
- for families in mourning, for widows and orphans: for solace and for bread for the orphaned;
- for those who believed it was their civil duty to ask for the just rights of the working people;
- further, for those who caused these miseries, so that God will forgive them and so we might also be able to forgive them;
- and also for the sake of those who have now accepted the responsibility for order, internal peace in our Motherland, and justice for all, so that in the difficult social and economic situation of the country, they can find proper avenues to bring peace and healthy development, faithful to their promises, with respect for human and civil rights.

The bishops ended their letter with an appeal for help: "We will support our prayers with donations, even small ones, which we will give as 'the gift of the altar' during today's services for the families who have lost their support. This shall be a sign of our Christian community and compassion."

In January 1974 in the Church of the Holy Cross in Warsaw, the Primate of Poland, Stefan Cardinal Wyszyński, delivered three sermons devoted to man and his relation to God as it related to economics and politics. According to Cardinal Wyszyński, economic rights and responsibilities, though important, were not the most crucial in human life, and they should not be separated from "the meaning of humanity: the dignity of the human person. . . . The goal of man's work should above all be man." Regarding the question of economic rights, Cardinal Wyszyński followed to a large extent the encyclical of Pope John XXIII, *Pacem in terris*. A man can demand an appropriate salaried job in his own country, and this "right is connected with freedom of choice to undertake a job. . . . Everyone has a right to working conditions such that his physical health is not weakened." Man has a right to work in dignified conditions. He also "has a right to undertake economic activity in accordance with his sense of duty," as John XXIII stated in his encyclical. This encyclical invoked by Wyszyński also spoke about the right to "wages established according to the dictates of justice" and about the right of private ownership "to the extent that it is necessary to guarantee the freedom and dignity of the human person." The primate spoke against the omnipotence of "economism" and "economic productivism" and reminded his readers that "the most valuable commodity in our country is a man."

In this sermon on *"homo politicus,"* the primate specified what he understood by the normalization of Church/state relations: "the most important element is the recognition of the presence of the Church in Polish society." He also recalled that "the Polish bishops were distressed at the attempt to integrate all of Polish youth in one monopolistic organization, and they said so. Such attempts impoverish and lessen the possibilities of social sophistication among the youth, especially among the academic youth. This will without doubt harm the national culture, and even social and political life. Wisdom dictates that the organization of society should not be based on the general application of a narrow scheme but on the facilitation of free and unimpeded work of various strata and social groups, according to their reasonable and healthy preferences. The courageous defense of freedoms and of the right to unite or to organize for one's aims is therefore absolutely necessary, as well as the freedom of the press, public opinion, publication, discussion, deliberation, and scientific research. These are the prerequisites for creating the wealth of cultural, social, national, and political life."

The Church conducted many occupational and group pastoral actions. These included pastoral activity among the academic youth, in which people participated in informational, cultural, and political activities independent of the authorities. The Church's program of summer youth camps was one of its most important educational activities. There were also important cultural activities: Christian Culture Weeks, youth festivals of religious songs, Sacrosong, and lecture series connected with pastoral activities. Pilgrimages to Częstochowa or to Piekary Śląskie were occasions for communal social, cultural, and religious experiences.

For themselves, the authorities had their own goals on "the denominational front": to limit the influence of the Church and impede its activities. Seminary students were drafted into the army, permits for the construction of churches were refused, and priests were scrutinized by the police for any incriminating evidence that could be used for blackmail. The state authorities were very interested in modernizing the Polish Church; they condemned its conservatism and helped organize anonymous actions for "renewal in the Church," designed to turn priests against the bishops. They also mailed out falsified texts of Cardinal Wyszyński's sermons in which he supported the achievements of the Polish authorities.

The party and state authorities were in no position to attack the Church directly and openly, although the director of the Office of Denominational Issues, Kazimierz Kąkol, spoke openly at party meetings about what had to be done. Because of the difficulty in realizing their large-scale goals, the authorities initiated small-scale political intrigues, which did them little good.

The State and Society

In the seventies, the percentage of the employed population working for the state sector was steadily increasing. The power of the state, and consequent dependence of society, was further strengthened through its control of the consumer market. The state thus possessed a virtual monopoly over society through control of wages, consumer pricing, and supply.

At the same time, the Communist party, with its hierarchical structure and strict control of an apparatus and rank-and-file, was in a prime position to tighten its grip on social affairs, which it did. Compulsory military service was an important instrument in this regard. Every year, more than a hundred thousand young men are drafted into the army for two or three years. Indoctrination (called "political education") takes place in the army under conditions of military discipline, facilitating the enforcement of orders. The army indoctrinates the young by equating socialism with patriotism, and patriotism with the interests of the Soviet Union. The projected modifications of the educational program in the seventies were designed with the same message in mind. The mass media, carefully controlled by censorship and the party, followed a similar course.

The budget of the Ministry of Internal Affairs grew steadily throughout the seventies, and according to official data it was larger than the budgets of the ministries of health, education, and culture combined.

The entire areas of production and distribution, local administration, the army, education, the mass media, and the political police were, with the help of the party apparatus, actively directed by the party leadership.

In the early seventies the expectations of Polish society were raised significantly. There were promises of the modernization of the economy, the building of a "second Poland," the development of the housing industry, the fulfillment of nutritional needs, and improved health and recreation services. At the same time, the policies of the authorities continued to discriminate against those areas considered "nonproductive," which included education and health service, and also against those areas viewed as productive but secondary, for example, agriculture. And at a time when those born during the baby boom of the fifties were entering the mainstream and cities were becoming even more overcrowded, housing construction could not meet the demand. The waiting period for a cooperative apartment often extended to ten years or more. In short, the authorities failed to quench desires they had awakened.

Polish society was at the mercy of the party-state and of the planners, who failed to meet their promises. When the economy they had constructed and directed began collapsing, there was no mistaking who was to blame and why.

Culture in the Early Seventies

The period after 1968 introduced a somewhat modified official language. For example, words such as "the nation" and "Poland" were officially used more frequently. As usual, some writers and publishers sought to exploit these changes for common cause. For various reasons, it was a pitiful period (although not the most pitiful in postwar Polish history).

However, it transpired that the times were conducive to the publication of certain historical works, both scientific and journalistic. The party's emphasis on national themes facilitated publications in, for example, the history of Polish philosophy and, especially, of messianism (for example, Andrzej Walicki's works on the history of social thought). Works were also published about the Polish federalist program in the Second Polish Republic and Prometheanism, that is, Polish support for separatist national movements in the Soviet Union. This tendency seemed to continue into the early seventies.

Two years after Paweł Jasienica's death, the third volume of his *Republic of Two Nations* was published, entitled *A History of the Agony.* This revived discussions about the causes of the eighteenth-century Polish downfall, which was not without contemporary relevance. Referring to Jasienica's book, people asked whether the Polish reforms at the time had not gone too far or whether Catherine the Great had not been needlessly upset. In *November Evening* (1972), Andrzej Kijowski reminded his readers of independence and revolutionary endeavors in nineteenth-century Europe, and especially in Poland.

Stanisław Barańczak, Ryszard Krynicki, Julian Kornhauser and others composing "generation '68" were permitted to publish their poems. Their poetry reported on the propaganda world of words and images and the pseudo-reality popularized by radio and television; it depicted meetings where by common order people expressed approval or condemnation. This fabricated reality of propaganda was a subject of derision and parody in the student theater.

In a collection of articles entitled *The Unportrayed World* (1974), Julian Kornhauser and Adam Zagajewski complained about the tendency of Polish literature to turn away from contemporary reality. They also wrote poetry and novels. Adam Zagajewski's novel, *Hot and Cold* (1975), was an attempt to present the life of a member of his youth generation—significantly, the novel ends at the beginning of 1968.

Andrzej Kuśniewicz and Piotr Wojciechowski continued to write about a half mythological past, which, in the case of Wojciechowski, occasionally provided a relevant allusion (the story of a blind helmsman who caused one in a series of nautical catastrophes, or about the long trial of young people threatening the state through some unspecified activity, both from the volume *Downpour, Comet, Pig Market.* 1974).

In 1973, the publication of *138 Poems* and a collection of feuilletons from *Tygodnik Powszechny* entitled *Presence,* brought Antoni Słonimski, the distinguished poet and feuilletonist who was vilified in 1968 by the party, back into the cultural scene.

The publication of a series of episodic poems by Zbigniew Herbert, entitled *Pan Cogito* (1974), was one of the most important literary events of the seventies.

Contemporary Polish reality was presented in a series of books by Tomasz Staliński (a pseudonym for Stefan Kisielewski). *Shadows in a Cave* (1971) and *People in an Aquarium* (1976) dealt with the contemporary and depraved Polish intelligentsia: their susceptibility to "newspeak" and their cooptation as contributors to the new reality. The subject of *The Investigation* (1974) was the difficulty in specifying the facts and the motive of the December events. These events were shown in a fog, beyond which there were suggestions of party and police conspiracies, intrigues, and provocations.

Postwar Polish history (including the December events) was presented in Andrzej Wajda's film *The Man of Marble*. Krzysztof Zanussi's films (*Illumination* and *Camouflage*) spoke of contemporary moral problems and preserved a connection with Polish social reality. New documentary movies were made, though they had difficulties reaching the screen.

In 1976–77, the development of an independent press meant that Polish writers could publish without the interference of censorship. But the drawbacks of publishing outside the reach of censorship prevented many authors from going over. The authorities were hostile toward the independent publications; the police searched for printing machines and confiscated freshly published editions. Writers who published independently were banned from state publishing houses and the mass media: one could publish either officially or unofficially, but not both. Yet in this way there was a certain official tolerance of the independent press, and a more daring and independent culture did develop. In the end, the growth of uncensored publications contributed to the lessening of censorship in 1980, though it was seen by the party as a temporary measure.

Political Polemics

In the course of the strikes from December 1970 through the early months of 1971, the workers formulated a political program. The workers demanded the lowering of food prices, wage increases, compensation for losses suffered during the strike, release of arrested workers, and punishment of the perpetrators of the massacres on the coast. There were demands for truthful information, for the rectification of lies in the press, for the legalization of strike committees, and for changes in the functioning of labor unions (for their real independence).

Emigré publications and periodicals, especially Paris *Kultura* and its library, published testimonies to these events and to the events of March 1968. The publication of these volumes was facilitated by the gathering of information inside Poland, and this meant that the political events and the repressions that followed had not taken place in secret and that the lessons could be shared.

In the June 1971 Paris *Kultura,* Leszek Kołakowski published "Theses on Hope and Hopelessness." This was Kołakowski's first analytic and programmatic text on socio-political issues since his departure from Poland. Kołakowski christened the political system "despotic socialism," and he observed certain "contradictions," in accordance with Hegelian-Marxist terminology, pertaining to the various goals of this system. In contrast to the altered system of "despotic socialism," Kołakowski believed in unadulterated socialism. He defined socialism mostly in contradistinction to "despotic socialism" and as a sovereign society: democratic, pluralist, ruled by law, liberal (that is, would respect individual freedoms), and assuming "control over the use and development of the means of production and over the distribution of the national income." Only this last characteristic (the control of the economy by society, presumably exercised through extra-economic means) could be considered a feature specific to socialism, that is, differentiating socialism from other systems.

In later polemics on this subject, only the validity of the feature specific to "socialism" was challenged.

In *Kultura* (1971, no. 9) B. Zawisza questioned the need to concede "that nobody should be allowed to concern himself privately with production that might compete with the production controlled by society. . . . It seems paradoxical to me that all theoreticians of socialism, beginning with Saint-Simon, discuss the means of production (that is, of industry), but nobody has thought to ask people closely connected with industry what they think about the subject. I know of no case (apart from the philanthropist Engels) of a man who was familiar with the mechanisms of the development and progress of modern industry and who advocated social control over all means of production." We might add that the demand for social control over the means of production (even when this demand is limited only to certain areas of production) does not determine the methods of control: whether this should be group control (which demands decentralization) or control by the entire society (which demands both centralism in management and democracy in the control of management).

The names bestowed on the political system in Poland varied, but the authors were aware of the nature of this system, of its dependence on external factors, and of the connection between the Communist party and the state, the role of the coercive apparatus (the police and the army), and the aspirations of the party leadership to omnipotence, to central and monolithic rule. It was known that the system in Poland was changing, but the experiences of October 1956 and December 1970 led to the growing conviction that social pressure was a necessary condition for any more permanent changes.

Some authors wrote about the prosaic problems of people who merely wanted to work without the results being wasted. For over a hundred years there were discussions in Poland about working for the good of society, sometimes called "organic work," and whether, and to what extent, such work made sense when one could not control its product. Eliza Prusińska (in a *Kultura* text, June 1972) defended the "attitude of organic work" as prudent but also oppositional: "It is an attitude which is based on an understanding of the need to serve the material and cultural requirements of our country under the existing conditions," but without condoning, even in the name of preserving certain cultural or material goods, "actions that terrorize or demoralize society . . . or tighten the screws of Communist control."

In April 1973, *Kultura* published an article on "The Polish Question" by Leszek Kołakowski. Kołakowski wrote: "The question in Poland is the fight against spiritual corrosion. . . . Right now this corrosion is the Sovietization of Poland which is in no way based on ideological indoctrination. . . . Sovietism is . . . a situation in which everyone is aware that in public speech nothing is and *nothing can be* 'for real,' that all words have lost their original meaning." Of course, one can ask whether the indoctrination of society—even with an ideology that is not generally believed—has not contributed to this situation. Kołakowski returned to the discussion of good work and "organic work" and argued that appeals for "survival," "the preservation of the Polish culture," and "for decent work, honesty and solidity" are misguided at best. "The national culture does not need preservation but active defense, and it is bad faith to argue that one does not know what this means."

In *Kultura* of July/August 1973, Mieroszewski broached the subject of an independent Polish policy in an article entitled "The Polish *Ostpolitik*." Mieroszewski attacked the tendencies of some publicists of the emigré National Party to reach an understanding with the Soviet Union. These publicists tended to ignore the demands of the Ukrainians, Byelorussians, and Lithuanians. Mieroszewski supported the acceptance of the territorial *status quo*, thus abandoning Polish claims to Vilno and Lvov.

In the next issue of *Kultura*, Mieroszewski wrote about the Polish *Westpolitik*. If the future Western alliances of Poland were to be effective, then, according to Mierowszewski, Poland must see to its relations with its Eastern neighbors, that is, with the Ukraine, Byelorussia, and Lithuania. This could lessen the possibility of an understanding between the Germans and the Ukrainians at the expense of Poland.

In *Kultura* of November 1973, there was an article by Adam Bromke, "The Polish 'Ost-West Politik,' " which was a polemic with Mieroszewski. Bromke appeared as an adherent of conciliatory policies (the reconciliation of Poles with their government and with the Soviet Union). Mieroszewski was rather an opponent of conciliation, especially if political emigrés were to participate in it. In his answer to Bromke ("Books of Conciliation and the Diaspora of Adam Bromke," *Kultura*, no. 11, 1974) Mieroszewski stated: "Nations in captivity always play two pianos: they have both those who want reconciliation and those who desire independence. . . . Conciliatory politics may be realized only inside the country, and if someone believes . . . this is the only way to serve Poland, he should go back to Poland." Mieroszewski ended his article by stating that Professor Bromke had "left the circle of those whom we welcome to publish in *Kultura*." The reaction was sharp, but the exchange helped to clarify the political alternatives, particularly important for any future actions.

On September 17, 1974, in the Warsaw Cathedral of Saint John, on the 35th anniversary of the occupation of Polish territories by the Red Army, a mass was celebrated for five brigadier generals who fell in September 1939. Father Jan Zieja delivered a sermon about the obligation of forgiveness and conciliation: "We hope that at some time in the future authorized representatives of the Polish nation will meet with authorized representatives of the Russian nation—and that both nations, basing themselves on the truth about their history and their future, will be reconciled." Father Zieja also asserted that before this happened Poles had also to remember the Lithuanian, Byelorussian, and Ukrainian nations: "Praying for the souls of our fallen and murdered soldiers, let us pray for a day of truth, of freedom and reconciliation, not only for us, but also for our brothers the Lithuanians, the Byelorussians, and the Ukrainians."

Father Zieja spoke about issues similar to those addressed by Mieroszewski. Despite their differences both pointed to the need for a reconciliation of Poles with their eastern neighbors: Lithuanians, Byelorussians, and Ukrainians.

The issues of social attitudes and internal policies were raised in an article entitled "Political Opposition in Poland," which was sent from Poland and published in *Kultura* in November 1974. The article stated that "political opposition in Poland has an antitotalitarian and independence-oriented character." Three institutions were singled out without which it would be impossible to talk about opposition in Poland. Those were the Church, informal groups, and the emigration—or, more exactly, emigré publications. The text suggested that opponents of the system in Poland should respect the law in their activities. This suggestion encountered reservations because, among other things, the precision of crucial legal formulations in the Polish law leaves much to be desired, and it was not easy to determine whether certain political or social actions were consistent with the law or not. This would be decided by a political power that was very likely to interpret deliberately imprecise legal formulations to the detriment of opponents of the system.

The opposition, the resistance movement, and a program for Poland were discussed in *Kultura* in 1975. Not everyone drew up programs of action; some only stated that such programs were necessary (for example, Marian Kowalski, "On the Need for a Program," *Kultura,* May 1975). There were also articles that spoke of the need for political thought (that is, of the need for something more general than a program). After reading several such texts one wants to suggest that the authors stop justifying the need for thought and start thinking instead. One can mention, in all fairness, that there were some texts where some thoughts were indeed formulated.

The term "opposition" was used more and more frequently. Some wrote about what this opposition was doing, others about what it should be doing. The discussions taking place in the emigré periodicals, especially in *Kultura,* during the years 1971–76, helped to develop an understanding of the problems both of internal and of international Polish politics (particularly relevant to planning for the future). People wrote about the need to exert social pressure, to demand and force changes. They wrote about the necessity of respecting basic values, even when one undertakes "organic work." There were quarrels about whether the opposition needed to obey the law. Authors distinguished the tasks of those who lived abroad and those who lived in Poland, and also the tasks of those institutions that existed legally in Poland (e.g., the Church, Catholic groups, the universities) versus the tasks of the opposition. The discussions were conducted with increased knowledge of the characteristics of the ruling system in Poland and of the historical conflicts between the authorities and society. Indeed, the social response during the turning points of postwar Polish history (such as December 1970) was immediate and, despite difficult conditions, exhibited a significant degree of maturity (expressed, for example, in the strikers' demands in 1970 and 1971).

Shortly before the next crisis, in May 1976, the program of the Coalition for Polish Independence (PPN) was announced.

The PPN, whose membership was secret, formulated the following goals, called assumptions: 1) the sovereignty of the nation, understood as an inalienable right of a national collective to decide its own fate; 2) equality under the law; 3) freedom for all religions, and, above all, nondiscrimination against the religious majority; 4) the extension of civil freedoms; 5) the maintenance of ties with the traditions and present developments of European civilization.

This program also included such goals as making all Poles co-managers of the country; the implementation of civil rights; institutionalizing a multiparty democracy in Poland; welfare measured in terms of people's attitudes; progress in the national economy without constant demands for sacrifice on the part of millions of working people; the free and pluralistic development of Polish science and culture; open access to the world; and freedom of travel and of cultural and informational exchange.

Based on these assumptions and goals, PPN presented a 26-point program. As the text asserts, every point "contains a short evaluation of the current situation and formulates postulates for change." Thus, for example, point 2 states: "All authority must come from the nation and must be continually responsible to the nation, since it must play a role of the servant."

Point 6 speaks of democracy: "The highest authority in the state is vested in the nation and is exercised through the free, secret, direct, and proportional election of representatives. Beginning with the Diet as the highest authority, on all levels and in all areas of state administrative and economic activity, the freely elected representatives of society and individual citizens have the right and the possibility to control the fulfillment of responsibilities and the application of the law."

Points 7 and 8 concern the reestablishment of freedom of speech and of assembly; points 9 and 10 concern the reforms in education and science:

"We demand schools free from lies, fear, and political and police pressures. . . . Polish universities must regain their autonomy. . . . The Polish Academy of Sciences must regain the status of a self-governing body composed of those scholars with the most valuable accomplishments and with the greatest authority."

Points 13 through 16 specify the directions of foreign policy. "13. Relations with Russia constitute the most crucial aspect of Polish foreign policy. . . . Only when these mutual relations are founded on honesty, the disclosure of inequities committed against Poland, and real sovereign equality, will it be possible to develop an authentic friendship between the Polish and the Russian nations and to heal the old wounds.

"14. We are not neighbors of Russia. The Ukraine, Byelorussia, and Lithuania are our eastern neighbors. . . . We have no territorial claims towards them. . . . We demand, however, that all governments ruling over the old territories of the Polish Republic . . . guarantee to the Poles living in those territories equal rights and the free preservation of the Polish language and the national culture."

Point 15, which deals with Polish-German relations, states that "full information and the free exchange of people and ideas constitute the only manner of solving age-old quarrels."

Point 16 speaks about the European Community: "this group of states, which . . . is our most important trading partner, is also our natural ideological ally."

After the PPN program, there were other extensive programmatic statements coming from other circles (for example, "Program 44," published on August 6, 1976). These texts helped to determine common goals, and professional sociologists, economists, lawyers, or journalists, despite their compromised positions, also contributed. The crisis-prone policy of the authorities played an important role in the development of independent social actions, which created the conditions necessary for solving the crisis and for realizing the sometimes difficult and remote goals set forth in the programs.

The Constitution

Constitutional law in Poland does not play a great role. The most powerful bodies as outlined in the constitution (the Diet, the State Council, etc.) bear little resemblance to what are in fact the most powerful bodies (the Politburo, Secretariat, and departments of the Central Committee). The civil rights guaranteed in the constitution (e.g., freedom of speech, assembly, and demonstration) are limited by particular laws and by the actual practices of the authorities.

Despite this, shortly after December 1970, the authorities publicly announced the need for changes in the constitution. In fact, constitutional reforms were introduced at roughly the same time in other satellite countries. Moreover, the changes were similar: there were new references to the socialist character of the state, emphases on the role of the Communist party, and there were inserts about friendship with the Soviet Union.

The "Central Committee's Guidelines for the Sixth Congress of the Party," which appeared in September 1971, contained a rather strong assertion of the need for constitutional changes. The guidlines were entitled "For the Further Socialist Development of the Polish People's Republic," and they included the statement that "the currently binding constitution of 1952 fulfilled its role during the period of the building of the people's state." Now, "there is a need to prepare a project of a new constitution," which, among other things, would contain "solutions concerning the leading role of the party." It was announced that "the party will undertake the task of preparing the new constitution and will present this project for wide discussion during the Diet electoral campaign" (point 93 of the theses). This announcement was not fulfilled. For the time being, constitutional changes were forgotten or postponed.

The issue returned four years later in the "guidelines" for the next Congress of PZPR. The guidelines of August 1975 noted that "the Constitution should affirm the historical fact that the Polish People's Republic is a socialist state in which power belongs to the working people of the cities and villages, and in which the United Polish Workers' Party is the leading force." In the discussion that followed, the Main Council of the Polish Episcopate pointed to formulations that "again testify to the totalitarian nature of the Marxist-Leninist ideology of the party and state authorities."

Shortly afterwards, 59 persons signed a statement, a copy of which was transmitted on December 5, 1975, to the Marshall of the Diet. This statement is often called "the letter of the 59," though, strictly speaking, it was not a letter, since it was not addressed to any specific person but to everyone.

The statement of the 59 emphasized the need to guarantee the freedom of conscience, religion, work, speech, information, and science, not only in the constitution but also in the laws based on the constitution: "Guarantees of these basic freedoms cannot be reconciled with the official recognition of the leading role of one party in the state system of power, which is now being proposed. This kind of a constitutional statement would confer on a political party the role of an organ of state authority, which would be neither responsible nor controlled by society. Under these conditions, the Diet could not be the highest executive organ, and the courts would not be independent."

The Seventh Congress of PZPR deliberated from December 8–10, 1975. Speaking on the first day of the congress, Edward Gierek stated that "we have to limit ourselves to the most necessary modifications of the existing basic law, and above all to reflect in it the socialist character of our state and the social, economic and political changes which have taken place in the process of building socialism." Thus, Gierek called for minor changes, the "most necessary" ones, and did not directly mention that the leading role of PZPR should be guaranteed in the constitution.

On January 17, 1976, the Diet adopted a new electoral ordinance, which stated: "Elections to the Diet of the Polish People's Republic and to the national councils shall take place on the basis of the program of the Front of National Unity. . . . The Polish United Workers' Party constitutes the guiding ideological force of the Front of National Unity" (Article 1.1).

PZPR began to squeeze its name into various laws. There were projects to assert that the party was the leading force in the state or the guiding political force in the society.

On January 23, 1976, the Diet Commission adopted a proposal for changes in the constitution. According to the proposal published in the press the following day, the PRL, which was formally described in the constitution as a "state of people's democracy" (Article 1.1), was now to be a "socialist state." The project also asserted that PZPR was "the guiding political force of society in the building of socialism," and that in its policies the PRL "strengthens its friendship and cooperation with the Union of Socialist Soviet Republics and with other socialist countries." One of the new laws also stated that "Citizens' rights are inseparably linked with the honest and conscientious fulfillment of responsibilities toward the Motherland."

The project of this law encountered one in a series of criticisms. On January 31, the writer Jerzy Andrzejewski addressed a letter signed by 101 persons to the Extraordinary Commission of the Diet. The authors stated that "democracy in general, and thus also socialist democracy, assumes that citizens' rights cannot be limited by any special conditions, especially unclearly fomulated ones that are open to arbitrary interpretation by institutions and particular individuals in power."

The final version of the changes was adopted on February 10, 1976. The statements concerning PZPR and the USSR were adopted in the form recommended by the Diet Commission. The article linking citizens' rights with their responsibilities was dropped, but there was a passage according to which "citizens of the Polish People's Republic should honestly and conscientiously fulfill their responsibilities toward the Motherland and contribute to its development" (Article 57.3).

The legal significance of these formulations is not always clear. For instance, what is meant by the assertion that a certain organization (e.g., a political party) is entitled to a "leading role" (guidelines of September 1971)? How does a "leading force" (guidelines of August 1975) differ from a "guiding force" (the final version)? One might ask about the difference between "the guiding ideological force" (the electoral ordinance of January 1976) and "the guiding political force" (the amendment to the constitution), or whether the leading force in the state (guidelines of 1975) means the same thing as "the guiding force of society" (the amendment to the constitution).

The inviolable fraternal ties, announced by Edward Babiuch, sounded rather dangerous. They were replaced by the obligation to "strengthen friendship and cooperation." But the constitution does not state what this obligation entails nor whether it is conditional or absolute.

Article 57.3 of the constitution was equally unclear. The law that citizens are supposed to fulfill their obligations becomes meaningless when the obligations are not defined. And why was there the need to assert that one should fulfill one's obligations? Probably this section of the law, like many others, should not be interpreted legally but as an expression of the paternalistic attitude of the collective author, that is, of the party leadership, which in the constitution chose to admonish society, "fulfill your obligations, or else!"

The adoption of the amendment concerning the obligation of friendship and cooperation with the Soviet Union was an expression of servility, the need for which was perhaps strengthened by analogical tributes in the constitutions of other Soviet bloc countries. The constitution of the GDR mentions eternal and inviolable ties with the USSR, while the Rumanian constitution refers to friendship and fraternal cooperation with socialist countries without mentioning the Soviet Union directly.

References to the leading role or guiding force of PZPR can be regarded as part of a need to legalize the existing state of affairs. The authors probably intended these formulations as a legal cover for party involvement in the state, the staffing of state positions being an example.

Party lawyers wrote that the revisions of the constitution should *record* or *have recorded* otherwise unspecified rights of the party. In this manner, they avoided the claim that the law had been altered, that the revisions of the constitution established different rights. According to party lawyers, nothing of the sort had happened. The constitution simply "recorded" what was already a practical fact. According to this interpretation, the constitution is a "record," even if only a dim one, of what was going on anyway—without the constitution.

The declarations of the party aimed at the legalization of its role, its servility to the USSR, and its paternalistic attitude toward society, all encountered protest. The party leadership decided it was time to "record in the constitution" its illegal practices, but for many people this did not alter their illegality. These people's protests probably contributed to the unclear form of the final revisions.

The voices of protest against constitutional revisions demonstrated that the people of Poland (as opposed to the authorities) were prepared to take the law seriously. The issue of subservience to the Soviet Union and to the local Communist party was raised regarding the constitutional changes and reappeared in the summer of 1980, when, during the talks with the Interfactory Strike Committee in Gdańsk, the government demanded a promise that the new labor unions would not undermine "the established system of international alliances" (a milder formulation than that in the constitution). They also demanded that the new unions accept that "PZPR plays a leading role in the state" (which was stronger than the assertion in the constitution, which even after the 1976 revisions does not mention the role of PZPR in the state).

Catholic Groups

For many years Catholic groups constituted one of the few enclaves of permitted and officially approved (and thus rather limited) independence in social and political life. When the authorities felt that this independence had gone too far they became insulted and angry, and sought revenge. For example, after 1964, when Jerzy Turowicz, the editor-in-chief of *Tygodnik Powszechny* signed "the letter of the 34," the authorities lowered the circulation of *Tygodnik Powszechny* from 40 to 30 thousand copies. When, two years later, the same Jerzy Turowicz defended the letter of the Polish bishops to the German bishops at a meeting of the All-Poland Committee of the Front of National Unity, Gomułka was reportedly furious. The authorities were even angrier in 1968.

On March 11, 1968, five deputies of the Znak circle addressed an interpellation to the premier in which they asked what the government was doing to "restrain the brutal actions of the police and ORMO (the secret police) against the students and to investigate who is responsible for the brutal treatment of these young people." At issue was "the democratic rights of citizens and the cultural policies of the government."

During the Diet session of April 10–11, 1968, the Znak circle was the butt of rather crude attacks by Premier Cyrankiewicz and other deputies. This was accompanied by a press campaign and rallies organized by PZPR as expressions "of the people's anger" towards the deputies of Znak. On April 11, Znak deputy Jerzy Zawieyski was removed from the State Council.

In 1967, Janusz Zabłocki, a member both of Znak and of the editorial board of *Więź*, funded a Center of Documentation and Social Studies (ODISS). ODISS published papal documents, including the encyclicals, and strongly emphasized its Catholicism. At the same time, the political views of ODISS, like those of Pax, were consistent with official perspectives.

In 1972, Tadeusz Mazowiecki was replaced in the Diet by Wacław Aulaytner. Thus, the second of the Znak deputies to sign the interpellation of March 11, 1968, after Jerzy Zawieyski, left the Diet. Of the remaining three, two had moved closer to the authorities, at least insofar as their stated opinions were concerned. In the vote on the 1976 constitutional revisions, Stanisław Stomma was the only Znak member to part company with the other delegates and abstain from voting.

During the next Diet session (after the elections of March 21, 1976), Stanisław Stomma was no longer a deputy. New Znak deputies were connected with ODISS.

On April 11, 1976, representatives of the Znak movement adopted a resolution stating that the new circle of Diet deputies, despite its name, was not acting with the mandate of the Znak movement.

On July 14, 1976, the Polish Club of Catholic Intelligentsia was created in Warsaw, where the Club of Catholic Intelligentsia, founded in 1956, continued to exist. The creation of a new club using the adjective "Polish" testified to the desires of the ODISS group to expand its organizational structure.

During the years 1976–1981, numerous activists of the Clubs of Catholic Intelligentsia and the contributors and editors of licensed but independent Catholic periodicals participated in activities that were unauthorized and to some extent oppositional. They were active in the Society for Scientific Courses, published their texts in underground periodicals, and later helped the Independent and Self-Governing Labor Unions (Solidarity).

The election of Karol Wojtyła as pope and his later visit to Poland greatly hampered the authorities. Plans to persecute or even to limit the influence of independent Catholic groups had to be postponed. New clubs of Catholic intelligentsia connected with the old Znak movement were created in late 1980 and early 1981. Znak was still absent from the Diet, but the ODISS group eventually abandoned the name and called itself The Polish Catholic Social Association.

Policies Toward Youth

On October 23, 1975, Stanisław Kruszyński, a fifth-year student of theology at the Catholic University in Lublin, was arrested for "distributing false information that could inflict serious harm on the interests of the PRL by presenting false and tendentious views on the political, social, and economic relations of the Polish state in letters to various persons written during the period from June to October 23, 1975." On the basis of private letters, Kruszyński was sentenced to ten months imprisonment.

A short time later, the rector of the Pomeranian Medical Academy in Szczecin expelled Jacek Smykał, a third-year medical student. The explanation of this decision is worth quoting as a testimony to the educational ideals of the authorities. The rector characterized the remarks of Smykał during political science classes as follows: "These remarks were full of aggressive dynamism . . . and must have destructively affected the worldview of Smykał's fellow students by raising unnecessary doubts in their minds or even creating a distorted image of our reality. Moreover, the accused displayed passive resistance by his nonchalant and disdainful attitude during the interrogation in the district police headquarters, and in this manner he exhibited a complete lack of civil discipline toward the employees of the security sector."

Information about the cases of Kruszyński and Smykał circulated among students, raising understandable concern.

In May 1976, over 600 persons (mostly students of Warsaw University) addressed a letter to the State Council protesting against the treatment of Kruszyński and Smykał. The authors asserted: "We appeal to the State Council to determine the causes that made such baseless and harmful decisions possible, and to undertake steps necessary to prevent similar decisions from being made in the future."

Meanwhile, PZPR was busy pursuing its goal of unifying the youth organizations. On April 28, congresses of the Union of Socialist Youth (ZMS), the Union of Socialist Rural Youth (ZSMW), and a national meeting of the activists of the Socialist Union of Army Youth (SZMW) were all taking place in Warsaw. During the meetings of all these organizations, the Union of Socialist Polish Youth (ZSMP) was created as the "common organization of the working youth."

A new ZMP (though with the increasingly ubiquitous letter "S" inserted) was created as a unified youth organization (excluding the union of students and scouts). Such a union had not existed at least since 1957. Signified by the abundant use of the adjective "socialist," the party was realizing one of its main principles and systemic properties: uniformity.

These party actions provoked vigorous responses in the universities. In 1973, students protested against the unification of youth organizations in institutions of higher learning. In late 1975 and early 1976, approximately 600 students and university graduates of Warsaw, Łódź, and Katowice signed a letter protesting the proposed changes in the constitution. When the changes were adopted, 92 students and faculty members of the Gdańsk and Lublin colleges protested in a letter to the marshal of the Diet.

Since the latter half of the seventies, Polish students have not only protested party ideas about organizations, they have also created their own organizations. When the June 1976 price increases were announced in Poland, students and university graduates supported the workers' demonstrations and observed court proceedings, thus cooperating in the creation of an independent informational and cultural movement. The first Student Solidarity Committee, independent from the authorities, was created in May 1977 in Cracow, and later in other cities. Students and university graduates worked in the independent publishing outfits and organized self-education activities. Youth communities were crystallizing around independent periodicals; for example, Gdańsk *Bratniak*, which in July 1979 announced the creation of the Young Poland Movement. The first Organizational Committees of the Independent Student Union were established in Poland in the summer of 1980. During the academic year 1980/81, students in many university centers went on strike in order to induce the state authorities to register the independent union and also to deideologize, relatively speaking, the school curriculum.

June 1976

The seventies brought about many administrative and organizational changes. In October 1972, the highest authorities granted themselves salary and retirement benefits with bureaucratic exactness. They also detailed the forms of party control over the most important, and even the somewhat less important, positions (in the Politburo documents concerning the "nomenclature"). The reform of the administrative system began with the elimination of villages in November 1972 and ended with the elimination of counties in late May and early June 1975. The constitution was revised in February 1976, and unification of the youth organizations culminated with the creation of the Socialist Union of Polish Youth at the end of April 1976. The success of these changes encouraged the authorities to make another bold decision, this time in the economic realm.

In December 1975, during the Seventh Congress of PZPR, Gierek asserted: "As far as our concrete plans are concerned, we will begin next year with the current price structure. But the problem of the price structure of basic food products demands further analysis, especially in regard to our economic situation and our reserves. The government should provide such an analysis during the next year; and following consultations with the working people, it should present appropriate conclusions. Obviously, these must be congruent with the basic assumptions of the social policy of the party and in particular must insure the growth of real income planned for the next five years."

Gierek's statement contained the assurance that there would be no price increases before the end of December. Even further, Gierek did not speak directly about price increases, but about the analysis of the price structure and the need to present appropriate government suggestions. In party language, however, all this amounted to a public announcement of price increases in the following year, which was mitigated somewhat by the concurrent announcement of some increases in real income. Gierek used the term "consultations," and it was to recur often in the months following. The presence of the term was directly proportional to the absence of the fact.

On Thursday, June 24, 1976, during a session of the Diet, Premier Piotr Jaroszewicz presented the projected government price increases. The Diet approved these projections, and the increases were to go into effect as of Monday, June 28. This did not stop the authorities from announcing that there would be consultations in workplaces.

But on June 25, workers in many factories went on strike. In Radom the strike began in the General Walter Metal Factory. The workers there notified other factories and formed a demonstration, which marched in the direction of the District Party Committee. A crowd gathered in front of the building and waited for representatives of the authorities. Some people entered the building, but they did not find the party authorities. What they did find in this rare visit to the center of local party decisions was a lavishly stocked buffet, including goods the prices of which had just been raised. This did not pacify the visitors. Around 1:00 P.M. the crowd began destroying the committee building; and at 3:00 P.M. the building was set on fire. The crowd prevented firemen from coming near the building.

In the afternoon, a group of people walked through the main shopping street in Radom breaking the store windows. Nobody stopped them, and the perpetrators were never found, although the broken glass was exploited by the propaganda to condemn the workers. The burning of the Party Committee building, however, went unmentioned in the official press: beyond the embarrassment, the obvious analogy with the burning of party buildings on the coast in 1970, which led to Gierek becoming first secretary, was evidently discomforting. But the circle was complete —a Party Committee building was again in flames.

Around 5:00 P.M., motorized detachments of Citizen's Militia (ZOMO) began their pacification of Radom. The police conducted mass arrests and beat up those arrested and detained. One of the methods used in the torture of the arrested were so-called "health paths": men were made to run a gauntlet between two rows of policemen, who struck the stumbling men with truncheons. Those who found themselves in the hands of the police were beaten whether or not there was any proof of their participation in the June 25 events. One might suspect that this indiscriminate use of physical repression was ordered by a rather high level of the power hierarchy. One indication of this is the simultaneous appearance of beatings by both the police and the prison guards.

On the morning of June 25, workers in the Metal Factory in Ursus near Warsaw went on strike. The workers demanded talks with representatives of the authorities. After the director of the factory rejected this demand, the striking workers went out to the nearby railroad and dismantled the tracks and derailed a locomotive, which made train traffic impossible between Warsaw and Poznań and between Warsaw and Łódź. In the evening, Ursus workers were attacked on the streets by the police, who also beat pedestrians. The degree of brutality in Ursus was comparable to that in Radom.

The strikes were not limited to Radom and Ursus. There were also large strikes in the petrochemical industry in Płock, in the Pomeranian Foundry Enamel Works in Grudziądz, and elsewhere. According to party reports, there was a so-called "strike situation" in many factories across the country, and there were threats to strike if the price increases were not repealed (in Łódź, Warsaw, and on the coast).

The events of June 25 caused the withdrawal of the price increases. On the very evening of June 25, Piotr Jaroszewicz announced on the radio and television that "the project developed by the government was presented to the Diet and to the society as a proposition and not as a final decision. This decision was to depend on the course of discussions and on the reaction of the working people." According to Jaroszewicz, during the day "consultations on these matters took place in most of the country's workplaces. . . . Many concrete propositions were presented, and they deserve thorough analysis. In this situation, the government believes that a new analysis of the entire issue is in order. This demands at least several months of work. Therefore, in the name of the Ministers' Council, and after consulting with CRZZ, I have asked the Presidium of the Diet to withdraw the government project."

The further course of events leads us to conclude that either there were so many concrete proposals that not only several months but even several years were not sufficient for a "thorough analysis," or that there was only one concrete proposal—to withdraw the price increases. This proposal was supported by such "arguments" as strikes, demonstrations, dismantling railroad tracks, and burning the Party Committee building in Radom. It was precisely these "arguments" which forced the government to regard "a new analysis of the entire issue" as necessary.

Immediately after the events in Radom and Ursus, groups of intellectuals, students, and university graduates expressed their solidarity with the workers. The first such declaration was announced on June 28, on the twentieth anniversary of the revolt of the Poznań workers. It was signed by fourteen signatories who had earlier signed the "letter of the 59" concerning the constitutional changes. It is interesting that seven of these fourteen people were later among the founders of the Workers' Defense Committee (KOR), which was created at the end of September, and two more of them joined KOR during the following year.

While intellectuals and students were expressing their solidarity with the workers, PZPR initiated its own brand of solidarity under the slogans, "we support the policy of the party and the government" and "we condemn those who disturb the public order." A campaign of sending letters and telegrams to Gierek and Jaroszewicz took place. People cabled, for example, "I am with the party, I am with you, Comrade First

Secretary. . . . The party does not let us down, and we, the workers, will not let the party down." Many such letters were published in the press on June 28.

Also on June 28, the national press finally made mention that something had happened in Radom and Ursus three days earlier. An editorial in *Życie Warszawy* stated that discussions "on the proposed new price structure" began in a "factual atmosphere. . . . Only in a few cases was the course of these discussions connected with a temporary abandonment of the workplaces. In two instances, in Radom and Ursus, emotions ran so high that some people took to the streets. But where the street becomes vocal, there is no way to conduct discussions."

At this time, rallies in support of the authorities were reportedly taking place throughout the country. The rallies proclaimed: "We support the policy of the party and the government," "We want to live and work peacefully," "Work, order, discipline—the basis of our success." Press commentaries referred repeatedly to "asocial groups" and "rowdy elements" devastating the common wealth.

On Wednesday, June 30, there was an official rally in Radom at the local sports stadium at which the president of Radom, Tadeusz Karwicki, delivered a long speech. In it he singled out the employees of "Walter" for particular condemnation: "The team of 'Walter,' whose wages during the last five months rose twenty percent over the same period last year, initiated the events. These events were fomented by those for whom the dignity of the Pole, the dignity of the worker, is an empty slogan. This is how we must evaluate a group of workers from the P-6 division of the metal works, where the average wages are above four thousand złotys. It was these workers who left work and took to the streets last Thursday. The workers' collective could not control the situation and could not isolate the members of this group, which does not deserve to work in a factory named after the legendary General Walter. This group dragged behind them some workers in other departments, and parasitic, hooligan, criminal, and anti-socialist elements joined them in the streets. In this 'choice' company, force was used to enter other factories in Radom. Workers in these factories were terrorized and forced to leave work." Karwicki also spoke about the crowds around the PZPR building. "Unruly groups pushed their way into the building. Drunken hooligans and hysterical women led the crowd. The expressions of anger and of condemnation should be directed against those who passively watched these excesses, which led the attackers to feel more impudent. There followed a systematic destruction of interiors, theft and looting, and setting the building and official and private cars on fire."

Karwicki estimated the total material losses "at 77 million złotys. Thirty million złotys worth of goods was stolen from demolished shops. Seventy-five police functionaries were wounded, eight of them seriously. Two participants in the riots were killed when they were run over by a company tractor."

Were there only two casualties? Evidence suggests that there were more such cases. One of the unclear incidents was the death of Jan Bro-żyna. At the trial that followed, the witnesses of his death were accused of committing the murder.

The speech of the president of Radom was intended to portray the workers' demonstrations as the actions of hooligans and troublemakers.

Karwicki said that the troublemakers would be "severely and deservedly punished." The prison sentences handed down in the Radom cases were in fact severe, if not deserved. In four trials of 25 persons in the District Court in Radom, there were eight sentences of 8 to 10 years of imprisonment, eleven sentences of 5 to 6 years, and six of 2 to 4 years. Nevertheless, in July 1977 the last prisoners convicted in the Radom trials were released. The authorities bowed to the pressure of public opinion.

The price rises too had to face the power of public opinion. According to Gierek: "Benefiting thoroughly from the discussions that have taken place, the government, together with the Central Council of Labor Unions, will prepare a modified project of changes in the price structure, as the prime minister has already asserted." The propositions for new price changes was not presented. This unresolved situation in the economy lasted until 1980.

Clearly, after the June events the party was not the only one making its views known. The 1976 declarations by the intellectuals, students and graduates of solidarity with the workers turned to active defense shortly after the strikes in Radom and Ursus. The events in June 1976 contributed to a more distinct crystallization of centers of public opinion independent from the authorities. The actions of the authorities were increasingly being discussed publicly. This was taking place through small editions of statements, pamphlets, and periodicals distributed outside the reach of censorship. Society was asserting itself, and the darkness in Poland was being dispersed.

Conclusion

The attempt to raise prices in June 1976 demonstrated again the economic incompetence of the authorities. The economic managers clearly could not meet their goals. The brutal reaction of the authorities to the strikes and demonstrations and the ensuing propaganda campaign further alienated society. The terrorist action of the police after June 25, 1976 was revengeful and illegal.

After the June events, the students and intelligentsia organized financial, legal, and medical help for the workers. Solidarity was no longer merely a matter of words. On September 23, 1976, fourteen persons signed an appeal to society and the authorities in which the creation of the Workers' Defense Committee was announced. Its goal was to help the victims of repression connected with the June events. The Workers' Defense Committee (KOR) began publishing information on persecution and on assistance. KOR also served as an intermediary in collecting and distributing funds donated to help the persecuted workers.

The first issue of *Information Bulletin* appeared in September 1976. As stated in the heading: "The goal of this bulletin is to break the state monopoly of information guarded by the existence of censorship in our country. The information published here serves the openness of public life and constitutes a chronicle of repressions used against citizens and the national culture. The distribution of this bulletin is an active gesture in defense of human rights, and it exemplifies the use of these rights."

The first issue of the literary quarterly *Zapis* appeared in the form of a typescript in January 1977, and it continued to appear regularly in the following years. The publication of *Zapis* was a demonstration of the independence of the writers' community. Independent publication supplemented the writers' demands for limitation of the censorship and contributed to a weakening of the state monopoly on the dissemination of cultural goods.

Those involved in the first independent information and literary publications faced harassment by the authorities. Also, counterfeit KOR communique's, which were clearly prepared by the police, appeared, while the police confiscated makeshift copying machines. But the authorities did not conduct mass arrests or use physical coercion on a mass scale. The intelligentsia was generally treated differently than the workers had been previously. This seemed to be in some degree the result of the authorities' fear of public opinion in the West, which to a large extent was financing the Polish economy. Also, blackmail and physical coercion used by the police was countered by their exposure in the *Bulletin* and KOR communiqués.

The need to extend these actions beyond giving help to the workers was growing in the opposition. On March 26, 1977, during a press conference at which foreign journalists were present, the creation of the Movement for the Defense of Human and Civil Rights (ROPCiO) was announced (in an appeal signed by 18 persons). The movement for defense was not a committee and did not have a membership. ROPCiO had a less defined structure than KOR—which coordinated the actions of various persons and provided information on these actions—it was a group of people who mostly participated in common activities. The movement began publication of a periodical, *Opinia,* and also started a network in the larger cities of consultation centers, where lectures and the distribution of independent publications took place. ROPCiO published statements on such issues as freedom of speech and freedom of religion. *Opinia* criticized the cultural policies of the authorities, exposed the illegalities taking place in the country and the economic wastefulness, and recalled officially forgotten events from the history of Poland.

In April 1977, some Cracow students received anonymous letters attacking their colleague, Stanislaw Pyjas, a KOR supporter. Students protested to the prosecutor's office: it was known that Pyjas was followed by the police. On May 7, 1977, Pyjas was found dead in the stairwell of a house in Cracow. On May 9, both KOR and ROPCiO spokesmen made statements that there were suspicions the security forces participated both in writing the slanderous letters and in Pyjas' death (which occurred most likely as a result of beating). On Sunday, May 15, a mass for Pyjas was celebrated in Cracow. That evening, students of Cracow announced the creation of the Student Solidarity Committee (later such committees were also created elsewhere). The goal of the Student Solidarity Committees was to defend student interests outside of the single official student organization (the Socialist Union of Polish Students).

After Pyjas' death the authorities attempted to limit the activities of KOR. Six members of KOR were arrested in May and charged on the basis of Article 132 of the Criminal Code, which referred to contacts with a foreign organization in order to harm the PRL. Four KOR collaborators were also arrested for other crimes. But KOR's activities continued unabated, and after two months, following numerous protests both in Poland and abroad, the members and collaborators of KOR were released from prison. At the same time, the last of the workers convicted for their participation in the June events were also released. These concessions (largely forced) made the situation of the authorities more difficult and helped to enliven the oppositional activities.

During the academic year 1976/77 twelve new members of KOR were accepted, enlarging the membership to 26. On September 26, 1977, 23 of them made an announcement concerning the widening of the goals and activities of the committee and the transformation of KOR into the Committee for Social Self-Defense-"KOR" (KSS-"KOR"). The goals of KSS-"KOR" were formulated as follows:

1. The struggle against political, ideological, religious, or racial repression and help for those suffering from such persecution.
2. The struggle against breaking the rule of law and help for the victims of illegality.
3. The struggle for institutional guarantees of civil rights and freedoms.
4. The support and defense of all social initiatives aimed at the realization of human and civil rights.

The fall 1977 witnessed a proliferation of independent periodicals. There was *Postęp* (*Progress*, which defended the creation of urban and rural independent labor unions), *Robotnik* (*The Worker*, which was the largest circulation independent periodical and was concerned with workers' issues), the socio-political monthly *Głos* (*The Voice*, which published political essays, feuilletons, and journalistic reports dealing with the possibilities for democracy in Poland and the need to create self-governing social institutions), *Spotkania* (*Meetings*, which was published by young Catholics and dealt with the spiritual issues and practical problems related to the official harassment of Catholics), the irregular literary quarterly *Puls* (which largely published younger authors than *Zapis*), the student periodicals *Indeks* and *Bratniak* (the later becoming connected with the Young Poland Movement in 1979), *Gospodarz* (*The Farmer*, connected with ROPCiO and devoted especially to the concerns of the private farmer).

The first publications of the Independent Publishing House (NOWa) appeared in the fall of 1977. During the following years NOWa published nearly two hundred pamphlets and books—novels, poetry collections, essays, and documents. It published both writers living in Poland and those living abroad, as well as translations of foreign works. These publications were copied by "small polygraphy" (beginning with hectographic copying and then adopting offset printing). Xerographic methods were also used. Similar publishing actions were also conducted by other independent houses: The Polish Publishing House, The Publishing House of the Third of May Constitution, "Klin," and others. This publishing activity was supplemented by the Library of Forbidden Books, which collected and made available works forbidden by the censorship.

The authorities attempted to crack down on these activities and confiscated printing equipment and suspicious books and pamphlets, but largely to no avail.

The Flying University began its activity in Warsaw in the academic year 1977/78. It organized lectures in private apartments on recent Polish history, the foundations of political science, economic policy, the history of literature, etc. On January 22, 1978, 61 persons (mostly scientists and artists) announced the creation of the Society for Scientific Courses (TKN), which sponsored the lectures of the Flying University. TKN also organized discussions on topics in the social sciences and humanities that were not dealt with in the censored science. Materials from colloquia of TKN appeared in book form: one dealt with the language if propaganda, another with the history of contemporary Polish literature. The police organized raids on these lectures of the Flying University, and TKN was eventually forced to limit them (but following the workers' revolt in the fall of 1980 TKN renewed its lecture activities on a much larger scale).

In 1978, several other periodicals were founded (mostly political, namely *Krytyka, Res Publica,* and *Aspekt*) and organizations were created to defend the interests of specific social groups. And in November 1978, the discussion club of Doświadczenie i Przyszłość (Experience and Future) was created by a group of scientists, journalists and publicists. The authorities soon forbade its club meetings, but it continued its activities by conducting questionnaire surveys on the current situation in Poland. The respondents to the questionnaires were in agreement in their criticism of the government's policy and described the catastrophic state of the economy and the incompetence and hypocrisy of the authorities. The dangerous consequences of these policies were noted, and the respondents made recommendations for changes to the authorities, for what it was worth.

The election of Cardinal Karol Wojtyła as pope on October 16, 1978, had a tremendous impact on Polish society. John Paul II's visit to Poland in June 1979 instilled a sense of unity among people and strengthened the solidarity, assurance, and independence of Polish society.

New organizations advocating Poland's independence were created in 1979. On February 10, 26 persons formed a Committee of an Agreement for the Self-determination of the Nation (which published the periodical *Rzeczpospolita*), and the Young Poland Movement was created in late July around the periodical *Bratniak*. On September 1, the creation of the Confederation of Independent Poland was signed by 34 persons. Their declaration mentioned the principle of national self-determination based on the "free expression of the will of society in matters concerning the state's international sovereignty, the social and state system, and the government ruling the state."

The oppositional activities between 1976–1980, which consisted basically of disseminating uncensored information and publicizing the abuses of law, gross incompetence, and private profiteering of public officials, forged the social links useful for the creation of Solidarity in 1980. In a society that had been systematically atomized since its postwar beginnings, the uncensored press facilitated social contacts and created the possibility for social action, as witnessed by the public commemoration of certain important Polish anniversaries that had been disregarded by the PZPR. There were certain differences between the various independent groups, but they ultimately shared a fundamental commitment to basic values such as democracy and the independence of Poland.

In July 1980 new food price increases triggered strikes lasting throughout July and August. On August 16, 1980, an Interfactory Strike Committee was created in Gdańsk, followed shortly afterwards by the creation of Interfactory Strike Committees in other cities. These committees formulated demands that went beyond the issues of prices and wages. Their demands included the right to self-organization, the defense of one's interests, safeguards against the authorities, and uncensored information. The August strikes ended with the signing of agreements between the government commission and the Interfactory Strike Committees in Gdańsk, Szczecin, and Jastrzębie. The signing of an agreement by the authorities with representatives of society was an unprecedented event in the Communist countries. Granted, the authorities were not particularly disposed to respect these agreements; nevertheless, with the creation of independent labor unions, Polish society increased its ability to exert pressure and ensure that the authorities honored their agreements. The institutionalized forms of social pressure made it difficult for the authorities to resist on legal grounds. The realm of social action tolerated by the authorities had widened, at least for a time, and uncensored union periodicals and bulletins proliferated. But freedom was won only to the extent society fought for it. Party statements about agreements, toleration, and the need for democracy were belied by the party's actions. The police arrested activists of the opposition, sometimes using physical force, and the mass media (especially the daily paper of the Polish army, *Żołnierz Wolności*) conducted a propaganda campaign against so-called "anti-socialist" and even "counter-revolutionary forces." All of this testified to official resistance against the widening of social freedom. And one might suspect, given the parallels to the Soviet propaganda during the Prague Spring, that force by the authorities was not to be ruled out, even at the price of the armed intervention of the Soviet bloc countries in Poland. Social solidarity and the threat of worker strikes complicated realization of the party's goals. Poland's catastrophic economic situation also added to the authorities' dilemma. The existence of effective social pressure opened a new chapter in the postwar history of Poland.

INDEX